PUBLIC ADMINISTRATION

PUBLIC ADMINISTRATION

POLICY-MAKING
IN GOVERNMENT AGENCIES

IRA SHARKANSKY
University of Wisconsin

Markham Publishing Company · Chicago

MARKHAM POLITICAL SCIENCE SERIES
Aaron Wildavsky, Editor

AXELROD, *Conflict of Interest: A Theory of Divergent Goals with Applications to Politics*

BARBER, *Citizen Politics: An Introduction to Political Behavior*

BARBER, ed., *Readings in Citizen Politics: Studies of Political Behavior*

CNUDDE and NEUBAUER, eds., *Empirical Democratic Theory*

COPLIN, ed., *Simulation in the Study of Politics*

GREENSTEIN, *Personality and Politics: Problems of Evidence, Inference, and Conceptualization*

LANE, *Political Thinking and Consciousness: The Private Life of the Political Mind*

LYDEN and MILLER, eds., *Planning-Programming-Budgeting: A Systems Approach to Management*

RANNEY, ed., *Political Science and Public Policy*

RUSSETT, ed., *Economic Theories of International Politics*

SHARKANSKY, *Public Administration: Policy-making in Government Agencies*

SHARKANSKY, ed., *Policy Analysis in Political Science*

STRICKLAND, WADE, and JOHNSTON, *A Primer of Political Analysis*

For my mother
Beatrice Mines Sharkansky

It is common within the academic profession for writers to say how their approach to a subject differs from the approaches taken by others. In this case, it is especially appropriate to make such a statement. This book *is* different from other texts in the field of public administration in that it emphasizes the political processes within and surrounding administrative agencies more than it stresses the management techniques that a budding administrator should master. It is written for the student who seeks to understand the operations of public administration in its political environment.

Public administration lends itself to contrasting approaches. At times, it is taught in the political science departments of liberal arts colleges. Presumably, those courses focus on the activities of administrative units in relation to other activities in the larger political process; the end product is more likely to be *understanding,* rather than *training* in the techniques of administration. Elsewhere, public administration is separated from political science and is offered to students as professional training. It is also subordinated to programs that offer instruction in the general field of "administration." A student at the American University in Beirut revealed his confusion about public administration in terms that are not too different from those used by Americans:

> I'm confused about Public Administration. . . . The Graduate School to which I applied in the U.S. teaches Public and Business Administration together and when Colonel Urwick was here he said the main study is management. But when Prof. Pollock was here, he said P.A. is a part of Political Science. Dean Reining told us he had a separate School of Public Administration, but Dean Stone has Public and International Administration together. How can I reconcile all this?[1]

[1] Keith M. Anderson, *Emerging Synthesis in American Public Administration* (New York: Asia Publishing House, 1966). Cited in Dwight Waldo, "Public Administration," *Journal of Politics,* 30 (May, 1969), 443–79.

Public administration has both "liberal arts" and "professional" clientele. Its textbooks can be written for a liberal arts college or for the professional school of a large university.

It is not only the differing perspectives of a liberal arts department and a professional school which generate disputes about public administration. It is marked with disputes among faculty members within the same organization. In many political science departments that consider themselves to be solidly implanted in the liberal tradition, courses in public administration may be offered from the liberal or professional perspective. Students who aspire to a government career are urged to take the courses; the instructor may have some administrative experience; and the text materials often provide information useful to a public administrator. A popular introductory text includes chapters on leadership; decision-making; personnel recruiting, examining, evaluating, and promoting; employee relations; the impact of computer technology upon public administration; preparation, authorization, and execution of the budget; and judicial review of administrative decisions. After his introductory course in public administration, an undergraduate can take additional courses in "public financial administration," and "public personnel administration."

Among political scientists, public administration specialists are set apart not only by their interests in administrative training, but often because their scholarship is "traditional," "institutional," or "non-scientific." To the practicing administrator in government, however, the instructor in public administration is often viewed as too "academic," "theoretical," or "impractical." The editor of the *Public Administration Review* has described the "Public Administrationist" as a man with

> . . . an ambiguous and often uncomfortable dual citizenship status: he is the academic's practical man and the public administrator's academic. . . .
>
> To the Political Scientist who is oriented toward the values and activities designated . . . as "behavioral," the Public Administrationist has not advanced to the frontier of the discipline: he has an old-fashion concern for institutions and programs; he is excessively normative and prescriptive, is at best a technologist rather than a scientist. . . . [He] is perceived as more or less oriented toward an external world of governmental affairs, rather than toward academic-disciplinary matters in a strict sense; and as being importantly, perhaps chiefly, concerned with preparing students to get and hold "government jobs."[2]

Another conflict divides those who study *public* administration as a distinct entity and those who agree that the proper inquiry is *adminis-*

---

[2] Waldo, *ibid.*

tration per se. Those who take the larger view see administration as a generic process. It may be divided into "public," "private," "business," "educational," "military," or other forms of administration. However, each segment is said to have less distinctiveness than the general process of which they are all parts. From this perspective, the study of *public* administration represents a distraction. To understand or to practice administration of any kind, one should devote himself to the examination of administration in several of its forms.

> Now, instead of a universally valid theory [of administration], there is a growing variety of part-theories—of business administration, public administration, hospital administration, educational administration, and other administrations. . . .
> Administrative science is establishing an identity and is gaining momentum. We firmly believe that there is in the making a rigorous science of administration, which can account for events in particular times and places and for the ethical or normative content of those events without itself incorporating the particular conditions and values of those events. The necessary theory must take such factors into account as variables. These variables must be broad enough to include the conditions and ethics found in all fields of administration and in all cultural contexts.[3]

This book does not resolve the questions about the generic nature of administration or about the distinctiveness of *public* administration. Its principal roots are in political science; and it seeks to bring together that information about administration that is most relevant to an understanding of the larger political process. Of necessity, much of this information concerns *public* administration. It includes information about the public's regard for government bureaucracies; about the personal characteristics of public administrators; about interactions among public administrators and political parties, interest groups, and the executive and legislative branches of government; and about interactions between public administrators and government officials from different units in the federal system. At times we consider some information about the behavior of administrators in non-governmental contexts. In dealing with decision-making within administrative organizations, for example, it appears that certain features of decision-making prevail in both public and private administrative organizations of a certain size. We also find some striking similarities in the social backgrounds of high-level administrators in both government agencies

[3] Peter B. Hammond, *et al.*, "On the Study of Administration," in James D. Thompson, *et al.*, eds., *Comparative Studies in Administration* (Pittsburgh: University of Pittsburgh Press, 1959), pp. 3–4.

and large business firms. For the most part, however, the focus is on those attributes and activities of *public* administrators. The emphasis is on the contribution of public administration to public policy-making. While some features of administration appear common to both public and private arenas, any detailed inquiry into their commonness or distinctiveness is secondary to our task.

The systems framework should clarify the policy roles of public administration and should highlight the significance of administration for other features of politics. This book deals with several features that seem capable of affecting policy-making in administrative units and—insofar as this is permitted by the available literature—describes the interactions among these features and the influence that each of them has upon the policy roles of the administrator. Among the questions that the book tries to answer are some of the classic inquiries of political science, as reformulated to make them relevant for a study of public administration:

- *Who gets what, when, and how from the decisions of administrative units?*
- *What share do administrators have in policy-making, as compared to elected legislators, chief executives, and members of the judiciary?*
- *How do administrators affect the benefits that citizens receive from governments?*
- *How do administrators affect the constraints on citizens' behavior that come from government agencies?*

The structure of this book highlights its use of the systems framework. After two introductory chapters that explain the systems concepts and describe the merits of comparison in the field of public administration, a group of three chapters deals with the *conversion process* of the administrative system. The conversion process converts the *inputs* of a system into its *outputs*. These chapters examine decision-making in administrative agencies; the structures of administrative agencies and their formal ties with other branches of government; and the personnel who staff administrative agencies.

Then a group of three chapters deals with several sources of inputs to administrative units: the political culture and its predispositions toward public administration; citizen demands; and demands and resources that come from the executive and legislative branches of an administrator's own government. Finally, two chapters examine the outputs that administrative units provide to other governments and to other actors in their environment.

Although this book departs from the typical model of a public administration text, the departure is more a matter of format and emphasis than a thoroughgoing revolution in content. Many of the topics considered in this book can be found in other public administration texts. However, the organization of this book places these topics in a different context. Instead of being introduced as tools for public management, they are considered components of the *administrative system*. For example, instead of having a separate chapter on "personnel administration," this book considers some topics related to personnel in Chapter 5 dealing with the selection of policy-level administrators and with their socioeconomic characteristics, skills, and values and considers some additional topics in Chapter 6 dealing with the public's conception of the administrative service. Since our focus is on policy-making, we omit many items of personnel administration pertaining to the selection and training of lower- and middle-level employees.

Another example of this different perspective is that there is no separate group of chapters on budgeting as such; but Chapter 8—dealing with relations among administrators, legislators, and the chief executive—describes budget-making in federal, state, and local governments. For a political scientist, budgeting appears less significant by itself than as an example of policy-making interactions between administrators and other branches of government. Budgeting provides the best examples of intragovernmental relations that occur on a regular basis. Chapter 8 is less concerned with a description of paperwork and deadlines that budget officers must meet, than with a discussion of the decisions that are made and the kinds of influences that shape them. Chapter 3 also discusses budgeting under the heading of decision-making. There it is used to illustrate some general aspects of policy-making behavior in administrative agencies.

ACKNOWLEDGMENTS

Many people have contributed to this book. Several hundred students in my public administration courses over a period of five years contributed their explicit and implicit comments to the outline and contents of this book as they evolved through each course syllabus and lecture. During the same period of time, a number of organizations provided me with funds to conduct research. The organizations are Ball State University, the Social Science Research Council, the Computer Center of Florida State University, the Office of General Research at the University of Georgia, the Graduate School of the University of Wisconsin, and the Center for the Study of Public Policy and Administration at the University of Wisconsin. The primary products of that research are published elsewhere; but this book reflects the impact of those experiences upon my conceptions of public administration and the political process in which it operates. Early drafts of the manuscript were read by Chalmers Brumbaugh, Marvin Druker, Barry Gaberman, Richard Hartwig, Michael Kagay, Martin Landau, Clara Penniman, Wallace Sayre, Frank Sherwood, Donald Van Meter, Aaron Wildavsky, Deil Wright, and Dean Yarwood. Mrs. Beverly Shaver and Mrs. Deanna Gervasi typed the manuscript. At home Erica and Stefan and my wife Ina accepted the domestic problems produced by another of Daddy's books. The dedication is for my mother who in times past administered a small organization that was very important in my life.

I. S.

Madison, Wisconsin
July, 1969

CONTENTS

Part One
THE CONVERSION PROCESS
OF THE ADMINISTRATIVE SYSTEM   33

PUBLIC ADMINISTRATION

1

INTRODUCTION

Public administrators and the features that influence their activities are vital subjects for political scientists and for other students who are interested in public affairs.

The importance of public administration is suggested by the broad scope of administrators' responsibilities. In the United States, they helped to spend $259 billion during 1966–1967. This was 33 percent of the Gross National Product, a commonly used indicator of our total national resources. More than 12 million civilians worked for public agencies during 1968; and another 3.5 million citizens were members of the armed forces. The physical strength of the military is one kind of power resource which use is influenced by public administrators. Other powers are shaped by administrators who design and implement programs for public schools and universities; allocate research funds to projects in medicine and in the natural and social sciences; negotiate with landowners about the price to be paid for a highway's right-of-way; develop health and safety standards for foods, drugs, cosmetics, automobiles, and airplanes; and test individual products for their compliance with these standards. Our lives and fortunes are governed by the agencies that regulate the economy. Many of us (20 percent of the labor force) are employed by government agencies; so our salaries, fringe benefits, and work assignments are subject to administrators' decisions. All of us live in an "administrative state"; many of our deprivations and benefits come from administrative agencies. However, we need not become nervous about this situation. There are administrative procedures designed to protect the rights and interests of individual citizens. Much of the "red tape" that is frequently a subject of derision is designed to monitor and control the decisions of administrators.

It is not feasible to describe the activities of a "typical" public administrator. Some administrators are concerned with routine tasks that have been detailed by actions of the legislature. In this category is the case-worker in the county welfare department who decides what benefits should be paid to an applicant under the provisions of a government welfare program. Other administrators manage routine operations. The case-worker's superior allocates work loads, processes vacation schedules, sees to the maintenance of his local office, and deals with clients who are not satisfied with the routine decisions of his subordinates. Still other administrators involve themselves in the most innovative work of government. They help to push forward the frontiers of social progress by drafting proposals for new laws and by lobbying in behalf of these proposals among members of the federal or state legislatures. Administrators must also implement innovative programs. The way in which an administrator uses his discretion can mean success or failure for a project involving many citizens. A field representative of the U.S. Office of Education who negotiates with school systems about racial desegregation is vital to his program's success. Schools do not desegregate by themselves, or simply in response to court orders. As well as having a personal commitment to the principles of equal opportunity, federal administrators· must have great sensitivity to the constraints operating on a local school board. It may be necessary for an administrator to balance sharply-conflicting interests in order to help local officials make a concession to "the government in Washington" without losing their local political support.

The label "public administrator" is used in different ways. In some contexts, it denotes all the employees of governments, except those in the legislative and judicial branches and the elected chief executive. Such a designation includes the file clerks and sweepers, as well as persons in high- and middle-range positions in government departments. In other contexts, the term is reserved for high-level employees of government departments or agencies, i.e., the personnel who make the non-routine decisions that set the standards to be carried out by their subordinates. For the most part, we shall concern ourselves with the latter conception of public administrators. Most of our discussions are about those officials who make important decisions within administrative units and who interact with officials in other branches of government. At times, however, we shall enlarge our focus and report some information about the larger group of administrative employees.

OUR APPROACH TO PUBLIC ADMINISTRATION

This book is for a student's first course in public administration. Its goals are both more ambitious and less ambitious than are those of many introductory texts. Its primary goal is to make the study of public administration relevant and interesting for the student of political science. As a result, the book is concerned only minimally with several of the topics that are included in other books about public administration. It concentrates on those components that appear to be most relevant to the political process and that have received the most thorough attention by political scientists. One factor that links much of the material in public administration with other fields of political science is their common concern with public policy.

The meaning of the term "policy" is ambiguous. Policy can refer to a proposal, an ongoing program, the goals of a program, or the impact of a program upon the social problems that are its target. The uses of the term include such broad phrases as "the United States' foreign policy" and "the domestic policy of Richard Nixon." In a more precise manner, it is used to denote limited aspects of complicated activities: "the policy toward oil depletion allowances advocated by the Treasury Department" or "the policies followed by a university in dealing with student demands."

A definition of policy which fits many of its uses by political scientists is: *the important activities of government*. An activity is "important" if it involves large amounts of resources or if it is relevant to the interests of many people. It would be misleading, however, to specify one definition of policy at this point. Throughout the book, various of the above connotations will be implied; but the context in which the term is used should indicate the intended meaning in that instance.

The *policy process* includes the formulation, approval, and implementation of government programs. It joins public administrators to numerous other actors who have a stake in policy; these include officials in other branches of government, private citizens, interest groups, political parties, and sometimes the spokesmen of foreign governments. Also, within the policy process are the ideas, resources, stimuli, and constraints which influence the participants. The policy process is dynamic and is affected by intense controversies. Participants argue about the proper goals of government, about the programs that are suitable for obtaining each goal, about the probable impact of government programs on various segments of the population, and about the implication of certain programs for other activities of government. Many of these arguments proceed with a surplus of emotion and a dearth of information. Policy-makers frequently make important decisions with nothing more than a "best guess" about the effects of these decisions on the problems they are designed to resolve.

In order to be successful in introducing a student to public administration and the policy process, a book should array its material in a framework that leads the reader to comprehend both the important features of the policy process and the relationships that make each feature important for the others. The framework of this book focuses on: (*a*) an *environment* that both stimulates administrators and receives the products of their work; (*b*) the *inputs* that carry stimuli from the environment to administrators; (*c*) the *outputs* that carry the results of administrative action to the environment; (*d*) a *conversion process* that transforms (converts) inputs into outputs; and (*e*) *feedback* that transmits the outputs of one period—as they interact with features in the environment—back to the conversion process as the inputs of a later time. All of these features interact with one another. Together they form the *administrative system,* as it is outlined in Figure 1–1.

Environment and Inputs

The environment includes the host of social, economic, and political phenomena which present the problems to the policy-makers and which subsequently assist or confound their efforts to resolve these problems. Within the environment are: the clients who are to benefit from a policy; a market which sets costs for the goods and services to be consumed by a policy; and interest groups and members of the public and of other units of government who show political support for—or opposition to—a policy. While some features of an environment facilitate policy-making and the solution of social problems, other features "harden" the problems and frustrate the policy-maker's efforts to cope with them.

Policy inputs are the tranmissions sent from the environment to the conversion process of the administrative system. Inputs include: demands for policy; resources; and support, opposition, or apathy toward the actions of administrators. People demand public goods and services for their own use, e.g., recreation facilities, education, transportation, and health services. They also demand the regulation of other people's behavior, e.g., by the police and the military. In addition, people demand the emotional satisfactions that derive from

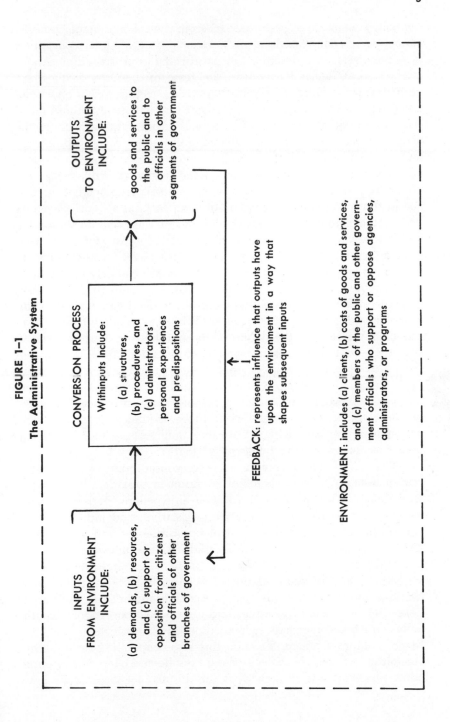

FIGURE 1-1
The Administrative System

INPUTS FROM ENVIRONMENT INCLUDE:

(a) demands, (b) resources, and (c) support or opposition from citizens and officials of other branches of government

CONVERSION PROCESS

Within puts include:

(a) structures,
(b) procedures, and
(c) administrators' personal experiences and predispositions

OUTPUTS TO ENVIRONMENT INCLUDE:

goods and services to the public and to officials in other segments of government

FEEDBACK: represents influence that outputs have upon the environment in a way that shapes subsequent inputs

ENVIRONMENT: includes (a) clients, (b) costs of goods and services, and (c) members of the public and other government officials who support or oppose agencies, administrators, or programs symbolic statements or gestures, e.g., from the celebration of patriotic, ethnic, or religious holidays. A "demand" is an analytic concept; it does not necessarily describe the nature of the citizen-administrator interaction. A demand may take the form of a routine request for service, such as filing an application with a welfare office or a state university; it may simply be a statement that an agency should introduce a new service; or it could be a public confrontation with all the hoopla of placards, civil disobedience, police, and tear gas. Resources include personnel, skills, material, technology, and money. Support, opposition, or apathy shows itself in the degree of willingness of a population to pay taxes, to accept government employment, and to accept the government's regulation of behavior; it is also evidenced by their patience in the face of adversity and by their sentiments toward administrative personnel. Sentiment toward administrators can range from the enthusiasm of "Support Your Local Police" to the animosity of a campaign to oust a school teacher or principal. Between these extremes are the more-typically passive attitudes toward government employees. Several research projects have investigated citizen attitudes toward government employees. While the results of these projects have varied with the nature of the questions that were asked or with the sample that was surveyed, they do agree in the finding that the status of public administrators in the United States is less than that of numerous other professional or technical groups. This finding has an implication for public personnel programs: because many people consider government service to be an undesirable profession, government recruiters may not attract a sufficient number of applications from highly qualified college graduates.

The private sector is not the sole reservoir of inputs to the administrative system. Other segments of government provide administrators with demands in the form of statutes, instructions, and requests or judgments from the chief executive, legislature, and judiciary. They also supply resources and support or opposition in the form of funds and discretionary authority. Some of these governmental inputs are informal, and some are not even expressed. Administrators receive suggestions and recommendations from legislators during legislative hearings and throughout the year as the legislators clarify their intentions behind enacted statutes. Moreover, administrators continually anticipate demands which they might receive from other branches of government. They do this by extrapolating from existing committee reports, court decisions, or public speeches. For example, administrators try to discern what the desires of another official will be or whether it is likely that an official will be so irked by a specific administrative action that he will invoke sanctions.

Conversion Process

It is not only inputs that influence the actions of administrators. Features of the conversion process itself affect their actions. These features are given a separate label in order to distinguish them from the inputs that come from the environment. Since they originate within the conversions process, they are called *withinputs*. Withinputs include: formal structures that are found within administrative agencies; the procedures used by officials to make their decisions; and the administrators' personal experiences and predispositions. Administrators must take account of numerous issues that are relevant to their major decisions and must find some way to assess the intensity, political support, moral virtues, and financial costs which are associated with each of the principal claims. Because each major issue is likely to involve a number of claimants from other units of government as well as from the private sector, there may be many situations in which the decision-makers feel badgered and thus may alter their procedures for making choices. Among the features that may be found in the conversion process are: conflicts between the formal rules of the organization and the personal values of administrators; clashes among administrators that increase the costs of an agency's outputs; decision-makers' use of routine procedures to simplify complex and numerous inputs; and tendencies toward rigidity in the face of innovative demands. An agency's leadership and staff may disagree about proper salaries, working conditions, and services to the agency's clients. Like other segments of government, administration is usually involved in some controversy. Indeed, it is partly because of its numerous relations with other social, economic, and political systems that administration is affected by differing assessments of its own proper activity. There is frequent conflict among administrators themselves, as well as between them and the suppliers of inputs or the recipients of outputs.

Outputs

The outputs that administrators provide to their environment include services, tangible goods, and behavioral regulations, plus gestures, statements, and activities which give symbolic messages to those who are tuned in. To the private sector, administrators provide many of the material and symbolic needs of the citizenry. Administrators also provide direct benefits to officials in other government units: information, technical advice, and concrete proposals that are necessary for policy formulation. Legislators and executives make their living by promising and delivering services to voters. Yet most of these services must ultimately come from administrative agencies. While the politician can supply the necessary resources to the administrator and can urge him to make the desired product for the public, it is the administrator who generally implements the precise statute that is enacted by the legislature or who makes the actual delivery of public service. The administrator's failure to provide desired services may offend both the citizen and the elected members of the legislative branch. Such failures are "negative outputs." They carry short-term deprivations for persons in the administrator's environment; and they threaten long-term deprivations for the administrators themselves.

Feedback

Feedback represents the influence of earlier outputs upon the demands, resources, and support or opposition (i.e., inputs) which an administrative system receives. Existing tax legislation influences the flow of economic resources into administrative agencies. Public services and regulatory policies directly affect citizens' satisfactions and thus shape the demands which they make. Past efforts to promote economic development may affect social and economic conditions in ways that influence both the resources provided by existing taxes and the demands and supports coming from the population.

Feedback mechanisms are evident in the continuity of interactions among administrators and the many sources of their inputs and the recipients of their outputs. Citizens, legislators, and the chief executive are seldom satisfied once and for all times. Some always ask for more. They may demand improvement of existing services, expansion of the magnitude of services to provide for increased population, and expansion of the scope of a program to provide for certain needs which are left unmet by present activities. The annual budget cycle requires an agency staff to defend its activities of the current year and its proposals for the coming year in hearings before officials in both the executive and legislative branches. On these occasions, evidence of program-accomplishments and of unmet-demands come back to the administrators in the form of program instructions and budget ceilings for the coming year. Groups that receive an agency's services or feel the impact of its regulations join with allies in the legislature and try to alter the legal authority of an agency or its level of appropriations. In less formal ways, client groups and legislators are always making some effort to get administrators to change their policies or their decisions in particular cases.

THE SYSTEMS FRAMEWORK

The environment, inputs, conversion process, outputs, and feedback relate to and interact with one another in the manner shown in Figure 1–1. An entire set of these elements *and* their interactions is called an *administrative system.* A system is not simply the administrative unit that is contained in the conversion process. An administrative system is the combination of the administrative unit and all of the elements and processes which interact with the unit: that is, the (*a*) environment within which the administrative unit operates and which influences and is influenced by the unit; and the (*b*) inputs to and (*c*) outputs from the unit which are connected to each other by the (*d*) conversion process and by (*e*) feedback mechanisms. A system such as this is a useful framework for treating individual items; it focuses attention not merely on a simple description of discrete parts, but on the importance and relationship of these parts to one another.

As a conceptual framework, an administrative system helps us think about public administration. It is not a fixed set of actors and activities. It can be used to guide our ideas about universal happenings (i.e., generalizations about administrative activities in all governments) or about particular happenings (i.e., administrative activities in certain settings). We can devise an administrative system to include the actions of most public administrators in the United States; this system would include legislative and judicial officials of state, local, and national governments, as well as all the principal interest groups that involve themselves in prominent issues. For other purposes, we might devise an administrative system to explain the actions of one agency. A system focusing on the Federal Bureau of Investigation, for example, would include a limited collection of resources, government officials, interest groups, and citizens.

By thinking about public administration in a systems framework, we should discipline ourselves to ask about the relevance of the individual components: What implications for outputs are to be found in the various features of the conversion process? How does the character of the conversion process respond to inputs from the environment? What kind of constraints over outputs are exercised by the amount of resources that come into the conversion process from the environment? This kind of questioning establishes the relevance of public administration to politics, to economics, and to other features of its environment which interest us as political scientists and as citizens.[1] The administrative system is not a set of fixed patterns in which administrators engage in documented relations with their environment. The system is a *conceptual framework* whose purpose is to aid the study of public administration. Inputs and feedback suggest the kinds of stimuli likely to influence activities in the conversion process; outputs are merely a label for that category of phenomena that reflect the products of administrators' work. As a conceptual framework, the system guides the selection and organization of information about public administration. With the system as a guide, we shall collect information about items that seem to function as conversion components, inputs, outputs, and feedback mechanisms. We shall then see how these items actually do interact with one another.

The linkages among environment, inputs, conversion, outputs, and feedback may appear to be a closed system in which decision-makers respond continuously to the impact which their own previous decisions have had upon their environment. Figure 1–1 may suggest such "closure" to some readers. However, the diagram only shows which aspects of a system interact with others; it does not portray the character of these relationships. There is much slippage among components of a system. In the real world, there are numerous features that can influence the decisions of the participants. New inputs continuously come from the demands of citizens and citizen organizations. Officials have many options in reviewing the feedback from their previous decisions: officials differ in the weight they assign to precedent, to the demands that come from citizens or from other officials, and to their own assessment about the success of current activities.

An administrative system may attain stability if its decision-makers succeed in satisfying demands and in living within the resources that are conveniently available. For the administrators who will be

---

[1] The theoretical work that is most frequently cited in connection with the systems approach to political science is David Easton, *A Systems Analysis of Political Life* (New York: Wiley, 1965). See also David Easton, *A Framework for Political Analysis* (Englewood Cliffs, N.J.: Prentice-Hall, 1965); Gabriel Almond and G. Bingham Powell, Jr., *Comparative Politics: A Developmental Approach* (Boston: Little, Brown, 1966); Thomas R. Dye, *Politics, Economics, and the Public: Policy Outcomes in the American States* (Chicago: Rand McNally, 1966); Richard F. Fenno, *The Power of the Purse: Appropriations Politics in Congress* (Boston: Little, Brown, 1966); John C. Wahlke, *et al.*, *The Legislative System* (New York: Wiley, 1962); and Karl W. Deutsch, *The Nerves of Government* (New York: Free Press of Glencoe, 1963).

A "systems approach" is not the only way to organize a book about public administration. For a discussion of the author's reasons for this choice, see the Preface.

described in this book, however, stability is—at most—an elusive goal. For some participants, the quest for stability is frustrated by an environment that provides not only shifting and ambiguous goals, but also resources and supports which change in response to numerous and complex determinants. For other decision-makers, stability is actually less desirable than is major change in their agency and its surroundings.

THE BORDERS OF ADMINISTRATIVE SYSTEMS

In order to examine the systems that link administrative units with their environments, it is necessary to mark the borders that surround the conversion process and that separate it from inputs and outputs. The conversion process includes units that provide services, collect taxes, and impose regulations. Administrative units are variously termed "departments," "bureaus," "agencies," "commissions," "offices," "services," or whatever label the designers of a unit consider appropriate. In the national government, for example, we can find the *Department* of Justice, the *Office* of Education, the *Agency* for International Development, the Public Health *Service*, the *Bureau* of Indian Affairs, the Interstate Commerce *Commission*, and the Selective Service *System*. Some writers call these the "line" units of government. They are distinguished in this way from the "staff" units that serve the chief executive and help him supervise and control the administrative branch. We consider line units to be within the conversion process of administrative systems. Excluded from the conversion process and assigned to the "environment" of our conceptual framework are the chief executive, legislators, judges, and their immediate supporting staffs. On the federal level, such institutions as the Bureau of the Budget and the White House Office are considered to be part of the executive (or "presidency") and are, therefore, in the environment of the administrative system. Along with other legislative, judicial, and executive units, these provide inputs to administrative agencies. Note that we distinguish the *administrative branch* from the *executive*. The executive is described along with other political phenomena that provide direction to administrators and seek to control their activities.

Admittedly, these borders are diffuse. Some of the work of administrative units bears close resemblance to the work of executives, legislators, and judges. The heads of numerous departments in state and local governments are elected by the voters and act as the executives of their own departments, separate from the chief executive. At all levels of government, regulatory agencies are charged with the formal responsibilities of legislating—and then adjudicating—their own regulations. Some organizations serve part-time as units of public administration and part-time as members of the private sector (e.g., government contractors). Administrators do not simply carry out decisions that are made in the legislative, judicial, and executive units of government. Administrators suggest policies to members of other branches and frequently write the bills that are enacted by the legislative branch. Administrators also exercise great discretion in carrying out assignments given to them. In describing the work of administrators, we shall be dealing with persons and institutions that make their own important contributions to the policies of government.

Despite the irregularity of the borders of the conversion process, it remains a valid subject for this book. Our focus is on the "fourth branch of government": those persons and organizations that are not usually included in the simple tripartite divisions of executive, legislative, and judicial.

Within the United States—which is the primary focus of this book —there are variations in the inputs received, in the nature of conversions, and in the outputs of administrative units at different levels of government. Within each level of government, moreover, important features of administrative systems may also vary from one agency to another. The use of a systems approach does not signify uniformities in behavior. It provides a framework that assists in the identification of general tendencies and deviant cases and in the understanding of those features that produce the deviations. On some occasions, we shall employ a system that has general application to administrative units. Elsewhere, we shall refer to a system that is relevant for only a limited number of administrative units.

THE ORGANIZATION OF THIS BOOK

Although this chapter focuses on the abstract categories of administrative systems, the book itself is not devoid of the dynamic, throbbing life of politics. Later chapters deal with the support given administrators by the political culture of the United States; with the social backgrounds of administrators and their own views about their jobs; with efforts they make to influence policy; with conflicts between administrative units that are ostensibly the subordinates of a common chief executive; and with methods that officials use to make decisions when their environment precludes a "rational" procedure. The systems framework shows itself most clearly in the book's overall structure.

Three consecutive chapters examine aspects of the conversion process; three chapters examine inputs; and two concluding chapters deal with outputs and feedback. Before these, however, a second introductory chapter explores the use of comparative research as an adjunct to the systems framework. It reports on comparsions of administrative systems within the United States and on comparisons of American administrative systems with some foreign examples. As noted above, understanding of the administrative system is not complete. The test of the systems framework for this book lies in the amount of clarity it brings to the subject, in the success with which it indicates important relationships among various components of the system, and—ultimately—in whatever research it provokes which helps to clarify some features of the system which presently are subjects of speculation or insufficient evidence.

2

COMPARISON IN THE STUDY
OF PUBLIC ADMINISTRATION

This book focuses on administrative systems within the United States. By concentrating on domestic materials, we can obtain depth of coverage. As a result, we must—albeit regrettably—sacrifice breadth in our treatment of the subject. Such a focus does not reflect any negative assessment of the rich and growing field of cross-cultural comparative public administration. The systems framework supports—and indeed requires—comparative analysis. Many studies compare administrative activities in various settings—both within the context of a single country and among different countries. By means of comparative studies, we see, for example, how administrators respond to different kinds of inputs and how outputs vary with the nature of administrative activities. This chapter illustrates some of the advantages that come to political scientists if they compare different administrative systems within the United States. It then examines briefly some features of administrative systems throughout the world. Some evidence suggests that certain features of environments have important influences on administrative units the world over.

A focus on the administrative systems within the national, state, and local governments of the United States does not signify any parochial attachment to the boundaries of this country. The inputs to and outputs from American public administration are global in scope. This is most apparent in the fields of diplomacy, international aid, and military policy. In other programs whose clientele are more uniformly domestic, there are also international inputs and outputs. In 1968, about 9 percent of the civilian employees of the federal government were stationed outside of the U.S. The U.S. Public Health Service concerns itself with diseases throughout the world. The U.S. Office of Education sponsors research into the educational programs of other countries—partly as an aid program for educators in those countries and partly to acquire information for this country about teaching techniques that have been developed elsewhere. Below the federal level, city planners and transportation experts study public housing and mass transit operations in cities throughout the world. They do this to broaden their knowledge of alternatives at home. It frequently happens that administrative actions have both international *and* domestic repercussions. This is certainly the case with research and development programs for weapons for the military. A new venture in this field gives signals to foreign governments about possible changes in our weapons strength and about likely offensive or defensive strategies; and such a venture simultaneously provides massive economic rewards to the American communities in which the weapons will be manufactured or based. One of the most controversial policy issues that connects administrative, political, and industrial sectors both within the United States and overseas concerns the "military-industrial complex." This is an alleged web of interconnected ambitions which is said to impel the United States toward high levels of military expenditure and dangerous international arms competition. Behind these expenditures, supposedly, are alliances of industrialists who want the profits to be made from building weapons, politicians who want military bases or industrial payrolls for their constituencies, party leaders who want the best "defense plank" for their candidates, and military officers who want power. (See below pp. 185–86.)

COMPARATIVE ANALYSIS OF ADMINISTRATIVE SYSTEMS IN THE U.S.

Within its domestic focus, this book makes a concerted effort to utilize the comparative method of analysis. As much as possible, it draws upon studies that are explicitly comparative in their examination of administrative processes in several agencies of the federal government or in several states or localities.

The comparative method indicates differences in form and process within varying contexts; identifies the range across which administrative phenomena vary; and demonstrates the patterns whereby certain features of administrative systems tend to occur together. As a result of comparative analysis, for example, we have learned a great deal about the influence of economic conditions—a feature of the environment—over the kinds of outputs that administrative agencies produce.

Thomas R. Dye provides the clearest statement of the argument that the level of economic development within a jurisdiction affects the nature of policy outputs.[1] The characteristics of the economy affect both the resources that can be made available to policy-makers and the demands for services that come to policy-makers from the environment. Dye and several other scholars have examined the impact of the economy on the policies of American state and local governments. High levels of economic development (measured by such items as the percentage of the state population living in urban areas, per capita personal income, median education level, and industrial employment) generally occur in states that show high levels of expenditures and service outputs in the fields of education, welfare, and health. (Service outputs in these fields are measured by teacher salaries, the rates of pupil attendance in schools, success on national examinations, average welfare benefits, and the incidence of medical facilities.) Economic development may provide the wherewithal to purchase these services, or may increase the service-demands of clientele groups.

In contrast to these findings, however, are results in the fields of highways and natural resources. In these two areas, economic development is inversely associated with levels of spending and services (as measured by completed miles of highway and by the magnitude of state wildlife and state park activities). That is, *high* levels of expenditures and service-outputs occur in states that have *low* levels of income, education, urbanization, and industrialization. Explanations are tentative and, in some cases, conflicting. Highway and natural-resource programs may draw their impetus from long distances between population centers and from wide-open spaces. The politics of rural states may facilitate the use of "pork barrel" or "log-rolling" techniques to authorize a dense network of roads between scattered settlements. In contrast, congestion produced by industrialization and urbanization may render highway construction prohibitively expensive and politically controversial. On the other hand, because urban

---

[1] Thomas R. Dye, *Politics, Economics, and the Public: Policy Outcomes in the American States* (Chicago: Rand McNally, 1966). See also Richard E. Dawson and James A. Robinson, "Inter-party Competition, Economic Variables, and Welfare Policies in the American States," *Journal of Politics*, 25 (May, 1963), 265–89; Richard I. Hofferbert, "The Relation between Public Policy and Some Structural and Environmental Variables in the American States," *American Political Science Review*, 60 (March, 1966), 73–82; and Ira Sharkansky, "Regionalism, Economic Status and the Public Policies of American States," *Social Science Quarterly*, 49 (June, 1968), 9–26.

highways transport many vehicles more efficiently than rural highways, industrialization and urbanization may actually reduce the cost
of roads that are adequate for demands.

Some additional research has examined the influence of the economy on policy under varying conditions. It finds that the economy
varies in its influence over outputs. This variation occurs among
different levels of government, at different periods of time, among
different kinds of public services, and at different levels of affluence.
One finding is that economic development has greater influence on the
outputs of local governments than it does on the outputs of state
governments.[2] Differences in economic resources and fiscal opportunities help to explain the fact that local governments have a greater
dependence on economic resources within their jurisdiction. Most
local governments must draw upon a narrowly-limited geographical
area for resources; in addition, they are confined to only one major
revenue source (the property tax) which of itself generates a great
deal of political controversy. State governments draw upon their
larger jurisdiction and can transfer resources from "have" to "have-
not" communities. State officials also have wider revenue options that
include taxes on income and retail sales. The state income tax and
sales tax appear to be less upsetting politically than is the local
property tax; and the state taxes appear to be less vulnerable to an
economic recession. As a result, state officials can escape many of the
constraints on policy which seem to originate in the economic sector
and to limit the policy discretion of local government officials. Among
the states, it appears that economy-policy relationships are *least important* in the middle-range of states whose economic conditions are
most similar and moderately wealthy. Under these conditions, peculiarities in non-economic inputs seem most important in determining
the kinds of policies that are produced. At the extremes of poverty,
state governments seem tightly confined by the small amount of
resources that are available. At the upper end of the economic spectrum, state governments may find it easy to pay for the varied demands of their residents, and they tend to meet those demands with
generous expenditures and service-outputs.[3] Officials of the national

---

[2] Compare the findings reported in Harvey E. Brazer, *City Expenditures in
the United States* (New York: National Bureau of Economic Research, 1959),
with those in Ira Sharkansky, *Spending in the American States* (Chicago: Rand
McNally, 1968), Chapter 4.

[3] John G. Grumm, "Structural Determinants of Legislative Output," a
paper presented at the Conference on the Measurement of Policies in the
American States, Inter-University Consortium for Political Research, Ann Arbor,
Michigan, 1968.

government do not appear to be hindered by economic constraints, partly because of their power to tax the resources of the wealthy areas of the country and partly because of their ability to borrow in the face of current deficits in the taxing-spending balance. Indeed, the national government operates numerous programs to control levels of employment, interest, and wages and, therefore, may be as much the master as the subordinate of the economy.

Presently, the influence of economic conditions on state and local government policies appears to be diminishing.[4] Policy-makers now have more opportunities to spend at levels above the "norm" for their economic conditions. Some of this increased flexibility may reflect growth in magnitude of federal aids. By transferring resources from "have" to "have-not" jurisdictions, federal grants-in-aid make up for some of the differentials among the states. Also, state and local governments now have a more flexible tax structure. With state taxes on personal incomes and/or retail sales now used by over 40 of the states (whereas no state used either tax at the beginning of the century) and with numerous local governments now also turning to these forms of taxation, policy-makers can tap an increasing proportion of the resources within their own jurisdictions. Even the poorest states (e.g., Mississippi, South Carolina, Arkansas, Vermont) have some pockets of wealth that can help support services in their poorest counties.

It is also apparent that economic conditions exercise less of a constraint on some kinds of policy than upon others. The political saliency of a policy is one of the factors that can lessen the influence of economics. To the extent that programs are made the subject of prominent disputes among individual candidates and political parties, such programs can provoke the use of substantially more resources than is normally associated with the jurisdiction's level of wealth. Officials "try harder" under the impetus of public demand. Under different conditions—when public sentiment runs counter to a program—there is less performance than would be expected on the basis of economic conditions.[5]

Another line of research examines the impact of economic resources as they affect different features of public policy: the *total*

---

[4] Alan K. Campbell and Seymour Sachs, *Metropolitan America: Fiscal Patterns and Governmental Systems* (New York: Free Press of Glencoe, 1967), p. 57.

[5] See Charles F. Cnudde and Donald J. McCrone, "Party Competition and Welfare Policies in the American States," *American Political Science Review,* 63 (September, 1969), 858–66; and Ira Sharkansky and Richard I. Hofferbert, "Dimensions of State Politics, Economics and Public Policy," *American Political Science Review,* 63 (September, 1969), 867–79.

service output of a jurisdiction and the *distribution of service benefits* among different income groups. The magnitude of resources in a jurisdiction seems to affect the total volume of benefits produced, more than it affects the distribution of these benefits to residents of different income groups.[6] We can speculate that policy-makers are sensitive to the total resources available when facing such issues as the number of teachers to be hired, the number of schoolrooms to be built, the miles of highway to be constructed, the number of acres to be purchased for state parks, or the amount of money to be spent on public welfare. Policy-makers may be more sensitive to non-economic political constraints when they consider questions of distribution: where to assign the teachers or to build the schoolrooms, which sites to select for the highways or the parks, or how much to pay different classes of welfare recipients.

Such findings about the influence of economic conditions upon the outputs of administrative systems may apply only to the United States, or they may also apply to analogous situations in other countries. The findings can be expressed in an interrogative fashion that would permit cross-national tests. Are the administrative units of national governments less constrained by economic conditions than are those of local or regional governments—owing to the greater jurisdiction of the national governments, to their opportunity to redistribute resources from "have" to "have-not" areas, or to their opportunity to exercise greater controls over their own economic development? Has the influence of economic conditions over policy declined in recent years—perhaps with increases in wealth and technological capacity? Does the politicization of an issue make policy decisions less dependent on economic resources? Are economic conditions less influential on the outputs of administrative systems among the middle economic range of countries, than in those countries that are at the extreme of affluence or poverty?[7] Does the total volume of economic resources in a country exercise more influence over the total outputs of its administrative systems than over the distribution of those outputs among high- and low-income groups? Questions of this detail have not been addressed in a sophisticated fashion in cross-national comparisons of administrative systems.

---

[6] Thomas R. Dye, "Income Inequality and American State Politics," *American Political Science Review*, 63 (March, 1969), 157–62; and Bryan Frye and Richard Winter, "The Politics of Redistribution," *American Political Science Review*, 64 (June, 1970).

[7] See Marvin E. Olsen, "Multivariate Analysis of National Political Development," *American Sociological Review*, 33 (October, 1968), 699–711.

COMPARATIVE ANALYSIS ACROSS NATIONAL BOUNDARIES

The remaining pages of this chapter employ the comparative method across national borders. These comparisons will not be as detailed as are those among American units to be found in this or in later chapters of the book. In part, this limitation is included by design. We hope to maintain the focus and depth of a domestic analysis. In part, too, the limitation is fixed by the lack of cross-national information. Although the field of comparative administration has progressed far in recent years, it has not yet provided the thoroughness or breadth of coverage that is available from intra-national comparisons.

This brief cross-national comparison provides some of the same benefits as are furnished by the more thorough domestic comparisons. It identifies the global range of differences in some administrative forms and processes. This exercise should convince the reader that there is nothing "natural" or "universal" about American public administration. It also suggests the utility of a systems framework for cross-national comparison. As in domestic analysis, the systems ordering of environment, inputs, outputs, conversion, and feedback can highlight the features of administrative systems which are related to one another. With this type of knowledge, we can gain some understanding of the processes that might bring about changes in administrative forms or procedures or in the outputs that administrative units provide to their clients.

At the present, comparative public administration has not progressed so far in its cross-national investigations as to define the numerous linkages that exist between administrative features and their environment. However, there is one environmental characteristic that often seems important to the nature of public administration: the level of "development." For many countries, the character of public administration corresponds with the place at which a society exists on a continuum of development.[8]

"Development" is a complicated concept. It is not a tangible commodity that a country either has or does not have. As the term is

---

[8] A number of labels have appeared for the "less-developed" countries. Some of the most common alternatives include "emergent," "transitional," "developing," and "expectant"; "underdeveloped" seems no longer popular, perhaps because it carries the onus of a connotation of permanence. Terms suggesting movement toward some more-developed stage seem to be the most acceptable.

used in the literature, it refers to an aggregate of economic, social, and political variables, each of which exists on a continuum ranging from less- to more-developed. An individual country may simultaneously exhibit some traits that appear to be developed and others that appear to be less-developed. Some features of public administration may likewise appear developed, while others in the same country—indeed in the same capital city—may resemble the administrative features of a less-developed country. At each pole of the development continuum there are differences in public administration that do not reflect the stage of development as much as they reflect peculiar historical experiences or cultural traits. Great Britain, France, Germany, and the United States, for example, are currently at about the same stage of advanced development. However, each of these nations demonstrates peculiarities in public administration that reflect its own evolution. The correspondence between development and public administration is not so close as to preclude other variables from having influence on administration. Development may not be so powerful a force that it controls the nature of administrative change in a society against counter-influences from cultural norms. Thus, a nation might experience development in its economy without seeing its administrative processes move toward the models developed in Western Europe or the United States. The discussion below shows the gross administrative differences between more- and less-developed societies and also presents some crucial differences within each major category.

Social scientists tend to disagree among themselves about the characteristics of development. To some, it is equated with the capacity to produce large amounts of tangible resources in relation to size of population—translated into industrial output, agricultural produce, raw materials, gross national product, and personal income. Others focus not so much on material production as on the forms of social and economic organization. They argue that *development* exists in societies that utilize *modern technology;* that assign rewards according to *personal achievement* and not according to family, caste, or tribal background; that use *specialists* in economic and governmental roles, instead of generalists who must provide their headship in a full range of activities; and that have governmental units that *can adjust* to social or economic change and acquire "new capabilities" to meet new demands.[9]

Each trait of development is a distinct variable. However, many

---

[9] The remainder of this chapter relies on materials in Ferrel Heady, *Public Administration: A Comparative Perspective* (Englewood Cliffs, N.J.: Prentice-Hall, 1966).

countries that score more-developed on one variable also score more-developed on other variables. Thus, the dimensions of development seem to reinforce one another. For example, the uses of sophisticated technologies seem to impel a society toward specialization and toward the distribution of rewards according to the criteria of personal achievement. Where there are complicated programs of medicine, agriculture, or industry, it appears to be necessary to allocate much of the educational resources to the training of technicians and professionals. In such a context, it is incongruous to give prestige and political power to religious and tribal leaders and not to those who have mastered both the sophisticated technologies and the large-scale organizations that seem to accompany these technologies. Also, in such a context, government units must be adaptive—partly to help supply the capital necessary for investments in sophisticated biological or physical engineering and partly to provide new social services to the individuals who are affected adversely by the changes in life style and family structure that accompany industrialization and urbanization.

Despite the tendency toward a clustering of the development characteristics, each of the most well-developed nations also shows some features of less-developed societies. Each has experienced some civil strife that reflects an inability to resolve the intense demands of certain social groups. Moreover, each has some "backward" regions that have been bypassed by some of the organizational traits and material wealth of development.

ADMINISTRATIVE SYSTEMS IN MORE-DEVELOPED COUNTRIES

When writers describe well-developed nations, they generally think about the most modern countries of Western Europe and about those elsewhere that have followed European models. The list typically includes Great Britain, France, Germany, the United States, Scandinavia, "white" nations of the British Commonwealth (Canada, Australia, New Zealand), and perhaps the Soviet Union, South Africa, Japan, and Israel. The features that are generally shared by these countries include the following:

1. The organization of government is patterned after the organization of the private sector, in the sense that there is a high degree of task-specialization and that roles are assigned according to the personal achievements of individuals rather than according to family status or social class.

2. Political decisions and legal judgments are made according to secular standards of rationality; traditional (e.g., religious or tribal) elites have lost any real power to affect major governmental decisions.

3. Government activity extends over a wide range of public and personal affairs; and it tends toward further expansion into all major spheres.

4. Popular interest and involvement in public affairs is widespread.

5. Those persons who occupy positions of political or governmental leadership are widely viewed as legitimate holders of those positions, and transfers of leadership tend to occur according to prescribed, orderly procedures.

Some of these five characteristics have counterparts in the nature of the public bureaucracies of more-developed nations:

1. The bureaucracy is large and has numerous, distinct subunits. Many of these units require highly specialized employees, and together they represent the full range of occupational specializations that are found in the society. This reflects both task-specialization and the wide range of government activities.

2. The bureaucracy tends to accept policy directions that come from other branches of government. This reflects both task-specialization and the legitimacy of elected officials.

3. The bureaucracy is considered to be professional, both by its own members and by other participants in the policy process. Professionalization is a sign of specialization among bureaucrats. It reveals itself in the educational requirements used by the bureaucrats when selecting new recruits and also in the acceptance by legislators and by the chief executive of policy information and recommendations provided by the bureaucracy.

Among the well-developed nations, there are considerable differences in bureaucratic forms and procedures which reflect peculiar historical experiences. One writer has likened public administration in France and Germany and has contrasted it with that in Great Britain and the United States.[10] Officials in the upper levels of French and German administration have achieved a distinct status, separate from other occupational groups in their societies. They undergo a long period of training in elite institutions of higher education. This train-

---

[10] Heady, pp. 44ff.

ing helps to maintain both the historic upper-class backgrounds of public officials and the anti-democratic bias in their norms. The separateness of public administration is enforced even further by elaborate procedures for administrative self-government. The recruiting of new officials is controlled by the administrators themselves; and upper-echelon administrators are selected by promotion from within the career service. Each of these countries has a system of administrative courts that is distinct from the civil-court system. Administrative courts hear charges brought against administrative actions by private citizens and charges brought by administrators themselves concerning their rank, salary, or pension.

In Great Britain and the United States, the tradition is to avoid any clear separation between public administrators and other occupational groups. In contrast to the continental model of distinctive training for high-level administrative positions, the British and American services recruit from persons with a generalized training. In some details of their selection procedures, however, the British and Americans diverge from one another. The British select recruits from among the graduates of elite universities, but not from curricula specifically designed for professional administrators. Graduates in literature or the classics have traditionally been favored by essay examinations in general knowledge. By contrast, Americans have a Jacksonian tradition that any citizen is fit to perform the chores of a public employee. Related to this is the practice—still observed in numerous state and local governments and for some federal positions—of filling government jobs on the basis of political appointments without regard to the details of a candidate's training. Both Britain and the United States have moved toward selection procedures that emphasize specialized competence in the administrative tasks to be performed. Yet neither has approached the French and German models of elite training schools for professional administrators, and neither emphasizes the distinctiveness of a government career to the extent emphasized by the French and Germans. In Britain or the United States, there is no pervasive concern among public officials to distinguish their rank and status from those of the citizen, and there are no separate administrative courts. On the matter of "distance" from the population, however, there are some important differences between the United States and Britain. By tradition, British civil servants have more typically come from the upper social class, while in America some effort has been made to ensure that civil servants are "representative" of the population. The British generally appoint high-level administrators from within the ranks of the civil service. At both federal and state levels in the United States, however, many high-level administrative positions are filled with "outsiders." American executives in government and in the private sector believe that the "transient" business-government administrator can infuse the government bureaucracy with an innovative stimulus from outside.

Some differences in British-American administrative practices seem to reflect differences in the political structures of the two countries. Britain has a parliamentary system of government, while the United States has a separation of powers—a system of checks and balances. The British chief executive officer (Prime Minister) is selected by the House of Commons and receives the support of his party colleagues in the legislature. There is less legislative-executive conflict in Britain than in the United States, and this affects the political position of high-level administrators. In Britain, these administrators are more likely to operate behind the scenes, under the "protection" of the politician who currently heads their ministry. American administrators do not work for superiors who have the strong support of a majority party in the legislature. Thus, being more on their own, they are more likely to identify themselves publicly with a policy and to engage in public disputes with members of the legislature. It is partly for this reason that the business-government transient is helpful in the American system. Business or professional men who enter government service at high-level positions often leave after a brief period (typically less than three years) and often cite disputes with Congress as a source of their dissatisfaction. In a system of this kind which generates legislative-bureaucratic conflict, it is helpful to have a large pool of potential recruits from the business world who may replace government administrators as they are used-up by conflict with the legislature.

ADMINISTRATIVE SYSTEMS IN LESS-DEVELOPED COUNTRIES

As might be expected, more differences in administrative systems are observed among the many less-developed nations than among the relatively few societies that qualify as more-developed. In part, this is merely a result of differences in numbers. It is also a result of the diverse cultures in which these two groups are found. Almost all of the more-developed societies are in Western European countries or in countries that are tied closely to the nations of Western Europe. They shared historical experiences with one another or were settled by immigrants who brought the governmental institutions of Western Europe with them. In contrast, the developing countries reflect a global range of political cultures. Some are in Western Europe (e.g., Portugal, Spain, and perhaps Italy); but others are in Latin America, Africa, and Asia. Most of these countries experienced a period of control by the colonial powers of Western Europe; but this period was too brief or too superficial to overcome the centuries of "traditional" (i.e., pre-European) cultural evolution.

Despite the peculiarities in structures and processes in individual countries, the following traits have been observed throughout less-developed countries:

1. Among political elites, there is a widely-shared commitment to "development." This commitment often takes on ideological trappings. The package of changes that are sought may vary from one country to another, but common goals are: increase in agricultural or industrial production; increase in personal living standards; improved programs for public health, education, and individual pensions; changes in the traditional roles of women or of the lower castes; and the change of one's loyalties from a tribe to the newly conceived "nation."

2. There is a high reliance on the public sector for leadership. Many developing countries have evolved structures that have a socialist or Marxist orientation. However, it is frequently a local variety of socialism, reflecting evolution of "Marxist" doctrines outside of the European working-class context. Agriculture rather than industry is the economic base; and the people who feel oppressed have ethnic ties rather than affinity for an industrial working-class. The proposals for specific reforms differ from one country to another. However, they typically seek rapid economic development and identify government bodies as the indigenous actors most capable of generating this development and guiding it along paths that are socially desirable. As will be seen below, not all sectors of government are equally well-developed in these countries, and the incidence of trained manpower in even the most well-developed sectors is less than the country needs. The typical results include a heavy reliance on the bureaucracy and a high incidence of frustrated goals and civil unrest.

3. The society suffers from incipient or actual political instability. This instability may be a carry-over of patterns that were developed within the native movements against a colonial power. In several countries, there was not only conflict between the colonial and native forces, but also internal strife among the native leaders. In many cases the "country" was an artificial creation of the colonial power who simply combined into one administrative unit the lands of distinct tribal or ethnic groups. During the campaign for independence, or perhaps soon after independence was achieved, conflicts between

these traditional groups erupted into violent confrontations. Also contributing to violence are the frustrations associated with unmet goals for development. Many campaigns for independence are coupled with rash promises made by the new elites. However, their limited economic resources and scarce supply of skilled manpower make these promises unfulfillable. Popular disappointments provide support for still-newer leaders who challenge those who steered the course from colonialism. When economic frustrations are coupled with feelings of discrimination among members of diverse tribal, linguistic, or ethnic groups, the stimuli for violence are present. One study of 84 developing countries found successful coups or serious attempts to overthrow the government in 40 of them.[11]

4. A gap exists between the modernizing and the traditional elites. This may actually be a series of differences—in social background, in orientations toward change, and in linkages to the mass of the population. The modernizing elites tend to be urban, Western-oriented, young, well-educated, and committed to economic, social, and political change; the traditional elites tend to be rural, oriented to local customs and to the indigenous religion, and opposed to change as a threat to these values. The new elites may control the technological skills that are vital to the nation's development; but the older elites may retain the intense loyalties of people in the countryside and the urban slums. The contrasting styles and orientations of the two elites may generate severe conflict between them and their followers.

5. There is an imbalance in the development of various political features. Former colonies tend to replicate the legislative, executive, and administrative forms of the former mother country. When these forms are imposed upon the institutions of the colonial and pre-colonial periods, however, they produce a wide gulf between formal procedures and actual practices. Legislative and executive branches often lack the ability to control the civil or military bureaucracies. The new bureaucracies usually show the most rapid development, often because the departing colonial power had already begun to staff its bureaucracy with natives. The administrative organization generally receives the most well-educated members of the new elite and thereby becomes the one institution with the expertise necessary to direct a program of social and economic development. The military sector may be even more well-developed (at least in its officer corps) than the civilian administration. The combination of a weak legislature and an inefficacious chief executive, plus a professional military, often results in government take-overs that are either engineered behind the scenes

[11] Fred R. von der Mehden, *Politics of the Developing Nations* (Englewood Cliffs, N.J.: Prentice-Hall, 1964), pp. 1–2.

by the military or are led openly by military personnel. Less-developed nations throughout the world may share no one trait as much as they share the experience of having a uniformed and bemedalled chief executive who either took over the government in an overt *putsch* or used an election format (perhaps without tolerating real opposition) to obtain office.

Several traits of administrative forms and procedures in less-developed countries reflect the attributes of their environment. A number of them are clearly indicated in the previous discussion: lack of sufficient skills in the bureaucracy which are required by the regime's program of development; conflict between the decision processes expected by Westerners and the traditional relationships that are expected by some members of the indigenous elite and by many citizens; and the tendency of former colonial territories to carry over the formal administrative structures that were acquired from the departed Europeans. Two other features of less-developed public bureaucracies are typically described as "problems": pervasive corruption and a marked discrepancy between the forms and realities of administrative procedures.

The corruption that exists in the bureaucracies of less-developed countries affects both small and large decisions and involves proportionately minor and major resources. It includes the small bribe that officials expect in exchange for "expediting" a decision on behalf of an individual; the willingness of officials to evade formal personnel procedures to hire their own relatives or fellow tribesmen; and the massive bribes from foreign investors that assure a favorable decision about mining rights, a utility monopoly, or a commercial concession. In some cases this corruption is so taken for granted that it is defended as "part of the system"—without which officials could not justify their decisions. Nepotism or tribal favoritism is a carry-over from traditional values and may disappear only when the norms that support them are no longer viable. The truly massive corruption may, in contrast, be a product of the colonial experience when outside investors bought concessions from traditional elites.

A discrepancy between form and reality is frequently the product of a combination of insufficient administrative resources and excessive aspirations. Governments establish procedures to resemble those observed in the capital city of the former colonial power or those prescribed by visiting American advisors. This trait has been labelled "formalism."[12] It has obvious implications for the citizens and elites of

---

[12] Fred W. Riggs, *Administration in Developing Countries: The Theory of Prismatic Society* (Boston: Houghton Mifflin, 1964), p. 12.

less-developed countries; it means that announced procedures may provide no reliable guidelines about the service to be rendered. Formalism rewards those who learn the informal procedures of administration and frustrates those who rest personal aspirations on the public promises of the government. Formalism also has important implications for the student of comparative administration. It means that he cannot accept as similar (or "comparable") institutions those which carry similar labels in different countries. An Interior Ministry may not only be—as in more-developed countries—the superstructure of the police service, but may also represent the single most powerful unit in the bureaucracy (perhaps excepting the army) and may even stand as the selector of the chief executive. The leading political party may not simply be the organization that currently has control of major government offices, but may also be the only real vehicle that integrates the programs of leading figures in the army, the civilian bureaucracy, and other branches of the government.

Since it can be misleading to compare administrative—and other governmental—institutions among less-developed countries merely on the basis of their labels, it is necessary to make comparisons according to the "functions" that various organs contribute to the political system. Gabriel Almond has suggested a series of functions that might serve as the framework of comparative analysis. His principal functions are: political socialization and recruitment; interest articulation; interest aggregation; political communication; rule-making; rule application; and rule adjudication.[13] To some, this list depends too much on the American pattern of legislative, executive, and judicial branches; to others is so general as to be of little help in clarifying issues for comparison among the less-developed countries. Fred W. Riggs suggests more detailed kinds of functions that might be examined comparatively within less-developed nations: the creation of agricultural markets; price-setting; and the establishing of quality standards for agricultural produce. According to Riggs, comparative-administration specialists should define features that coexist with various functional behaviors with the intent of understanding why various administrative units come to perform the kinds—and qualities—of functions that they do.[14]

The problem of formalism may also limit the extent to which the systems framework developed in this book lends itself to cross national comparisons. Recall from Chapter 1 (pp. 11–12) that the boundaries of our conversion process include administrative units found within

[13] Gabriel Almond and G. Bingham Powell, *Comparative Politics: A Developmental Approach* (Boston: Little, Brown, 1966), Chapter 2.
[14] Riggs, pp. 31ff.

the executive branch of national, state, and local governments in the United States. In order to compare the American conversion processes with those found elsewhere, it would be necessary to identify comparable units of public administration. This should be possible in most of the more-developed countries where there is a correspondence between the form and procedures within government structures. Even in the case of parliamentary governments, where the executive and legislative branches are merged to some extent, it should be possible to separate the "line" units of the administration and compare them and their environments with counterparts in the United States. In the case of many less-developed countries, however, the functions of "administration" as we know it here may not actually be performed in those units that are labelled as the line departments of government.

It would be misleading to end this discussion without asserting that a wide variety of administrative forms and procedures—both formal and informal—can be found among less-developed countries. As in the case of the more-developed countries, there is not a perfect correspondence between development and administrative forms and processes. Many factors peculiar to each country's history can shape its bureaucracy. Ferrel Heady suggests several categories of administrative types within the less-developed countries. The labels that he uses for some of these categories suggest the differences to be found within them: Traditional-autocratic; Bureaucratic Elite; Polyarchal Competitive; and Dominant-party Mobilization.[15]

Traditional-autocratic

This type is traditional in its style of rule, with dominant political elites drawn from families with monarchic or aristocratic status. Little economic progress and—unlike other less-developed societies—little commitment toward such development are expressed by the political elite. They rely on the military and civil bureaucracy to provide those changes in policy which are considered desirable and to inhibit those demands which are considered undesirable. Countries in this category include: Yemen, Saudi Arabia, Afghanistan, Morocco, Iran, Cambodia, Laos, Paraguay, Peru, Ethiopia, and Libya.

Bureaucratic Elite

In this type of system, traditional elites have been displaced from effective power, although they may retain some presence (perhaps as

---

[15] Heady, Chapter 6.

a figurehead monarch). Popular political participation is severely limited. Modernizing goals are proclaimed by leadership groups, but are not embraced by the general public. Political power is largely in the hands of the civil and military bureaucracy. Military officials are usually more prominent and are in positions of highest power, often as a result of having led a coup against the prior regime. However, the military depends on civil bureaucracy to carry out nonmilitary developmental projects. Countries in this category include: Burma, Guatemala, Indonesia, Iraq, Nicaragua, Pakistan, Paraguay, South Korea, Sudan, Syria, and Thailand.

Polyarchal Competitive

This form of system has political structures that resemble the models of Western Europe and the United States with respect to popular participation, free elections, interest-oriented parties, and policy-making authority granted to representative government institutions. However, there are occasional interruptions by military interventions, or there are other such lapses in representative government. Typically, these interruptions are claimed to be only temporary. The *poly*archal label denotes the existence of several political elites whose base of power may be spread among urban merchants, landlords, military officers, labor leaders, and professionals. There is greater social mobility than in the more traditional societies. Due to competing parties' search for "consensus," government programs emphasize "pragmatic" policies that are easy to understand and offer short-range benefits in such fields as education, welfare, and health. Countries included in this category are: Philippines, Malaysia, Jamaica, Chile, Costa Rica, Israel, Lebanon, Greece, Argentina, Brazil, Ceylon, Nigeria, and Turkey.

Dominant-party Mobilization

Within this type, there is little permissiveness in politics. The dominant party may be the only legal party, and it may assure its position with coercive techniques. There is usually a doctrinaire ideology and mass demonstrations of loyalty to the government. The elite group tends to be young, urban, well-educated, and secular. Often a charismatic leader dominates the entire movement in which the programs stress nationalism and development. A well-trained civil service is essential for the developmental goals of the regime; but there is frequent tension between the technical and professional people in the bureaucracy and the politicians who insist on the primacy of nationalism and loyalty to the current regime. Countries in this category include: Algeria, Bolivia, Egypt, Ghana, Guinea, Mali, and Tunisia.

It remains to be tested how closely the administrative structures, procedures, and outputs of the countries in each of these categories resembles other political, social, or economic features. Admittedly, the designations are loosely conceived. Insofar as some countries are put in more than one category, the categories are not mutually exclusive. The categories may be more useful as illustrations of variety among less-developed administrative systems than as tools for rigorous comparative analysis.

SUMMARY

The concentration on public administration within the United States should facilitate an in-depth coverage of this material. This choice should not disparage the exciting and rapidly growing field of comparative administration, nor should it suggest that the American model is any more "natural" or worthy of emulation than are those in other countries. The systems approach to the subject encourages comparisons. Throughout this book, we make an effort to employ the results of comparative research carried out *within* the United States. This permits us to identify some differences in structures and procedures among agencies of the federal, state, and local governments. In some cases, we can identify certain influences from the social, economic, or political environments that shape the administrative structures or procedures, or we can identify certain influences that administrative structures or procedures exert on other features of politics or the economy.

We have found that characteristics of economic development seem important for aspects of the administrative system. There is a growing body of political-science literature that shows the influence of economic development on outputs within the United States. When looking at administrative systems around the world, it is helpful to compare the more- and the less-developed countries. There are complex disputes—that this chapter has not attempted to settle—about the nature of "development" and about the place of individual countries on several measures of development. This chapter has attempted to illustrate the range of variations in public administration throughout the world and to suggest the importance of development as one influence that helps to shape variations.

Part One

THE CONVERSION PROCESS OF THE ADMINISTRATIVE SYSTEM

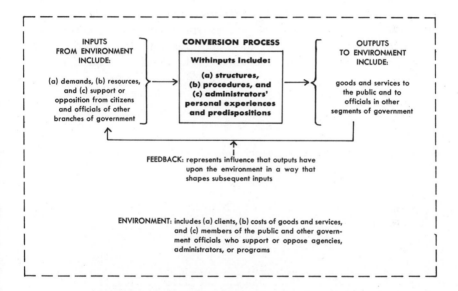

INPUTS FROM ENVIRONMENT INCLUDE:	CONVERSION PROCESS	OUTPUTS TO ENVIRONMENT INCLUDE:
(a) demands, (b) resources, and (c) support or opposition from citizens and officials of other branches of government	**Withinputs include:** **(a) structures,** **(b) procedures, and** **(c) administrators'** **personal experiences** **and predispositions**	goods and services to the public and to officials in other segments of government

FEEDBACK: represents influence that outputs have upon the environment in a way that shapes subsequent inputs

ENVIRONMENT: includes (a) clients, (b) costs of goods and services, and (c) members of the public and other government officials who support or oppose agencies, administrators, or programs

Chapters 3, 4, and 5 deal with the conversion process of the administrative system. The borders of the conversion process include the "line" agencies of government. These are variously termed "departments," "agencies," "administrative units," or "bureaus." As in the general literature, we use these terms interchangeably. One exception occurs in Chapter 4, where the terminology of the national government is used in distinguishing cabinet departments from other administrative units.

The order of these chapters is somewhat arbitrary and may be shifted at the option of the reader. Chapter 3 examines decision-making in administrative units. This topic is central to the systems framework. These decisions respond to inputs and withinputs; and they help to shape the outputs of the system. It is for this reason that the chapter on decision-making is placed at the beginning of this section. After reading Chapter 3, a student should be sensitized to the central position of administrative agencies in this system and should be more appreciative of subsequent discussions about other features of the agencies and about the inputs and outputs they receive from and send to their environment.

Chapter 4 deals with structures of administrative agencies and with control mechanisms that link the agencies with the legislative and executive branches. If a student is uncertain about what administrative agencies are or about where they fit into the larger governmental structures, he would be advised to look early at Chapter 4.

Chapter 5 considers administrators themselves. It inquires into the procedures used to select persons for policy-making positions in administrative agencies and then inquires into the nature of the persons who are selected, i.e., their backgrounds, personalities, and values.

3

DECISION-MAKING IN
ADMINISTRATIVE AGENCIES

Personnel in administrative units cope with the inputs from their environment and the withinputs existing in agencies by making decisions. As noted in Chapter 1, inputs are the stimuli from the environment of the administrative system which affect the decisions of administrators, and withinputs are stimuli that originate in the administrative organizations themselves. Inputs include such items as the demands of citizens and of members of the executive, legislative, and judicial branches of government. Withinputs include the formal rules of administrative agencies, the informal relations among members of the agencies, and the personal and professional norms that govern the actions of each administrator. *Decisions* are choices from among alternative courses of action; they help to shape the outputs that the units produce. The decisions in administrative agencies lie at the focus of our interest. They affect the contributions that administrative agencies make to political, social, and economic phenomena in their environment and that administrative agencies extract from their environment.

Note the careful choice of words in the opening paragraph. Administrators' decisions "help to shape" outputs; and they "affect" the transactions between administrative agencies and their environment. Administrators' decisions themselves are not the only outputs of an agency and are not alone in defining transactions between agencies and their environment. It is an oversimplification of systems analysis to say that the decisions within the conversion process are themselves the outputs. In the case of administrative systems, outputs reflect the interaction of many different decisions by administrators, of other withinputs of the conversion process, and of the social, economic, and political features in the environment. We shall return to this point when we discuss outputs in Chapter 10. Here it is sufficient to warn the reader that we are dealing with actions *within* the conversion process of the administrative system and not with the interface where those decisions encounter the environment.

Administrators are not free to make whatever decisions suit their fancy. To understand their decisions is not simply to understand the personal predilections that lead an agency official to make a certain choice. Administrators are subject to numerous demands and severe constraints. These include:

(*a*) The regard for public administrators in the political culture and the specific attitudes which citizens hold about public programs and government employees;

(*b*) Demands, resources, and political support from individual citizens, political parties, and interest groups;

(*c*) Demands, resources, and political support from the legislative, executive, and judicial branches of government;

(*d*) Demands, resources, and political support which come from individuals and institutions in other governments, through "vertical" or "horizontal" intergovernmental relations;

(*e*) The social backgrounds, skills, and values of the administrators themselves; and

(*f*) The structures, procedures, and precedents of administrative units.

The sheer number and variety of inputs and withinputs complicate the task of agency decision-makers. No simple procedure for making decisions can accommodate the factors that might be taken into consideration. In an effort to detail this complexity, we first describe a purely "rational" model of decision-making which urges administrators to "take everything into consideration." Then we identify several features that frustrate this kind of rationalism. Finally, we report some decision procedures that have evolved in various administrative units. These do not meet the standards of the purely rational model. Indeed, they are attractive to administrators partly because they permit administrators to ignore certain factors and thus to simplify choices.

A MODEL OF RATIONAL DECISION-MAKING AND ITS SHORTCOMINGS

Rationality is a value that has wide respect in our culture. As might be expected, public administrators like to be as rational as the rest of us. Certainly they are not going to admit that they make decisions "irrationally" or without taking into consideration all important issues. However, the demands of a completely rational decision are severe. It is costly to be perfectly rational, and few administrators seem to have sufficient resources to meet the price. It is unfair, however, to accuse administrators of making irrational decisions. This term implies that they make their choices in an undisciplined fashion, without paying heed to many of the considerations that most observers would consider to be important. As we unfold our description of administrative decision-making, we see that it is neither completely rational nor irrational. Complete rationality is an unattainable goal for administrative decision-makers in all but the most simple kinds of problems.[1] Yet most of their decisions appear to be disciplined and to be made after an assessment of several important issues.

We cannot extend this discussion further without a clear understanding of a rational model for decision-making. As noted above, this is a demanding model, against which the decisions of most administrative units score less than pure. According to one common formulation, a rational decision-maker would:

1. Identify his problem;
2. Clarify his goals, and then rank them as to their importance;
3. List all possible means—or policies—for achieving each of his goals;
4. Assess all the costs of and the benefits that would seem to follow from each of the alternative policies; and
5. Select the package of goals and associated policies that would bring the greatest relative benefits and the least relative disadvantages.[2]

Decision-makers who follow these procedures should inform themselves about all possible opportunities and all possible consequences

[1] Herbert Simon, *Administrative Behavior* (New York: Macmillan, 1961), p. 70.
[2] Charles E. Lindblom, *The Policy-Making Process* (Englewood Cliffs, N.J.: Prentice-Hall, 1968), p. 13.

of each opportunity. This is an enormous assignment. It assumes that an administrative agency has vast resources that can be used to gather intelligence about the environment and about the capabilities of the agency itself. It also assumes that personnel are sufficiently uncommitted to—or against—any one set of goals or policies and, thus, can make their decisions on the basis of information that is systematically collected. This rational decision-making model seems inappropriate for most public agencies which are under pressure to produce policies quickly and which operate in environments that impose commitments upon them. Political demands require that certain goals and policies be favored in agency deliberations and that other goals and policies be avoided. There are five major features of public administrative systems that block the fulfillment of rational decision-making by personnel in administrative units. These are:

1. The multitude of problems, goals, and policy commitments that are imposed on—or kept from—decision-makers by actors in the environment of an administrative unit;
2. Barriers to collecting adequate information about the variety of "acceptable" goals and policies;
3. The personal needs, commitments, inhibitions, and inadequacies of decision-makers which interfere in their assessment of goals and policies that are acceptable from their agency's point of view;
4. Structural difficulties within administrative units and involving their relations with legislative and executive branches of government; and
5. The deviant behavior of individual administrators.

These five items are not entirely separable. Each includes some features that are also apparent in others. However, each has been the subject of separate inquiries and has been shown to impose its own set of limitations on decision-makers who might—in an ideal world—desire to make rational choices. Aspects of Item 1 and Item 4 are inputs that affect decision-making in administrative units. The remainder are withinputs that operate largely within the borders of an administrative unit.

The Multitude of Problems, Goals, and Policy Commitments

This barrier to rational decision-making is actually a combination of two factors: the variety of problems and goals that can probably be selected as the target of administrative activity; and the commitments in the environment of an administrative agency that preclude a thorough assessment of each possible goal. Frequently, the full range of possibilities that are open to an agency are so great that even the task of defining one's problem (Step 1 in the sequence of rational decision-making) is obscured by the variety. A problem will, presumably, be signalled by difficulties perceived in the agency's environment. However, the difficulties perceived may not translate themselves directly into defined problems. One stumbling block may occur when officials try to distill a conception of "problems" from the "symptoms" which they see. What are the problems that lie beneath urban riots, student unrest, or protest meetings directed at American foreign policy? Are each of these symptoms to be treated by the selection of specific goals and policies? Are they indeed symptoms of underlying difficulties which are themselves the problems to be treated? If there are underlying problems, what are they? Is there a common problem which generates each of these symptoms? If there is a common problem, the way in which it is defined has important implications for which agencies will deal with the problem and how they will define goals and policies with respect to the problem. It can be a problem of dissatisfaction with the foreign policy of the national government; a problem of elementary, secondary, and higher education that is not adequately designed to meet the needs of certain clients; or a loss in the basic sense of community that once may have united the country. Each of these diagnoses has been made by observers of the contemporary scene. Without agreement as to the problem(s) that lies beneath perceived difficulties, it is not feasible to move through the goal- and policy-selection steps of a rational decision-making sequence. Problem-definition is, at best, a difficult and ambiguous process. Problems do not exist in reality, but must be defined through a process of observing, assessing, and abstracting from reality. This is done while under the influence of an agency's prior experiences and commitments. Thus, the process is somewhat less than "rational."

Once a problem is defined, there are additional difficulties involved in the definition of goals and policies. These do not flow naturally from one's sense of the problem. The definition of goals involves judgments that are as ambiguous as the definition of problems. Should a problem that is perceived as inadequate higher education, for example, be met with packages of goals and policies that envision changes in teaching techniques, the development of new curricula (e.g., courses in Black history), more financial aid for students, greater student-freedom from university controls, the "return" of universities to a preoccupation with liberal education, or the further refinement of specialization among institutions of higher education? The definition of goals involves a specification of what an agency will do in order to alleviate a problem. When a goal is defined, the agency personnel and actors in its environment (e.g., legislators, the chief executive, and interest groups) will receive signals about the future course of agency activity. With the variety of persons surrounding an agency who have something at stake in its activities, the choice of goals is not likely to produce a uniform reception. Disagreements will arise between members of the agency and those outsiders who feel affected by the agency. Even before the agency undertakes a course of action (i.e., before it chooses its policy), it may be set upon by actors who object to its goals.[3]

Limits on Information

The variety of problems that may be perceived in one's environment and the variety of specific goals that can be suggested for these problems are elemental facts of an administrator's life which complicate the tasks of rational decision-making. A set of factors which makes such decision-making prohibitive is the limits on adequate information. One limitation has been mentioned in the preceding section: information can have high political costs for an organization if it triggers disputes among people who might be content to cooperate on a project if each does not know the goals being pursued by the others. A second limitation is the sheer working time that can be devoted to analyzing an agency's environment and assessing the advantages and disadvantages that may be associated with each set of goals and policies, in addition to the costs of this working time in terms of lost opportunities for work on other projects. A third limitation is the ineradicable ignorance that may remain even after an organization has invested a great deal of its members' time and has risked offending individuals within the organization or its environment by looking into areas that are politically sensitive. The ignorance results from inadequate technologies for gathering information. Consequently, administrators must extrapolate from certain kinds of information in order to make inferences about the future. These inferences are called "predictions" or "anticipations." They require a leap beyond the edge of one's information. Some inferences are based on the assumption that past trends will continue into the near future; these are not too risky if the trend being considered is a simple one that has shown past consistency in repeating itself from one period of

---

[3] Richard M. Cyert and James G. March, *A Behavioral Theory of the Firm* (Englewood Cliffs, N.J.: Prentice-Hall, 1963), Chapter 3.

time to the next. On other occasions, however, extrapolations are complicated by the nature of the assumptions that must be made. Some of the most complicated statements about the future are those which depend on assessing both the intentions of individuals or organizations and the likelihood of changes in these intentions.[4]

Anthony Downs lists three conditions that generally restrict organizations from acquiring the type of information that is required by the rational decision model:

> 1. Information is costly because it takes time, effort and sometimes money to obtain data and comprehend their meaning;
> 2. Decision-makers have only limited capabilities regarding the amount of time they can spend making decisions, the number of issues they can consider simultaneously, and the amount of data they can absorb regarding any one problem; and
> 3. Although some uncertainty can be eliminated by acquiring information, an important degree of ineradicable uncertainty is usually involved in making decisions.[5]

Not all potential goals and policies can be examined for each of their implications. It is necessary for an organization to take some short-cuts. The important questions are: *When does an administrator stop gathering information? When does he stop assessing that which he has gathered?*

The answer to both of these questions may be: "Never!" Some administrative units never stop gathering and assessing information, but do not delay action indefinitely in the hope of obtaining complete information or a finished assessment. They precede with some activity, but they try to hold open the possibility of altering their actions if they acquire new information. Information-gathering and assessment may go into abeyance when a program actually reaches the operational stage. At this point an agency makes its commitments to action. The commitments may become increasingly strong as persons inside and outside the organization get used to the established practice. Although new information can alter procedures, established procedures may acquire a life-force of their own as they become ingrained in the expectations of officials and clients. Of course, different agencies cut off their active search procedures at different times. Some have greater staff resources that can be devoted to information-gathering; some may have greater tolerance for ambiguous or unresolved questions of

---

[4] Simon, Chapter V.

[5] Anthony Downs, *Inside Bureaucracy* (Boston: Little, Brown, 1967), p. 3.

policy; and some may experience greater conflicts (either internally or with external actors) that require a prolonged search for policies that appear bland to all protagonists.[6]

The multiplicity of information-gatherers within administrative units may present problems to the decision-makers. Each gatherer of information may have his own view of the problems facing the organization (and himself) and of the goals that are appropriate for each problem that he perceives; these problems and goals help to govern the information that he collects. Because it is not a single mind that is collecting information, no single mind can make the unique rational assessment of that information; this, too, limits a rational approach to the organization's problems and goals.

The Needs, Commitments, Inhibitions, and Inadequacies of Administrators

The administrative organization is more than the simple sum of its parts, insofar that a well-ordered group can accomplish more than if each of its members pursued his own efforts alone. When it comes to the selection of goals and the development of policies, however, the organization must face the individuality of its members. Each has his own values and attitudes; these tend to shape his perceptions of the organization and its environment and to create his own preferences about the organization's goals and policies.[7] These perceptions and preferences are among the withinputs of an administrative unit which help to shape the decisions of the unit. Moreover, the perceptions and preferences of individuals may gather strength through informal alliances among like-minded administrators.

The goals of individual administrators—and their alliances—may reflect professional training or personal predilections. Professional training provides norms as well as skills; and these norms affect both the professional's view of the problems he sees in the environment and the goals he adopts in order to confront those problems. Federal, state, and local administrators represent a wide range of professions, e.g., law, medicine, engineering, and various social and natural sciences. Not each member of a profession has a common "professional" view of the world. There are different schools of thought within each profession. These may generate disputes among the members of one profession within an agency at the same time that other disputes occur between

---

[6] Ashley L. Schiff, "Innovation and Administrative Decision-Making: A Study of the Conservation of Land Resources," *Administrative Science Quarterly*, 11 (June, 1966), 1–32.

[7] This discussion relies on Cyert and March, Chapter 3.

the members of different professions. Some disputes are nothing more than personality conflicts. Antagonisms developed in one context may carry over to other encounters between certain administrators and may generate severe arguments about the agency's definition of its problems or about its choice of goals or policies.

Because of diverse personal and professional interests within administrative organizations, the process of goal- and policy-formulation involves a continuing process of learning and bargaining. There is no once-and-for-all decision that reflects a "rational" assessment of problems, goals, policies, and the benefits and costs associated with each possible option. As changes occur in the organization's environment, it is necessary for participants to learn about the implications of these changes for the current set of goals or policies, and perhaps to renegotiate. Coalitions in an agency form around members of similar professional orientation or personal predilection. Yet the coalitions are not always homogeneous or continuous. Certain coalitions may be viable only for a segment of the agency's activities. Inputs of demands and resources may come from the environment to change conditions inside an agency. Also, the personnel of the agency change due to retirements, resignations, and new recruitment. Certain coalitions may grow; others may disintegrate and contribute their members to a new set of coalitions.

The bargaining among coalitions which often marks decision-making within administrative agencies puts a premium on some skills that are not considered in the rational model. These include a person's capacity to express himself clearly and his ability to resist the blandishments of antagonists. As arguments do not always carry their own weight, they may require a combination of tact, assertiveness, and humor, as well as wisdom, in difficult bargaining sessions.

Structural Difficulties within Administrative Units and Involving Their Relations with Legislators and the Chief Executive

Several structural difficulties hinder rational decision-making in administrative agencies. These include: (a) the administrators' need to interact with legislators and with a chief executive whose own relations are affected by a separation of powers and checks and balances; (b) limits on public administrators' control over subordinates; (c) standard operating procedures and red tape within administrative units which hinder innovation; and (d) conflicts between administrators in operating positions and administrators in positions of authority.

One incentive for administrators to avoid clearcut decisions about goals is the fear of alienating powerful legislators and the chief executive. The lack of announcement about goals and the difficulties in predicting the outcomes of policy can rebound to the administrators' benefit. Elected officials can support an administrator's policy, even though they would reject certain results the policy *might* produce. If the anticipated results remain ambiguous, a policy may receive support from representatives and from a chief executive whose own long-run goals are likely to be achieved, as well as from those who can only hope that their own goals will be achieved.

The efforts taken to protect the jobs of individual administrators further complicate the tasks of agency heads. Because of these features, agency heads are kept from directing the calculations about goals and policies that are required by the rational model. Unlike the managers of private firms, the heads of many public agencies cannot readily discipline a subordinate who does not accept instructions. Civil service sanction procedures are lengthy and threaten to disrupt morale within an agency when they are invoked against an employee. Many administrators feel that it costs more in heartache to attempt dismissal proceedings than it would be worth in greater efficiency. Sometimes a subordinate chooses to follow his own policy inclinations. The problem may not be incompetence, but independence. Such a person can shop around for a legislator to support his position or can seek public support from the mass media or an interest group (see pp. 177–90). A legislator may support an errant administrator with the intention of embarrassing an agency head or a chief executive who is a member of the opposite party. Because of the publicity involved, as well as the difficult procedures necessary to dismiss an employee who has civil service protections, a superior may not be able to fire his obstreperous subordinate or even to transfer him to a "harmless" assignment.[8]

Within administrative units, some procedures have a life force of their own and can resist changes in policy that might otherwise be dictated by an assessment of problems, goals, and policies. These are standard operating procedures. These procedures may be established in legislation, or they may only be the habitual practices of administrators. They are frequently designed to inhibit hasty decisions or to keep individual officials from making off with public resources in their own pockets. Such procedures are generally considered to be essential; but they often limit the flexibility with which an agency can cope with its environment. In the latter case, they lose the connotations of "safeguards," and acquire those of "red tape."

---

[8] Louis C. Gawthrop, *Bureaucratic Behavior in the Executive Branch: An Analysis of Organizational Change* (New York: Free Press of Glencoe, 1969).

Another structural problem in some administrative units is the conflict that occurs between specialists who are loyal to certain norms of their own profession and persons who exercise managerial authority.[9] There may be a lack of communication, cooperation, and coordination among individuals with different training and career experiences and different responsibilities in the organization. The specialist is encouraged by training and experience to look out for the interests of his own program; he usually seeks not only the resources that are sufficient to operate his program, but also autonomy in making decisions. Specialists may resist the pressures of an agency head who wants activities to conform with the needs of the larger organization. Such problems may be particularly acute during periods of scarce resources when the agency head must persuade several specialists to defer to the organization's needs. Since many agency heads themselves come from the ranks of specialists (see p. 122), conflicts between the specialist and the central authority may have a personal as well as an organizational dimension. The agency head may experience role conflict within himself as he moves from a position of specialist to a position of central authority. He must adjust for himself the demands of a specific program against the demands on the total organization.

The Deviant Behavior of Administrators

Another factor which hinders rational decision-making in administrative agencies is the behavior of certain individuals who preclude the kind of communication that is required by rational decisions. In each of the preceding sections, we documented a number of behavioral patterns that are non-rational according to our model. In this section, however, the focus is on behavior which is not simply non-rational according to the severe standards of that model. Here the concern is with individuals whose behavior is "unreasonable" in that it precludes cooperative communications among members of an organization. In effect, this kind of behavior prevents organizations from making appropriate adjustments and from making decisions that approach some, if not all, of the standards of the rational model.

Like other factors that affect decision-making, the deviant behavior mentioned here is not found equally in all administrative units. Undoubtedly some units are free of all deviant behavior, while others have more than their fair share. If some of these deviant actions occur in high places within an organization, then other individuals may be

---

[9] Victor A. Thompson, *Modern Organization: A General Theory* (New York: Knopf, 1964), especially Chapter 5.

more likely than otherwise to show such traits. The actions themselves may reflect stress within administrative organizations; and the stress generated by some deviancy may produce even more stress. The stresses include: the personal insecurity of organizational members; their inability to accept (either as superiors or subordinates) the status and power which adheres to hierarchical positions; and the gap between the authority incumbent in a formal position and the knowledge which the holder of that position may have about his responsibilities. Some deviant behavior actually derives from normal organizational behavior, but is an extreme manifestation of the normal activities. Such deviant behavior is called "bureaupathic," to signify its relation—but pushed to *pathological* proportions—to behavior which is "normal" in a bureaucracy.[10] Bureaupathic behavior includes: excessive efforts on the part of persons in leadership positions to maintain aloofness from their subordinates; ritualistic attachments to formal procedures; petty insistence on the rights of one's status within the organization; insensitivity to the needs of subordinates or clients; resistence to conflict within an organization; and resistence to change. Some measure of each kind of behavior may be commensurate with the normal requirements of administrative organizations: the need to have persons in positions of authority; the use of standard procedures for making certain kinds of decisions and a stability of these procedures; and the need to make some decisions about subordinates or clients that run counter to the feelings produced by personal relations. However the pathological variants of these activities hinder communications within the organization. These pathologies create distrust among members of the organization, and between the organization and its clients. They threaten the kind of rapport that is necessary for a reasonable discussion of goals and for a consideration of alternate policies; and, thereby, they hinder the explicit definition of goals and the assessment of each possible policy that is demanded by the rational model.

DECISION-MAKING IN ADMINISTRATIVE UNITS: COMPROMISES WITH THE RATIONAL MODEL

The failure of decision-makers to follow the rigorous prescriptions of the rational model does not mean that their decisions are frenetic, unpatterned, or made without benefit of human reason. The rational

---

[10] This discussion relies on Thompson, Chapter 8. See also Robert Presthus, *Organizational Society* (New York: Knopf, 1962), Chapter 9.

model demands a central decision-maker who can—with the cooperation of his subordinates—define problems, establish goals, and survey
all possible policies before selecting those that will maximize benefits
and minimize costs. Some of the factors that hinder this kind of
decision-making are features of the democratic process, i.e., a large
number of actors having a stake in administrative decisions, many of
whom have the political resources to block decisions that threaten
undesirable consequences. Other factors occur in private firms as well
as in public agencies: outside limits on information-gathering technologies and the high cost of information; a variety of goals that are
relevant to an organization; personal needs and commitments among
members of the organization; and the deviant behavior of individuals
who show pathological responses to the pressures of organizational
life. Decision-making according to the rational model seems inappropriate to most large and complex organizations. The finding of deci-
sion-practices which are not purely rational, therefore, is not a serious
condemnation of the ways decisions are made in administrative systems. Some of the features that preclude the rational model may also
preclude any other single mode of decision-making from attaining
universal use among public agencies. The variety of interests that are
brought to bear on the decisions of most agencies and the variety of
functions, resources, personnel, and clientele that one finds among
agencies are likely to create marked differences in the ways that
agencies make their decisions. In this section, we describe several
features that are observed in administrative decision-making. None
can claim to be the one way in which most decisions are made; but
each represents modes of decision-making that are widely found in
administrative systems. While none of these can claim to be rational
according to the standards of the purely rational model of decision-
making, they do represent *reasonable* ways for administrators to cope
with the numerous demands that come from their environment
or from within their own organizations. One set of terms for
labelling these different kinds of decisions is useful because it blunts
the sharp contrast in connotations between rational and non-rational.
The rational decision has been labelled an optimal procedure, i.e., one
that would be desirable in the most ideal kinds of surroundings. In
light of the problems described above, however, it is conceded that
administrators make do with *satisfactory* decisions. These may not be
ideal to all observers, but are said to meet the needs of participants in
a decision-making situation, after taking into account the information
about goals, resources, and alternative courses of action that it is

feasible for them to assemble.[11] There are "satisficing" techniques appropriate for each of the features that hinder rational or optimal decision-making.

Satisficing with Respect to the Multitude of Problems, Goals, and Policies

One of the practices used by administrators who must be content with satisfactory decisions is to define problems, goals, and policies that permit the use of existing agency resources and that are consistent with existing expectations of legislators, the chief executive, and interest groups. Administrators define problems, goals, and policies that do not reveal a marked departure from existing activities and that do not provoke challenges from those inside or outside the organization who might object to any explicit goals they had not already learned to tolerate.

Administrators are also skilled bargainers. They often settle disputes over goals and policies by accommodating diverse interests. Bargains are made between persons with different interests within administrative agencies, between agencies and officials in other branches of government, and between agencies and interest groups or even prominent citizens. The test of a good bargain is its acceptance by individuals and groups that have control over resources important to an agency. Such a test is not featured in the model of rational decision-making, but it is prominent in democratic political theory.

Another practice is to avoid making any explicit definition of problems or goals. This may avoid one source of severe conflict for the leaders of an organization, and still not preclude their mobilization of resources in behalf of certain policies. People who disagree over a definition of problems and goals might agree—each with their own conception of problem and goals—to work in behalf of specific policies. The announcement of an agency head's view of problems and goals may cost more in the antagonisms that it creates than is warranted by the benefits that it provides. Not only may it be possible, but it also may be necessary, for an organization to proceed with its policies without having a clear or agreed-upon understanding of its major goals and of the social or economic problems that these goals are designed to alleviate. Such a procedure departs from the norms of rational decision-making, but is consistent with the variety of problems, goals, and policy commitments that exist within and surrounding many administrative agencies. This satisficing technique may alle-

---

[11] James March and Herbert Simon, *Organizations* (New York: Wiley, 1959), pp. 140–41.

viate problems for a decision-maker which originate as conflicts within his agency, as well as those which reflect conflicts between members of his agency and legislators, the chief executive, or other political actors in the environment. Each of several participants may support a concrete policy without arguing with others about the long-range goals that the policy might—or might not—realize. Work on a policy can go forth despite potential dissent which may lie dormant throughout the life of the policy.

Satisficing with Respect to Limits on Information

Administrators often cut off their search for information about problems, goals, or policies when they discover a mode of operation that will involve the least profound change in their established programs.[12] They do not search all possible alternatives until they find "the one best" way. Instead, they search until they find something which "will work," i.e., provide satisfactory relief from the perceived difficulties without threatening undesirable unrest within the agency and among the legislators, executives, and interest groups who involve themselves in its affairs.

The reluctance of an agency to search fully results partly from the variety of goals held by agency personnel and by powerful outsiders, and partly from the sheer impossibility of finding one best solution that squares with all of these goals. Most large agencies delegate information-gathering for different projects to different individuals or units within the organization. Program specialization may govern the choice of information-gathers. The specialists in each of the agency's numerous activities search for and assess information that is relevant to their program. The use of numerous information-gatherers and assessors may have the benefit of facilitating some goal satisfactions for a wide variety of members.[13] However, the result may also be a lack of coordination. This lack of coordination is better suited to some contexts than to others. When an organization recognizes that it is in danger, it may coordinate information-gathering so that it will have an early warning of situations that are threatening. Yet it may be difficult to discern a harmful situation and to govern the flow of information so that the coordinator is not smothered in a mass of undigested data.

Fragmentalization of perception inevitably produces an enormous amount of "noise" in the organization's communications networks. The officials at the bottom must be instruc-

---

[12] Downs, p. 173.
[13] Cyert and March, pp. 36–38.

ted to report all potentially dangerous situations immediately so the organization can have as much advanced warning as possible. Their preoccupation with their specialties and their desire to insure against the worst possible outcomes, plus other biases, all cause them to transmit signals with a degree of urgency that in most cases proves exaggerated after the fact. These overly urgent signals make it extremely difficult to tell in advance which alarms will prove warranted and which will not.

There are no easy solutions to this problem. With so many "Chicken Littles" running around claiming the sky is about to fall, the men at the top normally cannot do much until "Henney Penney" and "Foxy Loxy" have also started screaming for help, or there is a convergence of alarm signals from a number of unrelated sources within the organization.[14]

Satisficing with Respect to the Needs, Commitments, Inhibitions, and Inadequacies of Administrators

The presence of personal conflict among personnel does not mean than an agency will be rent apart, or even that individuals will be miserable on account of the fray. Several mechanisms can protect both the organization and its individuals from the costs of conflict. These are *not* the mechanisms portrayed in the model of rational decision-making. They are, in contrast, mechanisms that permit the organization to make some decisions about goals or policy and to carry on its activity despite the conflicts that prohibit agency leaders from making integrated, rational decisions for the entire organization.

The mechanisms that protect administrative organizations from the worst consequences of internal conflict include: the selection of highly ambiguous or non-operational goals; the use of slack resources to "buy-off" members who might be unhappy with the goals or policies selected; and the acceptance of precedent (i.e., goal- or policy-selections made in the past) in order to narrow the conflicts to be faced in the present.

The selection of ambiguous or non-operational goals defers conflict by obtaining agreement on a diffuse statement that does not commit participants in favor of—or against—any activity that threatens their own goals. Conflict may come when subgoals—or actual policies—are selected. At that time, however, the choice may not involve the entire organization. The subunits involved might reach agreement about their own activities if they can deliberate without

---

[14] Downs, p. 190.

being the focus of widespread attention by a total membership who expects major goals to be chosen.

Organizational slack consists of resources that are not yet allocated, but that can be used to provide some rewards to administrators who are dissatisfied with goal- or policy-selections. The resources include money, status and other symbollic rewards, and policy commitments. When they are used in order to placate individuals who are miffed by major goal selections, they can be thought of as "side payments" which the organization makes in order to remain viable. Side payments can be an increase in salary or rank; a larger or more comfortable office or other amenities that make work easier or more pleasant; or a commitment to undertake a program that is tangential to the main effort of the agency. Such a program can be experimental or can be the continuation on a small scale of a project that had been larger. A side payment of an experimental program might be given to an officer who failed to have the organization adopt a massive effort in this new direction. A diminished continuation of a previously large activity may be granted to an individual who fought unsuccessfully to retain the program at its previous size.[15]

Many agencies use precedent to simplify the decisions they make about goals and policies. Decisions made in the past tend to stand until they are overturned or replaced. Precedents narrow the range of goal- and policy-questions which an organization must face. If a new problem can be defined in such a way as to make an existing goal relevant, then such a definition will spare the organization from the turmoil of a new goal conflict. We shall see in a later discussion of decision-rules that precedent has several manifestations in administrative agencies. For example, decisions can become "routinized," so that there is no longer any conflict over which criteria are used in making those decisions.

The mechanisms that protect the organization from the worst consequences of internal conflict also benefit individual members. When an agency selects ambiguous goals, it masks the threat to an individual of having been on the losing side in a confrontation. Reliance on precedent also permits many potential conflicts to pass unexamined. And the pool of slack resources provides some payoffs when an individual is faced with having lost a dispute over major goals. Individuals also have another protection from internal conflict: the tendency of specialists to focus their energies on a small fraction

---

[15] Cyert and March, pp. 36–38.

of the organization's problems. This permits individuals to identify problems and formulate goals which are only subproblems and subgoals for the larger organization. Other specialists may be pursuing subgoals that *might* come into conflict with one's own. However, as long as a confrontation does not occur, each group of specialists may pursue their own goals without regard for—perhaps without even knowing about—activities in other units of their organization.

Satisficing with Respect to Structural Problems

As in the case of other difficulties that are raised as barriers to rational decision-making, the response to structural problems within administrative agencies or between the agencies and legislators or executives in the environment is often to deemphasize overt decisions about goals and to permit policies to proceed without the centralized deliberation and clear choices that are prescribed by the rational model. Organizations often "factor out" goal-setting and policy-formulation to specialized units. Matters requiring new programs are typically assigned to program specialists, with the central authority satisfied with an opportunity to review their proposals. The difficulties of coordinating different specialized units can be met by keeping coordination to a minimum. The news that these specialized administrative units pursue duplicate, or even contradictory, programs reflects this lack of coordination. Central decisions about goals or policies may be made at the insistence of individuals within an organization or at the insistence of legislators and executives on the outside. Even when this occurs, however, decision-makers may not meet the demands of the rational model. An order to "make a decision" may not be acceptable where specialists within an organization could not live with the implications for their own activities. Such a decision may be so obscure or non-operational as to avoid imposing a threat on any of the specalists involved; it may require the devolution of subgoal- and policy-definition to specialists who will administer the eventual program.

THE USE OF DECISION RULES IN MAKING DECISIONS

Common to each of the satisficing techniques is the use of several kinds of decision rules. Three of these rules are prominent enough to merit separate attention. They are: administrators' reliance on *tensions* between established patterns and unmet needs to signal the need for a change in policy; the tendency to make *adjustments* to demands, rather than initiate decision processes that seek a clear definition of goals or policy; and the use of *routine procedures* to simplify the complex considerations that are potentially relevant to a decision-maker. Common to each of these features is the reluctance of administrators to make great departures from customary activities. This is not simply laziness, but represents their appreciation of the numeorus demands that are presented by members of their own organizations, by legislators and the chief executive of their own government, by officials of other governments with whom they have contact, and by their clients and other interest groups. It is seldom that everyone is satisfied with the current state of affairs. To change markedly from the current state, however, might arouse more unrest among the constuents than would be warranted from the benefits promised.

Reliance on Tensions

Administrative agencies wait for tensions to signal dissatisfaction with current activities. Some dissatisfaction is always present, insofar as the agency lacks resources to adequately serve all demands. There are several factors that prevent an agency from making an active search for unmet needs and then seeking to alleviate these needs. These factors include: a scarcity of personnel that could be used for these search processes; the desire to avoid provoking new conflicts within agencies or between agencies and other branches of government which might upset delicate agreements that have been reached on other matters; and a scarcity of resources needed to support new programs of service. By relying on tensions, administrators wait for problems to present themselves. When problems become sufficiently severe to cause a tension, administrators make some effort to respond. Tensions can be thought of as a screening device between an administrative unit and its environment; the members of the unit use it to determine when unmet demands are so severe as to require a response. The quality of the tension may indicate the source of the stress, the actors involved, and the intensity of their dissatisfaction.

> The tension network appears to have both independence and substance, as if, instead of a network of logical relationships, it were a large computer receiving dozens of demands for service and matching them with hundreds of alternative service capabilities. In this process it manipulates the composite of all demands against the total available capacity to meet them. Since demands for service typically exceed capacities, rough priorities are established by a set of values and agreements, evolved over the years. These priorities do not go into process . . . as a logical list of things to be pursued, against which an incoming request is matched and then

either accepted or rejected, but rather as a series of thresholds guaranteeing that the demand has a minimal amount of support. Thus, instead of a *rational structure of program values*, there is a series of barriers operating as thresholds; they screen the values that have meaning, relevance, and support from those that lack one of the requisites.[16]

Mutual Adjustment

An administrative unit that responds to tensions does not initiate policy-change according to any rationally-defined set of priorities; it waits until a change is demanded. A set of procedures for accommodating demands has been labelled "mutual adjustment." Like the reliance on tensions, the concept of mutual adjustment refers not to a rational assessment of priorities; mutual adjustment is a pattern of response and negotiation. One of the terms used to identify decision-making by mutual adjustment is "muddling through."[17] This term suggests a lethargic organism that would detour around an antagonism rather than meet it head-on.

The techniques of adjustment include: the delegation of decision-making to subunits; the representation in subunits of spokesmen for various interests; a reluctance to view any part of one's own position as inflexible; a willingness to bargain with a protagonist; the expectation that protagonists will negotiate in good faith and relinquish part of their demands in exchange for one's own concessions; and the view that goal-formation and policy-making is a continuing process, so that desires that are not satisfied in one period may be realized some time in the future.[18]

The use of decision-units representing diverse interests stands as a major departure from the centralized choices that are assumed by the rational decision model. These subunits may be special task forces set up to represent the constituents who are concerned with an issue or intra-agency committees that include spokesmen from different divisions. While these subunits may have only advisory functions, they often obtain agreement among their contending members and present their parent agency with a proposal that is accepted in whole or part.

---

[16] William J. Gore, *Administrative Decision-Making: A Heuristic Model* (New York: Wiley, 1964), p. 43 (italics added).

[17] Charles Lindblom, "The Science of 'Muddling Through,'" *Public Administration Review*, 19 (Spring, 1959), 79–88.

[18] This discussion relies on the works of Charles E. Lindblom, especially those cited in Notes 2 and 17 above, and "Decision-making in Taxation and Expenditure," in National Bureau of Economic Research, *Public Finances: Needs, Sources and Utilization* (Princeton, N.J.: Princeton University Press, 1961), pp. 295–336.

Flexibility in the face of others' demands is a primary feature of mutual adjustment. It represents an admission that decision-makers lack incontrovertible evidence that any one set of goals or policies is "the one best way" to resolve their problems. Intellectual search and discovery is less to the point of mutual adjustment than is the acceptance of certain demands. The number of individuals who support a demand, their intensity, their alliances with key officials, and the possibility of modifying their position so that it appeals to an even wider population are useful criteria for mutual adjustment. *Adjustment* is not simply a process of rewarding overt power, but is a system of recognizing that power and demands are held by numerous interests and that each can modify its position somewhat to make demands more acceptable to one another.

Another component of mutual adjustment is flexibility over time. Decisions are not made once and for all, but in a sequence of continuing interactions; later decisions modify the impact of earlier ones. Demands that are not met in one phase of the sequence return again, often in a different formulation and with different supporters. With some changes in content or style and with some additional changes in the context that might expand its appeal to other interests, a once-rejected demand can find wide acceptance and a generous provision of resources.

Routines

Routines are used by decision-makers in administrative systems to avoid the time-consuming, expensive, and impossible demands of the rational model. Routines are decision rules that specify which of the numerous inputs that might be relevant are actually considered in making decisions. Some routines are more elaborate than others and indicate the weight to be given each input; some even specify the response to be made under certain conditions. What routines share is their ability to select for the decision-maker those few considerations to be kept in mind from among the myriad that are potentially relevant. They simplify his inputs and, thereby, make his decision easier.

There are different types of routines in administrative systems. At the extreme of simplicity, an electronic computer uses a routine when it decides if the arithmetic is accurate on a citizen's tax return. At another stage, the computer uses a slightly more elaborate routine to determine if the citizen claims more for charitable contributions than is commensurate with his total income. If the citizen does claim more, the computer identifies the tax return for human scrutiny. When the auditor examines the tax return and other documents which the taxpayer is asked to present, he employs additional routines. These are more flexible than those programmed into the computer; but they likewise provide a screening process for the inputs. They identify the kinds of evidence that are acceptable—and unacceptable—for showing the citizen's contributions. Other routines help the tax agency determine from the circumstances whether the citizen will simply pay back-taxes with interest, pay a fine in addition to the taxes and interest, or be prosecuted for tax evasion.

Many of the routines used in administrative agencies reflect the working-out by subordinates of procedures that are designed in an explicit manner by their superiors. However, some routines are used in making policy decisions. These are the most interesting. They affect enormous financial, material, and personal resources. Often they are not pursued in a conscious manner. Decision-makers accept them because of their appeal as the simplifiers of complex situations. Like the routines mentioned above, those used by policy-makers select a few inputs from the many that face a decision-maker; and sometimes they assign a weight to each of these inputs or even prescribe the decision-maker's response to a certain kind of input. At the same time that routines simplify the tasks of policy-makers, they also help to stabilize the political system. They do this by screening out certain kinds of inputs, especially those which would produce marked departures from prevailing activities. Three policy-making routines will be illustrated here. They are: incremental budgeting; the tendency of state and local administrators to copy regional neighbors in formulating their own policies; and the tendency of policy-makers to seek an increase in spending when they perceive a need to improve their programs.

Incremental Budgeting

Incrementalism is a routine which is found in many types of government decision-making, but most clearly in the budgetary process. Budget-makers who follow an incremental approach fail to consider all of the alternatives that face them; and they do not make their decisions on the basis of all relevant information. Incrementalists do not debate grand social goals. Their most salient concerns are immediate appropriations for specific agencies, rather than long-run benefits for society. They generally accept the legitimacy of established programs and agree to continue the previous level of expenditure. They limit their task by considering only the *increments of change* proposed for the new budget and by considering the narrow range of goals embodied in the departures from established activities. Their expectations tend to be short-range and pragmatic.

More clearly than other decision rules, incremental budgeting reveals its function as a conservative force in administrative agencies. Budget-makers consider no single criteria so important as their own decisions of the recent past. They accept established levels of spending and focus their inquiries (and their budget-cutting) on the increments of change that are requested.

The power of incremental budgeting is apparent in the statistical relationships between current and previous levels of state government expenditures. When past and present spending are only three years apart (representing in most cases the expenditures of two consecutive budget periods), the correspondence is virtually perfect. Although state governments increased their spending during 1963–65, they remained in essentially their same positions relative to one another. The power of previous expenditures is strong in budget considerations and inhibits policy-makers from accepting major innovations. As the span between current and previous expenditures increases, the correspondence between spending positions lessens. There is an increasing opportunity for factors to enter the budget process which are remote from the situation in that past year. Yet even with increasing time between a current year and a past year, the expenditures of the past continue to be the nucleus around which later expenditures have grown. The high- and low-spending states of 1965 tend to be in the same relative positions as they were in 1903! Despite several major wars, population shifts, and transformations in the economy, there remains some resemblance in the spending positions of most state governments now and then.

There is some evidence that incremental budgeting is most confining in state and local governments. At the federal level, incrementalists seem willing to examine the changes in expenditure *and* service outputs that are requested for each agency.[19] In the state and local governments that have been studied closely, however, there is a more narrow concentration on the increments of dollars which are requested. In his study of budgeting in Illinois, Thomas J. Anton finds decision-makers relying on a simplistic set of rules that examine—and cut—budget totals with little concern for the impact on programs.[20]

---

[19] Aaron Wildavsky, *The Politics of the Budgetary Process* (Boston: Little, Brown, 1964), Chapter 3. This discussion of routines relies heavily on Ira Sharkansky, *The Routines of Politics* (New York: Van Nostrand-Reinhold, 1970).

[20] Thomas J. Anton, *The Politics of State Expenditure in Illinois* (Urbana: University of Illinois Press, 1966).

Administrators often must expand services by shifting funds within budgets that reveal minimal overall change.

John P. Crecine's findings about budgeting in Detroit, Cleveland, and Pittsburgh document how incremental budget-makers can parcel out annual increases in revenues without concern for program values.[21] When budget-makers expect a revenue surplus they distribute it among most agencies on the basis of fixed priorities that have no relation to programs. Salaries are given first preference; equipment gets the second rewards; and maintenance gets the remainder. A contrary priority is used when the forecast indicates a need to reduce budgets below present levels. Cuts are made first in maintenance, then in equipment, and only lastly in salaries. Those items which promise the greatest political appeal—regardless of program—receive the best treatment. (A more-detailed description of incremental budgeting and of its influences on the expenditures of administrative agencies appears in Chapter 8, pp. 222–33.)

Regional Consultation

Incremental budgeting is a routine that guides officials to take their decision-cues from within their own jurisdiction. The routine of regional consultation guides the administrators of state and local governments when they look outside their own arenas for decision cues. When administrators look elsewhere for a model policy to copy for their own jurisdiction, they do not survey all the possible models throughout the country—as the rational model suggests. Instead, they look within their geographic region—or, more typically, to a jurisdiction that borders directly on their own.

Many administrators believe that neighboring jurisdictions have problems similar to their own.[22] Because neighboring governments serve similar populations, it is likely that the people have common needs for public services and present similar demands to government agencies. The economies of the neighboring governments are generally alike, and they present to government agencies a comparable set of resources and needs. The political environment is also likely to be similar in neighboring jurisdictions. Politicians will probably support comparable levels of service, and there may be similar relationships among administrators, the executive, and the legislature. Southern

---

[21] John P. Crecine "A Computer Simulation Model of Municipal Resource Allocation," a paper delivered at the Meeting of the Midwest Conference of Political Science, April, 1966.

[22] Ira Sharkansky, *Regionalism in American Politics* (Indianapolis: Bobbs-Merrill, 1969).

states are said to be the archetype of American regions. They share certain geographical features that have affected their politics through the intermediary of the cotton-plantation-slave syndrome. They also shared historical experiences of racial heterogeneity, Civil War, Reconstruction, continuing poverty, and limited political participation and competition. Many government services in the South are distinctive; but the South is not the only distinctive region. States in the Great-Lakes and Rocky-Mountain areas, in particular, share traits that seem to reflect common features of population, geography, history, economics, and politics (see pp. 268–70).

It is not only policy-makers in administrative agencies who feel that regional neighbors are likely subjects of emulation. Politicians, journalists, and members of the public who take an interest in certain programs are accustomed to comparing efforts in their own state to those which are in their own circle of experience; and this circle typically is limited to the region. Thus, the inputs that come to an administrative agency often carry demands that are developed in a distinct regional context. State bureaus of research usually publish comparisons of their own state's demographic, economic, and public-service characteristics with those of regional partners. For example, the Georgia Statistical Abstract (published by the University's Bureau of Business and Economic Research) compares data for the state as a whole with a figure for the entire United States and with separate figures for Alabama, Florida, North Carolina, South Carolina, and Tennessee. When a study committee of the University of Wisconsin analyzed tax burdens in that state, the comparisons were drawn with Illinois, Indiana, Iowa, Michigan, Minnesota, and Ohio.

The professional activities of administrators also lead them to regional neighbors for policy cues. Policy-makers and professional employees of state and local governments belong to formal organizations according to their subject-matter speciality. There are now at least 46 of these groups. They include the National Association of State Budget Officers, the National Association of State Conservation Officers, and the National Association of Housing and Redevelopment Officials. They have both national and regional meetings that provide the opportunity for trading information about current problems and reinforcing friendships that had been formed at earlier meetings. State and local officials indicate that they are more likely to attend the regional than the national meetings of these groups and that they acquire many of their professional contacts at these meetings.

Since administrators have consulted in the past with their counterparts in nearby governments, they have learned who can be trusted for credible information, candor, and good judgment. Unless an official is committed to an extensive program of research before making his own policy decisions, he may be satisfied with making a few calls to individuals with whom he has dealt amicably in the past.

Several elements favor the development of nationwide similarities in the public policies of state and local governments. They include federal aids, improvements in transportation and communication, and the mobility of professional and technical personnel from schools or previous government jobs in one state to new jobs in other states. Yet regional patterns in policy have not succumbed to these influences. Distinct regional patterns remain in spending and service levels for the fields of education, highways, and welfare, in the nature of state and local revenue systems, and in the use of federal and state aids (see pp. 264–67). The presence of these regional similarities in policy remains as the single most prominent indication of the routine of regional consultation.

The Spending-Service Cliche

The spending-service cliche is a routine which leads policy-makers to equate levels of expenditure with levels of service-output. Like other routines, the spending-service cliche gets its support from the need of decision-makers for a device that will simplify reality. In the field of program development, there are five principal elements which add to the appeal of the spending-service cliche: (1) the large number of factors—and complex interrelationships among these factors—which actually have an influence on the character of services that an agency provides; (2) the lack of information among decision-makers about these service-factors; (3) the belief that some factors that influence the level of outputs are not conveniently subject to manipulation by public officials; (4) the commonality of money as an element that may influence many potential service-factors; and (5) a widespread belief among analysts and observers *outside* the decision-making arena that money is crucial among the factors that influence the level of service outputs.

Among the factors that can influence the nature of public services are: the nature of staff and leadership; physical facilities; the clientele who are to be served; the organizational structure of the service agencies; the economy of the jurisdiction receiving the service; and the political environment in which policy decisions are made. There is much folklore about the elements that will help to improve services; but there is little hard information about the results to be expected from certain combinations of ingredients under certain conditions. In a number of federal, state, and local agencies that have access to sophisticated staff assistance and electronic data processing equipment, efforts are being made to identify salient features that have a bearing on the level of services produced (see pp. 65–67). However, much of this work is still in the exploratory stage. It is not sufficiently widespread among government agencies, and its techniques are not sufficiently well-accepted for it to have broad application.

Among the elements that seem likely to influence service levels, a number of them appear unamenable to direct manipulation by government officials. Because of this, decision-makers may be dissuaded from a thorough analysis of service-determinants and may be led to rely on the simple routine which assumes a spending-service relationship. The preparation of clients, their motivation for making the efforts that are part of the services to be rendered, market costs, the level of economic development in a community, and the attractiveness of a community as a residence for professional and technical personnel can have a bearing on the services that an agency can render. Although each of these elements may be altered by long-range campaigns directed specifically at them, it is unlikely that these changes can be made the responsibility of service agencies who have other, more immediate goals.

In the face of the complexities which face the decision-maker who would undertake a thorough analysis of the elements that influence his agency's level of services, the routine of the spending-service cliche offers both simplicity and credibility. Although money, *per se,* does not affect levels of service, it seems reasonable to believe that money will purchase many of the commodities that do affect services. Money is not only a common denominator, but is also subject to manipulation by government officials. If the present level of service is not satisfactory, it is always possible—assuming sufficient resources or sufficient willingness to increase taxes—to spend more money. With additional dollars, officials can seek to recruit and/or train leaders and scientific-technical-professional personnel for their agencies; they can pay existing personnel enough money to make it difficult for them to accept employment elsewhere; they can offer financial inducements so that personnel will accept changes in organizational structure or changes in agency norms; and they can buy the material and talents necessary to construct and maintain attractive physical facilities. Unfortunately, the willingness to spend more money may not solve the service problem. Not only is it true that some service-determinants are not subject to alteration by current spending, but it is also unclear as to which of the commodities that are purchasable—and how much of each—will do the job that is desired.

One of the factors that helps to make the spending-service cliche attractive to administrators is its popularity among those who observe and analyze public policy. Journalists frequently rank state or local governments on some readily-available financial scale. Total spending, expenditures per client, or average salaries are favorite subjects of comparison. Several academic social scientists with solid reputations as scholars, consultants, and government executives also give high marks to the spending-service cliche. In much of the literature that examines government expenditures in the United States, we can find the assumption that spending provides the primary stimulant for public services.[23] Most writers who assume the expenditure-service correspondence fail to test their belief. On some occasions, they even overlook contrary data from their own tables.[24]

Opportunities for Innovation in Administrators' Decisions: Deviations from Routines

The use of routine decision rules does not fix the decisions that administrators can make. As it is noted above, routines are only one of several devices they use in making decisions. Others, like mutual adjustment, are more hospitable to innovative stimuli. Moreover, some officials recognize the biases in decision-makers' routines, and they devise strategies that play on the weaknesses of routines. Certain environmental conditions help to weaken routines and to permit innovative proposals to affect policy. Some officials are sufficiently won over to new ideas that they disregard their normal routines and make a new kind of decision.

Aaron Wildavsky identifies a number of strategies that are used within the confines of incremental budgeting. The following set of strategies, for example, defends the "base" (an agency's current budget) against attack from legislative committees.[25]

Cut the popular program. By anticipating legislative insistence on a pruned budget, administrators can cut their requests for programs

---

[23] See, for example, Robert C. Wood, *1400 Governments* (Garden City, N.Y.: Anchor Books, 1961), p. 35; Jesse Burkhead, *Public School Finance* (Syracuse: Sycracuse University Press, 1965), p. 50; and Philip C. Burch, *Highway Revenue and Expenditure Policy in the United States* (New Brunswick, N.J.: Rutgers University Press, 1962), p. 34.

[24] In Burkhead's book, for example, the author is not troubled by the lack of significant statistical relationships between four measures of educational expenditure and such likely indicators of service as the salary of beginning teachers, the insurable value of school property, and the number of full-time employees in such auxiliary services as student health and counselling. For a test of the spending-service cliche, see Ira Sharkansky "Government Expenditures and Public Services in the American States," *American Political Science Review,* 61 (December, 1967), 1066–78.

[25] Wildavsky, pp. 102ff.

that they know are popular. When this happens, it is more than likely that the legislature will restore the cut and, hopefully, not make up for the restoration with a cut taken elsewhere.

Claim that any cut in a program will require its sacrifice. Any cut will be too great to allow the program to be continued. The risk with this kind of claim is that the legislature might view such a program as existing on too tenuous a foundation and scrap the whole works.

Separate programs in the budget presentation. This makes it difficult for legislators to cut "across the board" in a way that takes funds from anonymous programs. By forcing the legislature to cut out of specific activities, an administrator can mobilize the supporters of those activities in opposition to the cut.

Wildavsky also identifies some strategies that administrators use to increase their budgets within the constraints of incrementalism. He calls them "increasing the base—inching ahead with existing programs."

Old stuff. Funds for new programs are difficult to obtain. Therefore, administrators say that their "new" money is for existing programs. "Our programs have grown a lot, but we have never begun anything we described as fundamentally new in the twenty years I have been [with the agency]."[26]

The transfer. Administrators maintain budget requests at constant levels, even though some older programs are phased out and have been replaced with others. This is one way of moving ahead in program development, while appearing to stand still.

The numbers game. An administrator claims that the *number* of his programs has remained constant. This may be true. But while he tries to focus attention on the number of his activities, the activities and the cost of each one can move ahead.

The wedge or camel's nose. This is a device that begins a new program with a sum that appears insignificant. Once this has been accepted, the administrator claims in the next budget period that the program has become part of its base and that it must increase expenditures in order to go ahead and finish the task it has started.

If this, then that. This is implied in the claim that a new activity is integrally related to an existing program. Thus, the implied obligation to go on with the old passes on to the new.

The backlog. This is the claim that existing activities have not accomplished the assigned tasks. Therefore, additional expenditures are necessary to clean up the backlog of unfinished business.

---

[26] Wildavsky, pp. 109ff.

The crisis. A proposed new program is identified with an event or set of circumstances which is widely viewed as a crisis: war, drought, depression, plant disease, social unrest. This strategy is related to the next device.

The defense motif. National defense has wide appeal. It often enjoys bipartisan support and a willingness to spend money that might otherwise be denied. It is not only the military that receives the benefit of the defense motif; other activities have tied themselves to this symbol with lucrative payoffs. The largest single highway program—and the costliest—in the nation's history is the "Interstate and Defense Highway System." One of the most generous and wide-ranging federal aids for education enacted during the 1950's is the "National Defense Education Act."

Historically, national crises have affected the use of such routines as incremental budgeting and the spending-service cliche. In particular, the Depression, wars, and post-war reconversions made untenable some of the factors which normally led officials to practice these routines. Intergovernmental aids can also upset the routines of recipient governments. And certain individuals, when elected to high public office, may be able to alter, at least temporarily, the routines of their governments while they implement policy.[27]

The Depression had its most severe impact on the routines of local governments. In many communities, the bottom dropped out of the real estate market, at the same time that there was unprecedented unemployment and industrial shut-downs. The combination of these factors resulted in a great loss in local-government revenues from the property tax; in some places, it led to the actual bankruptcy of the municipality. Under these conditions, incremental budgeting was a luxury; and many localities cut deeply into the expenditure base of existing programs. The Second World War and, to a lesser extent, the Korean Conflict also forced local, state, and *domestic* federal agencies to fall behind their previous year's expenditures. Both manpower and raw materials became less available for domestic purposes. The number of state and local government employees declined during World War II, and the magnitude of federal aids also declined.

The high levels of military expenditure that were reached during World War II seemed to lessen the willingness to continue with incrementalism and the spending-service cliche. In the executive branch, the reform movement which has now evolved to PPB got a

---

[27] This discussion draws on Sharkansky, *The Routines of Politics,* Chapter IX.

beginning in 1946 when the Navy Department reorganized its budget to emphasize the program components which its expenditures would purchase. In 1949, the Hoover Commission urged the adoption of "performance budgeting" within federal agencies. This style of budgeting—like the earlier innovation in the Navy Department— would call the attention of budget reviewers to the levels of program output that were promised by each agency's request. Service levels, and not simply spending, would be examined by budget analysts. This reform was initiated in the Budget and Accounting Act of 1950, and a number of federal agencies took steps to clarify the outputs that funds would provide. (For an additional discussion of PPB, see pp. 65–68.)

Grants-in-aid have some influence on the routines of state and local administrators. The sheer magnitude of grants coming into a state can distract state and local administrators from the routines of incremental budgeting. This is particularly true in the fields of highways and natural resources, reflecting the substantial amounts of the federal grants for these programs.[28] Federal funds represent "outside" money that is free from the constraints placed on additions to the base of state expenditures. Of course, the federal grant usually requires an outlay of "matching" state resources; but this can be justified by the amount of federal money that it "brings in" (see pp. 241–42). Also, some federal programs permit recipient agencies to match the grant with an "in-kind" contribution. This may be land, office-space, employees' time, or some other commodity that represents no visible outlay of state or local funds.

RATIONALIST EFFORTS TO REFORM DECISION-MAKING: THE CASE OF BUDGETING

The procedures that administrators use to make "satisfactory" decisions have evolved in the face of constraints that inhibit "optimal" or "rational" decisions. These procedures have some appeal for those observers who see insurmountable difficulties that block rational decisions. However, other observers are dissatisfied with existing procedures. They may not expect to mold decisions to the demands of the purely rational model, but they do want decision-makers to take more of a rational route to their decisions than has been the practice. Over the years, they have urged structural reforms for administrative systems—both on the agencies themselves and on legislative and execu-

---

[28] Ira Sharkansky, *Spending in the American States* (Chicago: Rand McNally, 1968), Chapters IV and VIII.

tive institutions in their environment. The reforms are designed to permit and encourage decision-makers to take more factors into consideration when choosing goals and when choosing policies that will realize their goals. If successful, these reforms would open policy decisions to a wider range of economic, social, and political inputs. The failures of many proposals and the sharp modifications of others when put into practice suggest the power of the features that hinder rational decision-making. Many of the reforms have focused on the budgetary process. They have resulted in the development of the Bureau of the Budget (see pp. 97–98), The Executive Office of the President (see pp. 96–98), and, more recently, planning-programming-budgeting.

PPB is actually an interrelated series of several devices whose description is clouded by the failure of advocates to agree on a common set of terms. Systems analysis, cost-benefit analysis, cost-effectiveness, and program budgeting have been used to describe the principal components. PPB seeks greater rationality in budgeting by clarifying the choice of means used to attain agency goals. Its decision stages are:

1. Defining the major programs in each area of public service;
2. Defining the principal "outputs" (goals) of each program;
3. Identifying the "inputs" that generate "outputs" (inputs include various combinations of personnel, facilities, and techniques of rendering service);
4. Computing the costs of alternative combinations of inputs and the value of the outputs likely to be produced by each combination; and
5. Calculating the cost-benefit ratio associated with each combination of inputs and outputs.

Presumably, PPB guides those who would employ public resources in the most efficient manner. If its practitioners are thorough, they should be able to identify the set of inputs that produces the lowest cost-benefit ratio of inputs to outputs.

The experience with PPB is too current to permit anything like a thorough assessment of its potential and limitations. However, some shortcomings may be inherent in the system. Indeed, they point to the continuing problems that have also shown through other attempts to make decisions rationally: an inability to assess the full range of political and economic issues associated with each major policy; and the failure of participants to subordinate their own loyalties to the recommendations that evolve from a new system.

A major criticism of PPB focuses on its inability to provide budgeteers with an evaluation of the political costs and benefits associated with their support of certain programs. Aaron Wildavsky is an outspoken critic of PPB who cites it for failing to provide information about three types of political costs:

1. Exchange costs—the costs of calling in favors owed and the costs of making threats in order to get others to support a policy;
2. Reputational costs—the loss of popularity with the electorate, the loss of esteem and effectiveness with other officials, and the subsequent loss of one's ability to secure programs other than those currently under consideration; and
3. The costs of undesirable redistributions of power—those disadvantages that accrue from the increase in the power of individuals, organizations, or social groups who may become antagonistic to oneself.[29]

An advantage to incrementalism is that it sharply limits the political costs that have to be calculated. When incrementalists accept the base of previous expenditures as legitimate, they excuse themselves from reviewing the whole range of tradition, habits, and prior commitments that are subsumed within existing programs. PPB threatens to perpetuate controversy (and discomfort for budget-makers) with its rationalist analysis of alternative approaches to each major program.

Another accusation directed at PPB is that systems analysis focuses on the ingredients of program inputs and outputs that are easy to investigate. Many of the systems analyses and cost-benefit analyses which have been published introduce their subject matter with an impressive list of potential service-determinants and likely products of the service. But the analysis itself typically deals with a few of the inputs and outputs, seemingly selected on no more substantial basis than the analyst's convenience. Thus, practitioners of PPB may base their recommendations on a routine that is *no more comprehensive* in its rationality than is incremental budgeting.

The usefulness of PPB may be greatest in the military, where the major goals are clear and widely accepted among the officials who

[29] Aaron Wildavsky, "The Political Economy of Efficiency: Cost-Benefit Analysis, Systems Analysis, and Program Budgeting," *Public Administration Review*, 26 (December, 1966), 292–310.

make budget decisions: deterrence of war, defense of country, and victory in war. Elsewhere, the goals of programs are subject to intense controversy. In many cases, different legislators and interest groups agree to support specific activities, even though bitter conflict would result if they had to agree about the long-range goals of the programs. Even in the case of agencies with relatively non-controversial goals, the value of PPB is limited by the extent to which the costs and benefits of programs can be measured. The life of an unlettered peasant in a foreign country, the value of an American soldier's life, or the payoffs of a research and development project must be considered in many phases of military planning; but they hardly lend themselves to simple or indisputable pricing. Some factors are worth more than their market price indicates. PPB also encourages centrallized decision-making (i.e., by officials who assess information relevant to goals, resources, and prospective performance). Yet a prominent characteristic of American government is decentralized decision-making, with spokesman of different government units or interest groups bargaining with one another. A participant's definition of a policy's feasibility is "a seat-of-the-pants judgment." The relevant "cost" questions are: "Will it 'go' on the Hill?" "Will the public buy it?" "Does it have political 'sex appeal?' "[30]

SUMMARY

The variety of features both within administrative agencies and coming from their environment, along with the changes that continually occur in these features, complicate the administrator's task. For one thing, this variety makes the prescriptions of rational decision-making impractical.

If an administrator were to follow the standards of the rational model, he would list and assess all goals that appear relevant to the problems he perceives, and would then do likewise for each of the policies that appeared capable of achieving each of the potential goals. On the basis of all relevant information about the probable advantages and disadvantages associated with each package of goals and policies, he would then select the one best goal-and-policy combination to become the program of his unit.

The rational model is widely respected by individuals and groups who comment about government activities. It presents a standard of "right thinking" which asks that officials take every issue into consider-

---

[30] Ralph Huitt, "Political Feasibility," in Austin Ranney, ed., *Political Science and Public Policy* (Chicago: Markham, 1968), pp. 163–67.

ation and make clear decisions that can then guide the actions of subordinates. The result promises to be integrated policies that complement rather than conflict with one another. However, administrators who would accept the prescriptions of the rational model find their way blocked by a number of constraints. These constraints are not alien to American politics. They reflect the heterogeneity and conflict which are considered—by many writers—integral components of the democratic process. The finding that they hinder rational policy-making is frustrating, however, and may account for part of the alienation that separates certain citizens—and even some administrators—from the procedures of administrative agencies.

The factors which stand in the way of rational policy-making include: the variety of possible problems that can be perceived in an agency's environment; the numerous goals and policies that are potentially feasible; the high cost of information; the personal, ideological, and professional interests of policy-makers; structural disharmonies that generate conflict among administrators or between them and other participants in the policy process; and deviant (bureaupathic) behaviors that occur in administrative units.

In the face of these problems, policy-makers tend to avoid centrallized decisions that are announced in an unambiguous fashion. They seek decisions that will be satisfactory rather than optimal. They avoid as many difficult choices as possible. Problems are avoided unless they appear with enough severity to generate tensions in an organization or its environment. Once tensions occur, an administrative unit may use the procedures of mutual adjustment. These include a combination of: delegation to subunits; negotiation among interested parties; flexibility on the part of each protagonist in the face of others' demands; and an expectation that problem-solving will be a continuing process. Mutual adjusters do not seek final solutions to social or economic problems, but recognize that the perception of problems as well as goals and policies are matters of dispute among reasonable individuals. They provide opportunities for dissatisfied interests to express their demands. It frequently happens that a demand raised and rejected in one context appears later under other conditions and receives some resources from decision-makers.

Another device that compromises some of the requirements of the rational model is a routine—a decision rule that identifies which of numerous inputs the official should take into account and that sometimes specifies how he should respond to specific inputs. Routines appeal to decision-makers because they simplify their choices. By limiting the kind of inputs that are likely to have an impact on policies, routines also help to stabilize policy and complicate the task of those who demand major innovations. The routines considered in this chapter are incremental budgeting, regional consultations, and the spending-service cliche.

Although routines bring some stability to policy-making, they do not choke off all innovation. As is evident in the strategies used in federal budgeting, participants can innovate within the constraints of a routine. Stimuli associated with national crises (e.g., wars, post-war reconversions, and depressions) have occasioned major departures from routine policy-making. Intergovernmental aids can also generate innovations in the policies of recipient agencies. And occasionally a powerful official may upset—at least temporarily—the routines of entrenched officials. Moreover, reformers have not resisted the temptation to enhance the components of rationality in existing procedures. Although the results of their most recent effort—PPB—are not yet clear, this reform, like many others, seems destined to compromise its expectations in the face of continuing pressures which inhibit pure "rationality" in administrators' decision-making.

4

ADMINISTRATIVE ORGANIZATION AND ADMINISTRATIVE CONTROL UNITS: STRUCTURES AND THEIR INTELLECTUAL ROOTS

ADMINISTRATIVE ORGANIZATION AS POLITICAL CONTROVERSY

As we have defined the conversion process of the administrative system, it is outlined by formal structures. It includes those agencies of government which are in neither the executive, legislative, nor judiciary, but which produce the goods and services that government provides to its citizens. The description of administrative organization is not a simple matter that can be accomplished in the manner of a tourist's guide. Agencies—and their relations with other branches of government—are designed partly by reference to theories that claim to have general application and partly by the politics surrounding the individual programs and the interests which either support or oppose them. Issues of administrative organization erupt prominently over the creation of new government agencies, over the elevation of existing federal units to "cabinet rank," over the transfer of a program from the auspices of one agency to another, over the design of powers that will strengthen or weaken the ability of the chief executive or legislature to control agencies, over a change in procedures that link "line" and "staff" agencies, or over the alteration of budgeting or other devices that are used to govern administrative units.

The model that is used most often to describe administrative organizations in the United States is the hierarchy. The typical organi-

zation chart shows several department heads who are directly responsible to the chief executive and whose own departments fan out
beneath them to include several layers of leadership and ultimately
the personnel who actually provide the services or impose the regulations which are the department's major tasks. The pinnacle of the
hierarchy is the chief executive who reputedly exercises control over
the department heads and through them reaches the activities of all
administrative personnel. However, this simplified hierarchy is so
often violated in practice that it hardly qualifies as a model of public
administration.

The hierarchy is qualified by several features that weaken the
chief executive's control over the department heads and that make the
heads (and their own "subordinates") responsible to numerous actors
besides the chief executive. Each of these features represents a desire
to broaden control of administrative units beyond the interests who
would be represented by the chief executive and his appointees. Those
wanting a say in the policy-making of administrative units—and
willing to violate hierarchical principles—include: legislators; the
clients of agencies and the interest groups who represent them; employees of the administrative units; and citizen groups who feel
strongly about the use of special procedures (e.g., the "merit" selection of employees) for the control of administrative units.

One of the features that violates the model of the heirarchy is the
direct popular election of department heads. This device is employed
by all of the state governments for at least some of their department
heads and is used by most of the states for the positions of attorney
general, secretary of state, auditor, treasurer, and superintendent of
public education. These administrators become politicians in their
own right and may be independent of the governor in both party
membership and policy orientation. At the federal level, the president
is not bothered by subordinates who are elected independently; but
he must cope with other mechanisms that are designed to impede his
control of administrative departments. One of these is senatorial confirmation of his appointees (e.g., cabinet officers and the heads of
major agencies). Another is the Civil Service Commission, whose
members are appointed by the president, but whose fixed terms of six
years signify the concern of the Commission's founders to keep federal
hiring outside of the president's control. State and federal legislators
also destroy the symmetry of a simple administrative hierarchy by
their control over the legal authority and the budgets of administrative agencies and by their desire to influence specific decisions in
certain programs. Legislatures are not content to write general pol-

icies and let the chief executive and his subordinates administer their departments accordingly. The history of legislative-executive-administrative interaction has seen countless devices employed by the legislature to retain detailed control over those aspects of program administration that interest them. These devices include: specific recommendations in committee *Reports* that administrators are expected to follow; detailed questioning during annual budget hearings on the minutiae of program administration; special investigations into the operation of agency field-installations; and statutory amendments designed to prohibit certain practices that legislators have found distasteful. At the federal level, Congress has established under its own auspices the General Accounting Office in order to supervise the expenditures of administrative agencies. This institution—large enough to employ about 4,500 persons and to spend $54 million in 1968—is a staff-arm of the legislature and has the power to question and to disallow individual items of agency expenditure.

Another factor that qualifies the model of the hierarchy in administrative organizations is the disinclination of some chief executives to operate in a hierarchical manner. President Franklin Roosevelt often ignored the niceties of hierarchical etiquette. He dealt directly with bureau chiefs without going through their department heads; and he purposefully generated conflict within the administration so that the noise of battle would inform him about the issues that his subordinates debated. He guaranteed conflict by appointing likely antagonists to positions in which they had to deal intimately with one another. He also divided what appeared to be single jobs into multiple positions so that different officials would contend with one another in their operations. Another device that Roosevelt used to infiltrate the hierarchy was the freewheeling personal assistant. Harry Hopkins was in and out of several formal positions in the Roosevelt Administration, but his most important assignments were *ad hoc* assignments that permitted Roosevelt more direct contact with significant decisions than he would have had if he relied upon the traditional hierarchy.[1] A more recent counterpart of Harry Hopkins was Robert F. Kennedy. In formal position, he was the Attorney General in his brother's Administration. But he served beyond the boundaries of the Justice Department and was an analyst and advisor in fields of defense, international relations, and domestic politics.

If the hierarchy is not the perfect model for public administrative organization, there is no single model which serves better. The vari-

---

[1] See Robert E. Sherwood, *Roosevelt and Hopkins* (New York: Grosset and Dunlap, 1948).

eties of administrative organization are numerous and reflect the peculiar turns that have been taken by controversies surrounding individual agencies and programs. We can better understand the varieties of organization which do exist after we have examined four intellectual roots of administrative organization. One of the four roots lends its support to hierarchical forms of organization. These roots have not operated in isolation. They are frequently compromised for reasons of political expediency. Their influence is evident, however, in the administrative units of national, state, and local governments.

INTELLECTUAL ROOTS OF ADMINISTRATIVE ORGANIZATION

Four intellectual roots are prominent in the structures of administrative organizations in the United States. Each is built on the assumption of certain political goals that are inconsistent with the goals assumed by other roots. If nothing else existed to insert controversy into the construction of administrative institutions, the attempts to obtain some of the benefits from each of these goals would guarantee that conflict. The four roots are: (1) the desire to maintain political accountability in public administration; (2) the desire to maintain the traditional equilibrium among the three constitutional branches of government by preserving the system of separation of powers and of checks and balances; (3) the desire to insure that professional and technical skills are brought to bear on relevant matters of policy formulation and implementation; and (4) the desire to maximize the efficient use of resources by means of a hierarchical form of organization.

Political Accountability

The political accountability of public administration is a general principle that has included several tenets and has been pursued in radically different ways. Indeed, there are such sharp controversies between the proponents of different forms of "accountability" that they could be termed distinctly antagonistic approaches to administrative organization. One approach—which can be termed "traditional" by virtue of its historical lineage—maintains that elected officials should have the final say over the activities of administrative agencies. This means that agency programs are defined by laws subject to the approval of the legislature and the chief executive. Moreover, annual or (in the case of many state governments) biennial budget requests are subject to similar law-making procedures and require the approval of the legislature and the chief executive. An element that sometimes accompanies this form of political accountability is executive and legislative control over agency personnel. At the extreme, this has meant both control over individual appointments by the political branches and the insistence that all administrators be contributing members of the party in power. The excesses of "Jacksonian" patronage are no longer evident at the federal level and are decreasingly apparent in state and local governments. Yet for many years, public bureaucracies experienced mass turnover with a change in party control of the executive. Although Jacksonianism is often equated with patronage for the sake of maintaining party strength, it was first presented to the country as an integral component of democratic political theory. President Andrew Jackson felt that the administration had become the possession of an elite class, and he sought to bring it within reach of the common man. He said:

> Office is considered as a species of property, and government rather as a means of promoting individual interests than as an instrument created solely for the service of the people. Corruption in some and in others a perversion of correct feelings and principles divert government from its legitimate ends and make it an engine for the support of the few at the expense of the many.
>
> The duties of all public officers are, or at least admit of being made, so plain and simple that men of intelligence may readily qualify themselves for their performance; and I cannot but believe that more is lost by the long continuance of men in office than is generally to be gained by their experience.
>
> In a country where offices are created solely for the benefit of the people, no one man has any more intrinsic right to official station than another. Offices were not established to give support to particular men at the public expense. No individual wrong is, therefore, done by removal, since neither appointment to nor continuance in office is a matter of right. . . . The proposed limitation would destroy the idea of property now so generally connected with official station, and although individual distress may be sometimes produced, it would, by promoting that rotation which constitutes a leading principle in the republican creed, give healthful action to the system.[2]

By now, a series of administrative reforms has all but eliminated the spoils system in the federal civil service and has curtailed it

---

[2] Paul Van Riper, *History of the United States Civil Service* (Evanston, Ill.: Row, Peterson, 1958), pp. 36–37.

sharply in most state and local governments. Yet several features still testify to the remaining strength of this element in administrative organizations. Senior positions in many public agencies are filled by the chief executive's appointment of an "outsider" brought in from private life, rather than by a person who has devoted his career to the agency.[3] In this way, administration is thought to remain responsive to the wishes of the "people"—either because the elected chief executive makes the top appointment or because the appointee himself is a citizen rather than a professional bureaucrat.

A different approach to political accountability is direct client-participation in agency decisions. This feature has recently attracted considerable public attention as it has been implemented through community action programs of the U.S. Office of Economic Opportunity. As these efforts began, there was direct clash between the two principal forms of political accountability. Elected officials—especially state governors and local mayors—felt their own control over administrative activities would be undercut by citizen selection of policy-making councils and citizen control over the selection of agency personnel. This was a clear instance of intense political conflict over the design of administrative structures. Charges were made on the part of elected officials that the "extreme" device of citizen participation would not only threaten their own capacity to supervise and control government activities, but would also put untrained and irresponsible persons in charge of public resources. They predicted that huge sums would be siphoned off for the support of new "political organizations"; that untrained supervisors would waste resources in poorly conceived and poorly managed programs; and that cadres of new revolutionaries would gain control of these programs and use them to challenge established norms. From the other side, the spokesmen for citizen participation alleged that existing programs for welfare, health, and education were poorly conceived to assist those people who were most in need and that recipients were the best qualified to formulate policies for their own benefit.

The recent political uproar over citizen participation in administrative systems suggests that this is indeed a revolutionary form of structure; but this is not the case. Several old and respectable government programs include provisions for client control. State programs to

---

[3] Prominent exceptions are the military and the police, but even in these cases top policy-makers are "civilians" (i.e., non-professionals) appointed by a popularly elected chief executive or by a commission that is itself appointed by the chief executive.

license and regulate the professions and trades, for example, typically include members of the regulated group on the policy-making boards. A board of physicians typically oversees the regulation of the medical profession, for example; and boards of barbers, plumbers, or electricians supervise the regulation of their trades. Several of the federal agricultural programs established in the 1930's include boards of farmers that make the crucial decisions about local operations. County Committees for Agricultural Stabilization and Conservation, for example, pass on farmers' applications for acreage allotments in the different crops of the region and for federally assisted conservation activities.[4]

Separation of Powers—Checks and Balances

A second intellectual root of administrative structure is that which maintains a separation of powers and checks and balances. The framers of the U.S. Constitution implemented this mode of organization and established it as a tradition to be followed by the builders of state and local governments. In the federal government, the separation of powers takes the form of a bicameral legislature, a separately-elected chief executive, an independent judiciary, and a further division of powers between federal and state governments. Along with this division, each branch was given some tools to protect itself against the others: the chief executive was given a veto; the legislature was given the opportunity to override the veto with an extraordinary majority and the opportunity—in the Senate—to review major presidential appointments; the judiciary was given a vague grant of authority which it interpreted (in *Marbury* vs. *Madison*) as the right to review the actions of other branches for their constitutionality. Finally, the personnel of each branch faced the threat of impeachment if they violated certain prohibitions on their own behavior.

Each of the state governments adopted the separation of powers and the checks and balances, although with slight variations in the nature of individual branches. Indeed, if any general statement can be made about the structures of state governments, it is that they are even *more divided and beset with internal checks* than the national government. In contrast to the opportunities of the president to appoint all the major officers in his administration, each of the governors must work with high-ranking department heads who are separately elected or are appointed by quasi-independent boards or commissions. In contrast to the freedom with which the U.S. Congress can deter-

---

[4] Douglas H. St. Angelo, "Formal and Routine Local Control of National Programs," *Southwestern Social Science Quarterly*, 47 (March, 1966), 416–27.

mine its own prerogatives on matters of legislation, most of the state legislatures are limited to short sessions, are prohibited from borrowing sizable funds in a convenient manner, and have numerous other constraints against the types of legislation they may approve (see below, pp. 105–6).

The pervasive attachment of American constitution-makers to the separation of powers and to checks and balances has several implications for administrative organizations. *First,* control of administrative units is not given entirely to any one of the constitutional branches. *Second,* this concern to divide the leadership of administration precludes the use of a simple administrative hierarchy in which control of the hierarchy is given to the chief executive. The chief executive must share his prerogatives over administration with the legislature and the judiciary. The judiciary hears cases that aggrieved citizens bring against administrators and may void or restrict certain powers that the administrator had exercised. The legislature has many opportunities to affect the structure, procedures, and programs of administration. They include: review of new program proposals; periodic review of agency budgets; the approval of key personnel appointments; special legislative investigations into the operation of certain programs; the legislature's ability to initiate (and to pass over the executive's veto) new programs or to make changes in existing programs;[5] and informal arrangements in which administrators seek the approval of key legislators for certain kinds of decisions. *Third,* each administrative unit may be subject to demands from competing superiors. A committee in the upper or lower house of the legislature and the chief executive may send conflicting directives to the administrator. While at times this may benefit the administrator—by providing him with the excuse of conflicting instructions to explain his lack of compliance with any one of them—the conflict between superiors also presents problems for administrators. Each potential superior may have his spokesman within an agency; the unit may be affected by internal conflict over the choice of superiors. Multiple loyalties within a department can upset the department head's control over his own agency at the same time that they inhibit clear control by either the chief executive or the legislature.

Professional Expertise

Another root of administrative structure is that which seeks to elevate professional and technical competence to secure positions in

---

[5] The Taft-Hartley Act is a prominent example.

each agency. This root has had diverse manifestations, some of which have generated severe conflicts with the spokesmen of contrasting forms of organization. One prominent manifestation is the civil service movement. Several reform organizations have sought to protect federal, state, and local employees from patronage, the spoils system, or political control. Its most prominent success was the Pendleton Act, passed by Congress in 1883 and amended numerous times since then. Over 90 percent of the positions in the federal administration are now covered by merit provisions, as are an increasing number of positions in state and local governments. This has not been an easy process, however, as each major extension has removed patronage appointments from the control of the legislative and executive branches.

Employment on the basis of merit is only part of the more inclusive concern with technical competence. The merit programs merely remove the criteria of partisanship from personnel decisions; they have not—except in quite recent developments—been concerned with the development of recruitment, selection, and training programs to increase the level of technical competence in administrative agencies. These later movements reflect the increased preoccupation of administrative agencies with natural and social scientific programs that require highly trained specialists. Yet this concern with professionalism has its political opponents. The motivation for citizen participation in welfare and education administration comes partly from those who feel that established professions are insensitive to needs of certain clients. Another kind of conflict sees the spokesmen of hierarchical organization doing battle with those who want professionals in charge of their own administrative structures. Where this happens in a university, it is called "faculty" versus "administration." That part of a professional's training which leads him to make his own judgments about a client's needs clashes with the principles of hierarchical management that lead a superior to assert agency policies upon the decisions of his subordinates. Where the manager and the professional employees do not share similar professional training and norms of service—or where the manager has acquired managerial values since leaving day-to-day work as a practicing professional—the intra-agency clash may find professional workers on one side and the management on the other.

Hierarchical Management

Although the administrative hierarchy is often violated due to other "principles" or to the exigencies of special demands, it does have its own intellectual justification. It enjoys the support of a manage ment theory that corresponds closely with some "principles" of managing large private firms. Its proponents describe their work as leading to "the one best way" to organize administrative personnel for the purpose of maintaining control over subordinates and maximizing the efficiency of their performance. This body of theory is responsible for the hierarchical outline which is evident in the organizational charts of most governments and private business firms in the United States. Its principles are:

1. Activities should be grouped by purpose, process, clientele, place, or time and made the responsibilities of small units under the direct control of a supervisor.
2. Work units should be organized hierarchically, so that several units are grouped under the control of a single supervising unit (or supervisor) which is subsequently grouped with other supervisors under the control of a yet-higher supervisor.
3. There should be a narrow "span of control," with a limited number of subordinates under each supervisor. In this way, supervisory personnel can give sufficient attention to each subordinate unit or person.
4. There should be a clear "chain of command" and "communications through channels," so that superiors will have full information about the activities of subordinates and be assured that their directives will control their subordinates.
5. Executives should have sufficient authority to appoint and remove their subordinates.
6. Personnel appointments and promotions should be made on the basis of competence with no interference from "politicians" seeking to reward fellow partisans.
7. Executives should control the expenditures of administrative units.
8. There should be sufficient staff services that provide the executive with the information necessary to understand and control the activities of subordinates.[6]

These management principles have enjoyed strong support in the reports of prestigious commissions charged with proposing administrative reforms: President Taft's Commission on Economy and Efficiency; President Franklin Roosevelt's Committee on Administra-

---

[6] Albert Lepawsky, *Administration: The Art and Science of Organization and Management* (New York: Knopf, 1949), Chapter 8.

tive Management; and the two Hoover Commissions set up by Presidents Truman and Eisenhower.[7] However, recent investigations have challenged several of their basic assumptions.

We have noted above that certain assumptions of the hierarchy are violated by persons in the executive and legislative branches who wish to exercise special controls over administrators. An increasing body of literature also finds that hierarchical structures face difficulties in private industry, even where there are no outside intruders with the status or power of an elected executive or legislature. The hierarchy is no longer in vogue among organizational theorists who concern themselves with the private sector. Among the major shortcomings of a hierarchy in both a private and a public organization are: its failure to account for complex motivations of employees; conflict within administrative units; and the executive's inability to master all the information necessary to control his subordinates. For a hierarchy to operate according to design, subordinates must accept their superior's definition of organizational goals. However, employees come to their task with a variety of personal and professional interests.[8] It is no easy task to win their loyalties for any common goal. Indeed, it is often difficult to define the common goal because department heads themselves may not agree with their own superiors on the proper tasks of their organizations (see pp. 42–43). Conflict within a hierarchy may reflect the imperfect knowledge which the chief executive had about the department head when he appointed him to office; the department head's need to compromise his own desires with those of his subordinates; or the diverse nature of the department head's own interests and his willingness to accept some, but not all, of others' goals for the department. Although the theory of managerial hierarchy prescribes strict adherence to the decisions of a superior, that is a difficult standard to obtain. The result of different goals, different levels of motivation, and different loyalties is often the inability of an organization to clearly articulate its goals. It may be easier to "muddle through" on the strength of agreements about specific programs without raising the spectre of long-range goals. A result, of course, is the lack of clear normative standards against which an executive can

---

[7] See Frederick Cleveland and A. E. Buck, *The Budget and Responsible Government* (New York: Macmillan, 1920); Arthur Smithies, *The Budgetary Process in the United States* (New York: McGraw-Hill, 1955); and Barry Karl, *Executive Reorganization and Reform in the New Deal* (Cambridge, Mass.: Harvard University Press, 1963).

[8] James March and Herbert Simon, *Organizations* (New York: Wiley, 1958), Chapter 2.

screen his prospective subordinates or can test their loyalty once they are employed.[9]

The designers of public organizations have been motivated by a combination of political accountability, separation of powers and checks and balances, professional competence, and principles of hierarchical management. At different times and in different minds, each of these roots have seemed more or less important. There is no *prevailing mode* apparent in the organizational schemes of administrative systems in the United States. If the basic outline is a hierarchy, that outline is frequently compromised. By describing the basic features of administrative organizations at national, state, and local levels, plus the governmental institutions that are designed to control these organizations, we should reach some understanding of what can happen when four notions of administrative structure coexist and some understanding of the stimuli that motivate the designers of particular administrative units.

ADMINISTRATIVE ORGANIZATION IN THE NATIONAL GOVERNMENT

The hierarchical component in the national administration is evident in the organizational chart that is shown in Figure 4–1. Note that cabinet departments are connected by a heavy black line of authority to the Executive Branch. At the head of this is the president whose Executive Office contains a number of staff units designed to facilitate his control of the administration. As noted in Chapter 1 (see pp. 11–12), these staff units—as well as the president himself—are considered members of the "executive branch," and therefore external to administrative units. We examine several of the executive staff units below when we deal with the control mechanisms of the national administration. Most "independent offices and establishments" stand in the same formal relation to the president as do the cabinet departments. If the chart were large enough, most of them would be connected with a separate heavy black line of authority to the president. The model of a hierarchy is continued within the cabinet departments and independent offices. Figure 4–2 is a typical organizational chart for a cabinet department—in this case the Department of Commerce. Note that several units with staff functions are directly under the

---

[9] Charles Lindblom, *The Policy-Making Process* (Englewood Cliffs, N.J.: Prentice-Hall, 1968).

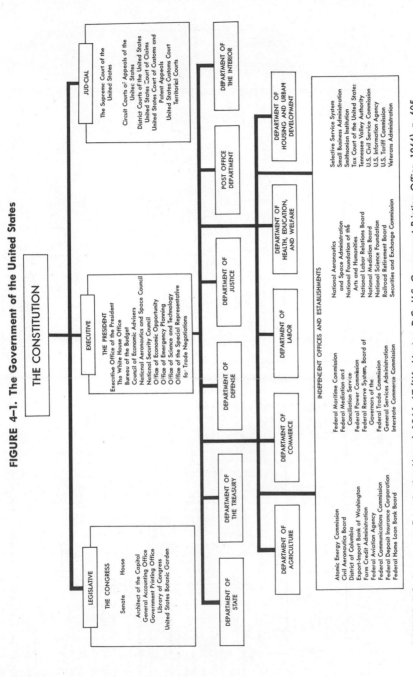

FIGURE 4-1. The Government of the United States

THE CONSTITUTION

LEGISLATIVE

THE CONGRESS

Senate   House

Architect of the Capitol
General Accounting Office
Government Printing Office
Library of Congress
United States Botanic Garden

EXECUTIVE

THE PRESIDENT
Executive Office of the President
The White House Office
Bureau of the Budget
Council of Economic Advisers
National Aeronautics and Space Council
National Security Council
Office of Economic Opportunity
Office of Emergency Planning
Office of Science and Technology
Office of the Special Representative
for Trade Negotiations

JUDICIAL

The Supreme Court of the
United States

Circuit Courts of Appeals of the
United States
District Courts of the United States
United States Court of Claims
United States Court of Customs and
Patent Appeals
United States Customs Court
Territorial Courts

DEPARTMENT OF
STATE

DEPARTMENT OF
THE TREASURY

DEPARTMENT OF
AGRICULTURE

DEPARTMENT OF
COMMERCE

DEPARTMENT OF
DEFENSE

DEPARTMENT OF
LABOR

DEPARTMENT OF
JUSTICE

DEPARTMENT OF
HEALTH, EDUCATION,
AND WELFARE

POST OFFICE
DEPARTMENT

DEPARTMENT OF
THE INTERIOR

DEPARTMENT OF
HOUSING AND URBAN
DEVELOPMENT

INDEPENDENT OFFICES AND ESTABLISHMENTS

Atomic Energy Commission
Civil Aeronautics Board
District of Columbia
Export-Import Bank of Washington
Farm Credit Administration
Federal Aviation Agency
Federal Communications Commission
Federal Deposit Insurance Corporation
Federal Home Loan Bank Board

Federal Maritime Commission
Federal Mediation and
Conciliation Service
Federal Power Commission
Federal Reserve System, Board of
Governors of the
Federal Trade Commission
General Services Administration
Interstate Commerce Commission

National Aeronautics
and Space Administration
National Foundation of the
Arts and Humanities
National Labor Relations Board
National Mediation Board
National Science Foundation
Railroad Retirement Board
Securities and Exchange Commission

Selective Service System
Small Business Administration
Smithsonian Institution
Tax Court of the United States
Tennessee Valley Authority
U.S. Civil Service Commission
U.S. Information Agency
U.S. Tariff Commission
Veterans Administration

SOURCE: *U.S. Government Organization Manual, 1966-67* (Washington, D.C.: U.S. Government Printing Office, 1966), p. 605.

84

FIGURE 4-2. Department of Commerce

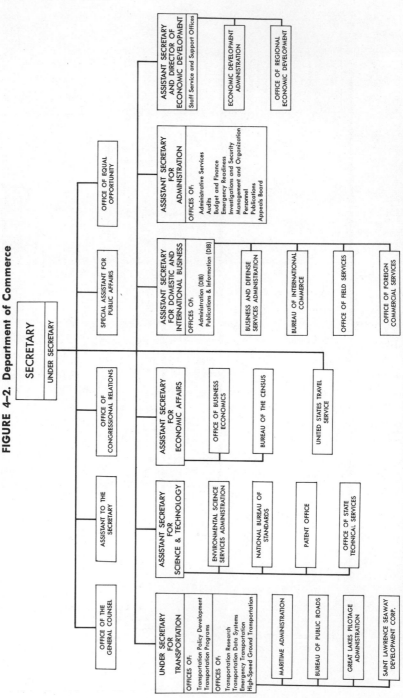

SOURCE: *U.S. Government Organization Manual, 1966–67* (Washington, D.C.: U.S. Government Printing Office, 1966), p. 619.

secretary (counsel, assistant, congressional relations, and public affairs); these units offer advice or services that are useful for the administration of the entire department. The high position of the Commerce Department's Office of Equal Opportunity suggests the importance that the secretary is expected to give to this function. The other functions of the department are arrayed below this secretarial level; and each is supervised by an undersecretary or assistant secretary who is—according to the hierarchical model portrayed in the chart—responsible to the secretary for the operation of his subordinates.

Cabinet Departments and Independent Offices

There is—as indicated in Figure 4–1—a visible distinction between cabinet departments and independent offices and establishments. However, it is sometimes difficult to distill the tangible from the symbollic differences. The principal distinction appears to be one of prestige and importance, as determined by the president and Congress. This determining seems motivated by political desires to reward certain programs with "cabinet status." It has little to do with any roots of administrative structure that are described above. The president's cabinet is a group of officials who may advise the president on matters of policy; but this group is *not* defined solely as secretaries of cabinet departments. In recent years, presidents have invited certain officers who were not cabinet secretaries to attend the sessions of the cabinet on a regular basis. The vice president and the ambassador to the United Nations have been regular participants at cabinet meetings. The heads of certain independent offices have also participated in cabinet meetings. Robert Weaver was a regular participant in John F. Kennedy's cabinet when Weaver was the Administrator of the Housing and Home Finance Administration—before that body became the Department of Housing and Urban Development.

It is questionable whether the president's cabinet has any importance as a policy-making body. President Eisenhower had frequent cabinet meetings and viewed it as a mechanism to obtain important advice from senior government officials. Presidents Franklin Roosevelt, Kennedy, and Johnson, however, spent relatively little time in formal cabinet meetings. They relied heavily on advice received privately from individual members of the cabinet, from officials holding non-cabinet posts in the government, and from trusted private citizens.

In their number of personnel and the size of their budgets, the cabinet departments are generally larger than independent offices.

However, this difference is not uniform. In 1968, two independent offices—the National Aeronautics and Space Administration and the Veterans Administration—had expenditures that were larger than seven of the twelve cabinet departments. The expenditures of the Veterans Administration were surpassed only by those of the Defense, Treasury, and Health, Education and Welfare Departments. In number of employees, the Veterans Administration is topped only by the Defense Department and by the Post Office. The organizational chart of the Veterans Administration—shown in Figure 4–3—suggests that its functions are every bit as broad in scope as those of most cabinet departments. Its units deal with services in the fields of education, health, real estate, insurance, and pensions. The agency's principal clientele are veterans of the armed services, plus their dependents, widows, and orphans who qualify for special services. With peacetime conscription and periodic wars, the Veterans Administration will probably remain in business as an important segment of the national government, even if it never does attain cabinet rank.

With the exception of those few units that were already established at the time of the Constitutional Convention in 1787 (the Departments of State, War, and Treasury),[10] all of the cabinet departments began their organizational lives as independent offices or as components of other cabinet departments. When they became cabinet departments in their own right, it signified a victory for themselves, for clientele groups, and for other supporters who sought the increase in prestige. It is felt that the increased visibility of a cabinet department gains more support from the White House, from Congress, and from citizens' groups and helps the agency in getting more legal authority, personnel, and funds. The elevation of some units to cabinet status has been opposed by congressmen or interest groups who were apprehensive about the growth of certain programs. Conservatives opposed the elevation of the Federal Security Agency to the Department of Health, Education, and Welfare and the elevation of the Housing and Home Finance Administration to the Department of Housing and Urban Development. The Housing and Home Finance Administration faced an additional hurdle when President Kennedy proposed it for cabinet rank: its Administrator, Robert Weaver, seemed likely to become the first Negro in the cabinet.

Within both cabinet departments and independent offices, there have been additional controversies over the placement of units in one agency or another or over their status in the hierarchy of a certain

---

[10] The Department of War was reorganized and merged with the Department of the Navy in 1947 to form the Department of Defense.

87

FIGURE 4–3. Veterans Administration

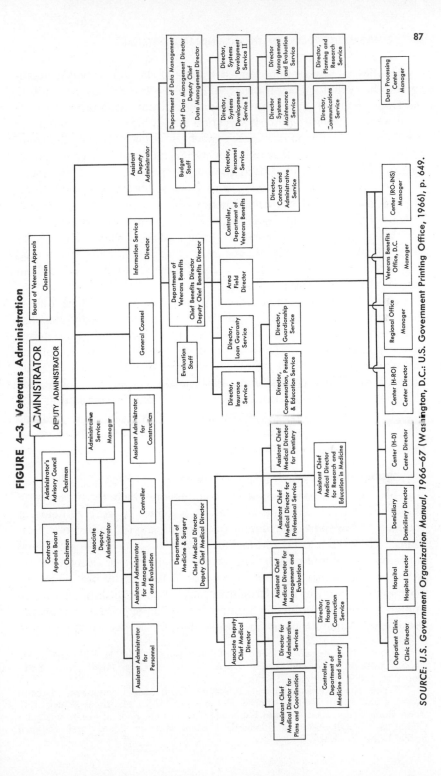

SOURCE: *U.S. Government Organization Manual, 1966–67* (Washington, D.C.: U.S. Government Printing Office, 1966), p. 649.

agency. Some conservation-minded friends of the Forest Service managed to have that agency transferred from the Interior Department to the Department of Agriculture. They argued that the Interior Department was less interested in conservation than in providing resources to commercial foresters and livestock ranchers. Friends of the Childrens' Bureau sought to have that unit elevated in the hierarchy of its parent agency. They wanted it shifted from a component unit of the Social Security Administration—which was one level below the top leadership in the Federal Security Agency—into a position of its own directly below the top leadership. They wanted the Bureau in a position of greater prominence and independence, where it would be more visible, more likely to attract congressional and presidential support, and more able to develop its programs without having them limited by administrative superiors.[11]

Aside from the cabinet departments and independent offices, there are several other kinds of organizations that enjoy peculiar relationships with the president, with Congress, and with other actors in the political system. These units exist near the "borders" of the conversion process in the administrative system. They include independent regulatory commissions, government corporations, federally aided corporations, government contractors, plus several additional "hybrids" that defy even a general label. We describe some of these units in order to illustrate the full range of organizational forms which exist in and near the federal administration.

"Independent" Regulatory Commissions

The independent regulatory commissions include 10 units in charge of setting rules and regulating activities in several fields of commerce, transportation, finance, communications, and labor relations.[12] They differ from "normal" departments and offices in several ways, but it is tempting to exaggerate their uniqueness. Each of them is headed by boards of several members instead of by one secretary. Furthermore, fixed terms of commissioners, bipartisanship, and vague guarantees of job protection promise some "independence" from the presidency. Commissioners are appointed for terms ranging up to

---

[11] See "The Transfer of the Children's Bureau," in Harold Stein, ed., *Public Administration and Policy Development: A Case Book* (New York: Harcourt, Brace, 1951), pp. 15–30.

[12] The commissions include: Interstate Commerce Commission, Federal Power Commission, Federal Trade Commission, U.S. Maritime Board, U.S. Tariff Commission, Securities and Exchange Commission, Federal Communications Commission, Civil Aeronautics Board, Federal Reserve Board, and National Labor Relations Board.

fifteen years; their terms overlap in a way that makes it unlikely that any one president can staff an entire commission with his appointees; and the members of each commission must include a "balance" of members with different party affiliations. Members of several commissions cannot be removed by the president except for certain "causes" which include inefficiency, neglect of duty, or malfeasance. Yet these protections do not protect commissions from being made the subject of public instructions by the president, of investigations by Congress, or of budgetary controls by both the president and Congress. Moreover, the fixed terms of commissioners are not foolproof protections against "stacking" a commission by the president. Many commissioners resign before their terms expire and thereby make their posts available to the next appointee of the incumbent president.

The peculiar structure of the commissions seems to fit their often-delicate assignments. They make rules within the broad grants of discretion provided by the statutes, apply their own rules to specific cases, and adjudicate cases where parties appeal the commission's first decision. Because they seem to be more independent of the chief executive than are other agencies, the regulatory commissions take on some of the reputation of judicial bodies. This may win the acceptance of business firms that must endure adverse decisions. The commissions' independence of the president may also lessen the president's concern with their budgets and program development; thus they may become more subject to legislative control. This increases the appeal of regulatory commissions to congressmen who might otherwise object to government regulation of private industry. Again, however, it is possible to exaggerate the uniqueness of the independent regulatory commissions. Other units within cabinet departments or independent offices likewise make rules, apply their own rules to specific cases of business regulation, and hear first appeals from dissatisfied firms. The unit that looks most like an independent regulatory commission—without the peculiar structure of a commission—is the Food and Drug Administration. It is headed by a single administrator who is appointed (and subject to removal) by the president. The FDA regulates the manufacture, advertising, and distribution of food, drugs, and cosmetics, and it determines which commodities or practices should be removed from the market. There is no clear theory of explanation for the trappings of the independent commissions being given to some regulatory units, while others—like the Food and Drug Administration—are indistinguishable from other agencies. Perhaps some political contexts lend themselves to the development of elaborate safeguards against presidential dominance of a control mech-

anism—along the lines of the independent regulatory commission—
while others permit regulation by a standard type of agency.

Government Corporations

Several corporations are wholly-owned by the federal government. They are subject to budget and basic-policy controls of the
president and Congress, but enjoy some of the freedoms of private
firms. Their activities include banking, insurance, scientific research,
electric power generation, and land development.[13] Their boards of
directors are appointed by the president with approval of the Senate,
and they are subject to the formal budget controls of the president
and Congress. However, much of their funds comes from the sale of
products or services in the private sector. The corporate format is said
to permit them to use economic as opposed to political criteria in
making their policies about pricing and the nature of products and
services.

The business-like status of government corporations does not
protect them from political controversy. The Tennessee Valley Authority began in the 1930's as a major departure for the federal
government. It undertook comprehensive programs for conservation,
flood control, navigation, and electric power generation throughout
the seven-state area that is drained by the Tennessee River and its
many tributaries. During its formative years, the TVA was engaged in
controversies with individual landowners whose land would—or
would not—be taken for an Authority project; with producers of
electricity, fertilizer, and other commodities or services who felt that
the TVA would move into their market with an unfair price advantage; and with local governments who felt that their tax base was
"eroded" by tax-free TVA facilities or by the flooding caused by the
TVA dams. A recent report suggests that the TVA remains controversial. Some of the charges reflect a change in status from a new and
revolutionary agency to one which has made enemies by its programs;
other charges are almost identical to those of 30 years ago:

> Conservationists in Tennessee and North Carolina accuse
> TVA dams of spreading pollution and of eliminating wild rivers
> and trout streams.

---

[13] They include: Commodity Credit Corporation, Export-Import Bank of
Washington, Federal Crop Insurance Corporation, Federal Deposit Insurance
Corporation, Federal National Mortgage Association, Federal Prison Industries,
Federal Savings and Loan Insurance Corporation, Panama Canal Corporation,
Smithsonian Institution, and Tennessee Valley Authority.

TVA developments are charged with providing an unjust advantage to private land speculators. It is alleged that the Authority makes excessive purchases of the land surrounding its reservoirs and sells this land to private developers.

TVA's insistence on cheap coal to run its generating plants is seen as a major incentive for strip-mining operations. It is alleged that TVA does not provide complementary incentives to have the coal industry clean up after a strip operation, replace the terrain to an attractive condition, or control stream pollution.

Local governments in the TVA region continue to charge that its payments in lieu of taxes for inundated lands is inadequate.

Other units of the federal government with overlapping responsibilities have engaged in conflicts with TVA over their mutual jurisdictions. The U.S. Army Corps of Engineers, the Fish and Wildlife Service, and the National Park Service overlap with the TVA on such matters as the development of wilderness areas and streams for navigation, flood control, wildlife, and recreation.[14]

Federally Aided Corporations

Even more ambiguous in their relations with the president and Congress are several institutions labelled "federally aided corporations." Several of these are housed for organizational purposes in the Department of Health, Education and Welfare. They include the American Printing House for the Blind, Gallaudet College, and Howard University. Ostensibly these are private institutions whose boards of directors, executive officials, and personnel are free from the customary selection by the president and approval by the Senate. However, each institution receives funds from the federal treasury; and their officials submit to the annual review of the Budget Bureau and Appropriations Committees. Each defends its peculiar relationship with the federal government by virtue of the socially desirable functions that it performs. Yet these are not the only institutions in the society performing desirable functions; their continued support rests on tenuous agreements with persons having budget responsibilities in

---

[14] See John Egerton, "TVA: The Halo Slips," *The Nation*, July 3, 1967, pp. 11–15.

the White House, in the Department of Health, Education, and Welfare, and in Congress.[15]

Government Contractors

Government contractors are almost thoroughly members of the "private sector," but serve important supplementary functions for government agencies. They build weapons for the military, construct post offices and other buildings for lease to the government, provide janitorial and protection services for government installations, and conduct research in numerous fields of social and natural science. What some agencies do for themselves, others (or the same agencies under other conditions) hire out to a contractor. Some decisions to contract are motivated by the agency's desire not to tie its funds up in capital construction. It takes less of an outlay for the Post Office to lease a building than to build one itself. At times, the temporary nature of a program will lead an agency to contract for services rather than to enlarge its own staff. In the case of scientific or technical jobs, a contractor can pay higher wages and more easily attract talent than can government agencies, due to his freedom from the salary scales of the U.S. Civil Service Commission. Contractors have some freedoms from federal standards that offer them flexibility in certain aspects of personnel, budgeting, and pricing. On other features, however, they are subject to official procedures. Contractors must accept equal-opportunity provisions in hiring and may not segregate their employees on the basis of race. They are also subject to audits by the General Accounting Office and may have details of their expenditures and profits made public by that unit.

Many contracts serve numerous purposes besides those for which they are obviously intended. Federal contracts with university professors for scientific research also funnel money into other features of higher education: to support the graduate students who get part of their training while apprenticed to the principal investigators and—by providing "overhead" money to the universities as part of the research contract—to support the general programs of the university. Federal contracts for the construction of public works or military hardware also serve an economic function. On occasion, these contracts are made with a weather eye to levels of unemployment; and specific projects or firms are selected for their likely contribution to economic conditions.

Several kinds of controversy may affect a university, private re-

---

[15] Ira Sharkansky, "Four Agencies and An Appropriations Subcommittee: A Comparative Study of Budget Strategies," *Midwest Journal of Political Science,* 9 (August, 1965), 254–81.

search laboratory, or business firm that accepts a government contract. Even though the contractor is only partially a member of an administrative unit, he is identified by some observers as part of the policy-making team. Students and faculty members who have objected to the activities of the Defense Department, the State Department, or the Central Intelligence Agency have been militant in their insistence that universities sever their contracts with these units. For similar reasons, industrial firms that make armaments have been picketed by citizens who object to the use of those arms by the military. The status of "government contractor" does not protect an institution from the political disputes that center on the agencies with which it does business. The boundaries of administrative organization are somewhat wider than the departments, offices, and agencies that are officially a part of the administration. Any attempt to assess the impact of government hiring practices, for example, must take account of the equal opportunity practice standards which apply to federal contractors. And any assessment of the goods and services produced under the auspices of the federal government must include the numerous business firms, research organizations, and universities that do part of their work under government contracts.

Administrative Hybrids

Two varieties of administrative hybrids are illustrated by the Office of Economic Opportunity and the Selective Service System. The Office of Economic Opportunity acts very much like the typical "line" agency of the federal government. It provides services directly to the public and administers grants-in-aid to state and local agencies and to non-governmental organizations. Its major programs are Job Corps, VISTA, and Community Action Programs. What is curious about OEO is its location (as of 1969) in the Executive Office of the president. This is generally reserved for staff units that facilitate the president's control over operating agencies. OEO's location in the Executive Office makes it a hybrid of administrative and executive features. It testifies to the fuzziness in the classic administrative concepts of "line" and "staff." As they are customarily used, these refer to administrative units with substantive, service-producing functions (line) or to units with planning, budgeting, or other functions designed to facilitate the executive's control of the administration (staff). The inclusion of the OEO in the Executive Office shows how an organizational innovator can flaunt the hierarchical model and place a unit where it "shouldn't be" in order to facilitate policy-making. There are several reasons for putting an innovative agency, like OEO, in the Executive Office of the president. It's location may signal the president's concern for its programs and may provide the agency with some protection from opponents in Congress or among the state and local authorities who are affected by its programs. Its prominent site might also make OEO more susceptible to control by presidential aides and, thus, might provide its opponents with some feeling of assurance that its "radical" programs will be governed.

The Selective Service System shows how fuzzy are the boundaries between the administrative systems of national and state governments. The Director of the System is appointed by the president and confirmed by the Senate. However, the operating units of the System are controlled by the states and coordinated only in a loose way by the national office. The state directors are formally appointed by the president, but only after the governor's recommendation. These state directors coordinate the activities of local boards. The members of these local boards—who actually classify the registrants and hear first appeals within their jurisdiction—are appointed formally by the president, but again only after the governor's recommendation. State appeal boards are also staffed by the president, but again on the basis of the governor's recommendation. Many other units of the federal government have intimate relations with state and local governments by virtue of grants-in-aid they provide or program standards that they supervise. The Selective Service System illustrates a highly federalized organization that does not rely on cash as the nexus of intergovernmental relationships. It is a minor-league consumer of federal funds (approximately $60 million in 1968); but no one can deny that this hybrid federal-state-local organization has a pervasive affect on its clients.

Another kind of administrative hybrid is the presidential commission that is named to investigate a particular crisis.[16] Examples include the "Warren Commission," named to investigate the assassination of President John F. Kennedy, and the "Kerner Commission," named to investigate urban riots in the summer of 1967. These are hybrids in the sense that they contain representatives of numerous sectors of government and private affairs. The Warren Commission was headed by the Chief Justice of the United States Supreme Court, and the Kerner Commission by the Governor of Illinois. Presidential commissions

---

[16] On the Selective Service System, see James W. Davis, Jr. and Kenneth M. Dolbeare, *Little Groups of Neighbors: The Selective Service System* (Chicago: Markham, 1968). Some observers would quarrel with the definition of this Advisory Commission as an "administrative hybrid" and would claim that it—and similar bodies—are more properly considered in the environment of the administrative system. See the essays in Thomas E. Cronin and Sanford D. Greenberg, eds., *The Presidential Advisory System* (New York: Harper & Row, 1969). See also pp. 195–97 below.

typically include members of the federal Congress and administration, prominent officials of state or local governments, and distinguished private citizens. Each also has a staff which carries the burden of interviewing witnesses, taking testimony, and compiling the interim and final reports. At least for the short time of its existence, a commission may represent a considerable investment of human resources. Insofar as the crisis that provoked the commission has sufficient meaning for large numbers of people, commission reports are "important." In the case of the Warren Commission, its importance seemed to lie in the publicity given to the alternative explanations for the President's assassination and in the legitimization of the "Oswald-as-single-assassin" explanation. In the case of the Kerner Commission, an important product was the creation in several states and localities of "little Kerner Commissions," which were assigned the task of discerning local relevance from the major report, making a local investigation, and producing some recommendations. These commissions perform several of the information-gathering and proposal-generating functions of other units in the administrative organization. They lack any permanence or responsibility for program implementation, but they do have prestige and national prominence. These attributes may warrant the creation of special units that are partially outside the borders of established agencies.

Each of the units described above exists among—or on the borders of—the administrative organization of the national government. In systems terms, they are components of the conversion process in the administrative system of the national government. Some hold only a tenuous membership as administrative units; this is especially true of the federally aided corporations, the government contractors, and the administrative hybrids. The common link between each of these, however, is the resemblance between their tasks and those of cabinet departments and independent offices; they perform important supplementary tasks or, in some cases, identical tasks as the departments, but under peculiar organizational arrangements.

ADMINISTRATIVE CONTROL UNITS IN THE NATIONAL GOVERNMENT

Now we look to the environment of the national administrative system for a number of actors that have the responsibility for controlling units in the conversion process. Each of the three constitutional branches of the federal government, plus one additional institution that does not fit neatly into any of the branches, help to control the administration.

Executive Units for Administrative Control

The Executive Office of the president includes the control mechanisms of the executive branch, plus an occasional administrative unit (like OEO) whose traits as an innovative and politically sensitive institution seem to require the special protections of presidential proximity. The Executive Office developed out of some recommendations of President Franklin Roosevelt's Committee on Administrative Management. According to that Committee, the President needed help in administering the sprawling collection of departments and independent offices that had grown up during the Depression. By 1968, however, the Executive Office itself had grown to nine units with a total expenditure of about $32 million.[17] Executive Office units that figure most prominently as mechanisms of administrative control are the White House Office, the Bureau of the Budget, and the Council of Economic Advisors. Other units have information-advisory-coordinating responsibilities for a limited range of activities. These include the National Security Council, the Central Intelligence Agency, the National Aeronautics and Space Council, the Office of Emergency Planning, the Office of Science and Technology, and the Office of the Special Representative for Trade Negotiations.

White House Office

This office includes the most intimate of the presidential aides: the press and appointment secretaries for the president and his wife; the president's physician; and other members of his personal staff. More important from a policy-making point of view, the White House Office includes several key individuals whose formal titles are unrevealing (e.g., Special Assistant, Legislative Counsel, Special Consultant, Special Counsel, or Administrative Assistant), but whose duties involve them in bill-drafting, in speech-writing, or in negotiations with legislators, administrative agencies, business firms, or foreign governments. The responsibilities of these assistants are not prescribed in any formal document. The White House Office is a flexible mechanism that permits the president to assign trusted individuals to major tasks of intelligence-gathering, policy-formulation, or negotiation. Before the White House Office was established, presidents were forced to do without some of these services or to employ private citizens (often without compensation) as their informal spokesmen. Private citizens (or government employees hired in other capacities) still

---

[17] This figure excludes the service and grant-funds spent by the Office of Economic Opportunity and the secret funds of the Central Intelligence Agency.

advise the president and perform other services for him. However, the opportunities provided by the White House Office may have lessened the president's need for auxiliary helpers.

Bureau of the Budget

The Bureau of the Budget (BOB) is the executive unit with the most awesome collection of formal powers vis-a-vis the administrative system. Its major powers are financial, but it also enjoys controls over the substance of departmental programs which reinforce its financial roles. During the annual budget cycle, the BOB screens administrative requests before they are transmitted to Congress. Indeed, it is the BOB's recommendations that the Congress considers! The rules of procedure prohibit any administrator from making a financial request of Congress that has not been cleared through the BOB. There is no prohibition against Congress granting more funds for a unit than had been requested by the BOB, so it sometimes happens that an administrator's budget will be larger after the congressional phase. In this event, the Budget Bureau has another weapon: it controls the allocation of funds from the Treasury to the agencies, so it can prevent an agency from spending funds in excess of the Bureau's earlier recommendation. The Bureau can use this same control over allocations to hold spending below the level that the Bureau itself had recommended. The Bureau has used this authority when economic conditions have signalled a decrease in expenditures or when a change in demand or policy has made certain programs appear less urgent.

Outside the financial area, the Budget Bureau has certain controls over the statutory authority of each department. Before any administrator can formally initiate a request for new legislation, or even reply formally to a congressman's inquiry about new legislation, he must clear his communication through the Budget Bureau's Office of Legislative Reference. This unit circulates the proposed communication to other agencies whose programs might be affected by the proposal. It then cumulates opinions and defines the implications of the proposal for the "president's program." Without a favorable evaluation from the Budget Bureau, a government agency cannot formally support a measure being considered in Congress. The Budget Bureau cannot stop Congress from granting powers to departments that the Bureau had not initially approved. However, the Bureau has an opportunity to act again after Congress has acted. While a measure is awaiting presidential action, the Bureau circulates it to relevant agencies, gathers their opinions, and then prepares a recommendation for the president's veto or approval.

Along with its formal powers, the Budget Bureau has earned a reputation for inviolability from members of Congress and interest groups. Congressmen respect the Bureau's efforts as a reviewer and distiller of agency budget requests, and they hesitate to impose their own desires on the Bureau in order to avoid setting a precedent that others might follow. Interest groups have failed to receive a sympathetic hearing from the Bureau, and the rules of their game assign it an "off limits" label. One manifestation of the political isolation of the Budget Bureau is the obscure nature of its decision processes. The Bureau has not welcomed outsiders to study its processes. Despite its obvious importance in the policy-making process, political scientists have learned very little about its activities.[18]

Council of Economic Advisors

The Council of Economic Advisors (CEA) consists of three professional economists, plus a staff of assistants. The three professionals are appointed by the president with the consent of the Senate. The CEA traces its origin to the Employment Act of 1946 and is one of the instruments established by that Act to give the federal government responsibility for supervising—and hopefully controlling—the nation's economy.[19] The most prominent activity of the Council is the annual *Economic Report of the President* which is submitted to Congress early each January. In this and other reports, the Council assesses the current state of economic growth and stability, balance of payments, and other international matters; appraises likely impacts on the economy from certain policy proposals; and recommends corrective measures for economic distress. The Council has no direct role in the implementation of policy. However, its advice on the economic implications of current (or proposed) activities affects decisions of the president and the Budget Bureau, and through them affects activities within administrative agencies.

Congressional Mechanisms for Administrative Control

The major control mechanisms in the legislative branch are the committees of the House and Senate, plus a unit that has all the earmarks of an administrative agency but is located in the legislature's jurisdiction: the General Accounting Office. The tools which the com-

---

[18] For significant exceptions, see James W. Davis, Jr., and Randall B. Ripley, "The Bureau of the Budget and Executive Branch Agencies: Notes on their Interaction," *Journal of Politics*, 29 (November, 1967), 749–69; plus other literature cited in that article.

[19] See Walter W. Heller, *New Dimensions of Political Economy* (New York: Norton, 1967).

mittees use to control administrative units include: statutory provisions, budget limits, formal recommendations in committee *Reports,*
and informal suggestions that are made by committee members.

Three types of committees perform control functions with respect
to the administration: legislative committees, appropriations committees, and special committees. In the first category are those committees
that consider the substance of program legislation; they govern the
scope and detail of departmental activities and typically review departmental operations as they consider proposals for adding to or
amending the statutes that authorize the operations. Some programs
are authorized for a limited period of time; so legislative committees
must re-examine the administrators on a regular basis. The labels of
most legislative committees suggest their responsibilities, e.g., Agriculture, Armed Services, Banking and Currency, Education, and Labor.
However, committee labels do not always specify the activities in the
committee's jurisdiction. The Committee on Banking and Currency,
for example, considers legislation that is concerned with public housing and urban renewal.[20] The label of the House Ways and Means
Committee bears little resemblance to its major responsibilities: tax
legislation and the social security program (i.e., Old Age, Survivors,
Disability, and Health Insurance).[21]

The Appropriations Committees have the most regular opportuni
ties for examining administrative activities. Once each year the heads
of administrative units present their requests for the coming year and
defend these requests (plus their performance during the past year)
before subcommittees of the House and Senate Appropriations Committees. It is the subcommittees which make the crucial decisions on
matters of appropriation. The subcommittees' budget recommendations are typically passed on unchanged to the full House or Senate by
their parent Appropriations Committees.[22]

The subcommittees of the Appropriations Committees are divided
according to those departments whose budgets they review; some
subcommittees review the budgets of more than one department. The
Appropriations Committees grant seniority privileges to the members
of their subcommittees, so that the individual members can remain

---

[20] A link between the committee's label and the substance of housing–urban-
renewal lies in the ingredients found within much of this legislation for financing
provisions, the role of lending institutions, and the guarantees on loans that
are provided by the federal government.

[21] The link between tax and social security legislation lies in the provisions
for financing the social security program: a special payroll tax.

[22] See Richard F. Fenno, *The Power of the Purse: Appropriations Politics in
Congress* (Boston: Little, Brown, 1966).

on their subcommittee from one year to the next and accumulate information about agency programs. Subcommittee labels indicate their responsibilities:

> Department of Agriculture and Related Agencies
> Department of Defense
> District of Columbia
> Foreign Operations
> Independent Offices
> Department of Interior and Related Agencies
> Departments of Labor and Health, Education, and Welfare and
>   Related Agencies
> Legislative
> Military Construction
> Public Works
> Departments of State, Justice, and Commerce, the Judiciary, and
>   Related Agencies
> Departments of Treasury and Post Office and the Executive Office

The committee structure of Congress is not static. It changes as members perceive new developments that require their attention. At times, Congress establishes special committees for the purpose of investigating certain institutions or events. A classic example was the committee that investigated the Japanese attack on Pearl Harbor. The committee's voluminous reports and conclusions are cited as justifications for "preparedness" policies followed by the military in the later periods; and the reports had a direct effect on the careers of individual officers.

The General Accounting Office (GAO) is the principal auditing unit of the federal government. Although the chief officer of the GAO (the Comptroller General) is appointed by the president, his term of office (15 years) guarantees considerable independence from the executive branch. The reports of the GAO are made to the presiding officers of the House and Senate, and it is formally responsible to these institutions.

Because of the role that spending plays in administration, the GAO is in a crucial position to enhance the legislature's control over the administrative organization. The GAO has auditing responsibility both for all expenditures of the federal government and for the spending of federal funds by state and local agencies that receive grants or loans. This is an enormous task; and the GAO has simplified it by letting the operating agencies audit their own expenditures under approved procedures. The GAO reserves the right to disallow Treasury payment for any expenditures that are not within the provisions of Appropriations Acts. Moreover, the GAO makes extensive studies—either on its own initiative or at the request of Congress—of administrative procedures. Where it finds these practices to be ineffective, inefficient, or uneconomical (but not necessarily illegal), it makes a report to Congress and proposes reforms.

Judicial Mechanisms for Administrative Control

The control mechanisms of the judiciary differ from those of the executive and legislative branches in their relative passivity. The federal judiciary does not seek out those instances of administrative behavior that it wishes to stimulate or curtail. This is not to say that the courts are weak partners or that they exercise no choice over their involvement in administrative control. Yet it is the nature of the federal judiciary that it waits upon a case being brought to court by a party who considers himself wronged by an administrative decision. Then, depending on circumstances, the court's decision may be a narrow opinion that is relevant for only one instance, or it may be a sweeping judgment that governs administrative actions in many similar instances.

The basic units in the federal court system are the 89 Federal District Courts. Their jurisdiction covers most of the problems raised by administrators' decisions. There is at least one District Court in each state, and another in the District of Columbia. Citizens bring cases to the Federal District Court if they feel that a federal administrative action is not consistent with the statutes, if they feel that the statutes which underlie an administrator's actions are inconsistent with the Constitution, or if they feel that the actions of a state or local administrator are inconsistent with the federal statutes or Constitution. There are also special courts which address themselves to limited concerns. These include: the Court of Claims, which is concerned with compensation for the taking of property, with construction and supply contracts, and with the salaries or perquisites of government employees; the Customs Court, which is concerned with actions arising under tariff laws, reciprocal trade agreements, and other matters dealing with imported goods; the Court of Customs and Patent Appeals, which reviews certain decisions of the Customs Court; and the Court of Military Appeals, which is the final appellate court for military court martials. The Tax Court operates as an independent agency in the executive branch; but it functions in much the same way as a judicial unit. It tries and judges controversies arising between taxpayers and the Commissioner of Internal Revenue. The decisions of the Tax Court, like those of other specialized courts and the Federal District Courts, are subject to review by higher units in the federal judiciary, i.e., by the Courts of Appeals and/or the Supreme Court.

The Civil Service Commission

The Civil Service Commission consists of three commissioners and an extensive staff whose functions are to formulate personnel policies for administrative departments, to supervise the implementation of these policies by the departments, and to perform some personnel services for the departments. In many state and local governments (and in national governments of other countries), the personnel function is assigned to the chief executive. In the U.S. national government, however, the Civil Service Commission grew out of a 19th-century reaction to the excesses of the spoils system. The reformers of that time established the principle that control over federal personnel policies should be isolated from the chief executive. The Commission is not affiliated with either the executive, legislative, or judicial branches of government. The president appoints the commissioners; but no more than two of the three commissioners may be members of the same political party; moreover, their terms of six years each are staggered so that no president can fill more than two of the seats in one term (barring the premature retirement or death of a commissioner). We shall leave until Chapter 5 a further discussion of personnel procedures. At this point, however, it is appropriate to list the principal activities of the Civil Service Commission and, thereby, to show the scope of controls that it exercises over administrative units. The principal activities are:

1. Recruiting and examining candidates for positions in the departments;
2. Developing standards to be used by the departments for the selection, classification, training, promotion, and dismissal of employees;
3. Developing standards for employee safety procedures, health and life insurance, vacation provisions, and retirement plans;
4. Developing employee incentive programs to be used by the departments;
5. Supervising the departments' use of the standards and procedures which have been approved by the Commission;

6. Enforcing provisions of the Hatch Acts which limit the political activities of government employees;
7. Adjudicating the appeals of individuals and agencies which involve rights and interests of federal employees arising under laws, rules, or regulations administered by the Commission; and
8. Examining and making recommendations about the departments' efficient use of their personnel.

ADMINISTRATIVE ORGANIZATIONS OF STATE GOVERNMENTS AND THEIR CONTROL MECHANISMS

In their gross outlines, the administrative organizations of state governments and their executive and legislative controls resemble those of the national government. Each has a number of departments that administer the major programs of the state. The structures of most resemble a hierarchy that culminates in the governor's office. Also, as in the case of the federal government, there are numerous compromises with hierarchical principles. As with the federal hierarchy, these compromises reflect the intellectual roots of political accountability, the separation of powers and checks and balances, and professional competence, as well as particular concerns relevant to each program. What distinguishes the administrative structures of state from federal governments is the extent of these compromises. The architects of state governments have been hyper-sensitive to the notion of political accountability and to the principle of separation of powers and checks and balances. The results show themselves in the top levels of administrative departments and in governors and legislators whose controls over administrative units are weaker than their counterparts in the federal government.

The separation of powers and checks and balances and political accountability are highlighted in most state governments by severe limitations on the authority of the chief executive to govern his administration. This takes the form of direct elections for the heads of major departments, the selection of other department heads by boards or commissions over which the governor has only partial control, the governor's obligation to share budget-controls with individuals who are not directly responsible to him, and more severe restrictions on the governor's tenure than those faced by the president.

In over half of the states, the following positions are held by separately-elected persons: Attorney General, Treasurer, Secretary of

State, Auditor, and Superintendent of Education.[23] Other major appointments are made by boards or commissions (over whom the governor has limited power of participation or appointment). Because governors have little direct control over several important department heads there is a high probability of internal tension and discord in the formulation of state policy. At times the tensions break out in dramatic relief. During a period of party division between Republicans and Democrats in Wisconsin's legislative and executive branches, the Republican treasurer refused to honor the salary voucher of a man appointed to a state commission by the Democratic governor. Because the Republican attorney general also opposed the governor on this appointment, the "chief executive" had to obtain private legal counsel in order to press his case within the administration.

The budget powers of most governors are woefully inferior to those of the national chief executive. Whereas the president formulates his administration's budget with the assistance of an expert Budget Bureau headed by his personal appointee, several governors must share budget formulation with persons who are politically independent. In Florida and West Virginia, the governor is chairman of a budgeting board that includes the separately-elected secretary of state, comptroller, treasurer, attorney general, superintendent of public instruction, and commissioner of agriculture. In Mississippi, North Dakota, and South Carolina, the governor is chairman of a group containing separately-elected administrative heads, plus the chairmen of the legislature's finance committees and members of the legislature named by the presiding officers. The governor of Indiana has only indirect access to the formulation of the budget; his appointee sits on a board with legislators appointed by the presiding officers of the House and Senate. In thirteen other states, the governor works with a chief budget officer who is either separately elected or chosen by the legislature or Civil Service Commission.

In about half of the states, the governor faces restrictions on his tenure. Seventeen states prohibit the governor from succeeding himself in office, and six other states limit the governor to one re-election. This tenure barrier may limit the expertise that the governor develops;

---

[23] This section on state administrative units and their control mechanisms relies on Joseph A. Schlesinger, "The Politics of the Executive," and Thomas R. Dye, "State Legislative Politics," both in Herbert Jacob and Kenneth N. Vines, eds., *Politics in the American States* (Boston: Little, Brown, 1965); tabular materials presented in Council of State Governments, *The Book of the States, 1964–65* (Chicago: Council of State Governments, 1964); and John G. Grumm and Calvin W. Clark, *Compensation for Legislators in the Fifty States* (Kansas City, Mo.: Citizens Conference on State Legislators, 1966).

and it restricts his power in bargaining with the legislature. When it is clear that the governor's term will end soon, individual legislators may be less inclined to accept his persuasion. A study of state budgeting in Illinois summed up the financial powers of the governor with a crisp analogy:

> The budget document may be compared to a huge mountain, which is constantly being pushed higher and higher by underground geologic convulsions. On top of the mountain is a single man, blindfolded, seeking to reduce the height of the mountain by dislodging pebbles with a teaspoon. That man is the Governor.[24]

The institutions that restrict the governor's control over the state administration are mirrored in further restrictions on the legislature's controls. State legislatures lack several of the features that enable the federal Congress to supervise and regulate administrative provisions These include strong committees bolstered with seniority provisions and staff units that can spend full-time on the tasks of administrative oversight.

In the legislatures of some states, committees are weakened by procedures that allow relatively new and inexperienced members to occupy chairmanships. The lack of a seniority system means that committee assignments and chairmanships are up for grabs at the beginning of each session. A 1950 study found that 76 percent of the committee chairmen in the senate of Alabama, 50 percent in the senates of Maryland and Kentucky, and 43 percent in Georgia had only one previous term of experience. In the lower houses of state legislatures, there was even less of a tendency for chairmen to be senior members: 50 percent of the chairmen in Vermont, 44 percent in New Hampshire, 100 percent in Alabama, 83 percent in Kentucky, and 43 percent in Montana, Tennessee, and Nevada had no more than one previous term in the lower house.[25] Without seniority provisions, state legislatures are unlikely to develop any expertise among their members. Where committees do not provide tenure and an opportunity for members to learn their jobs, they are likely to become highly dependent upon the recommendations of administrative agencies.

The lack of viable seniority provisions in state legislatures reflects the unattractive nature of state legislatures and the high turnover of their members, as well as the lack of effort to build strong legislative

---

[24] Thomas J. Anton, *The Politics of State Expenditure in Illinois* (Urbana: University of Illinois Press, 1966), p. 146.

[25] G. Theodore Mitau, *State and Local Government: Politics and Processes* (New York: Scribner, 1960), p. 29.

institutions. The prestige, salary, and perquisites of state legislators
are markedly inferior to those of federal congressmen; and a turnover
rate of 40 percent (much of it voluntary) is not unusual. Half of the
states pay their legislators less than $4,000 per year, and nine of the
states pay less than $2,000. The expense allowances and the clerical
and professional staffs of legislators are similarly inadequate. In several states, the legislators have no office or secretary of their own. Few
of the states provide their legislators anything like the expertise that is
available to U.S. congressmen in the form of committee staffs or the
General Accounting Office.

State legislatures are restricted further by the length of time they
are permitted to sit and by the nature of decisions they are allowed to
make. Only nine of the 50 state legislatures can stay in session for as
much as four months every year without going through procedures to
call a special session. In contrast, Congress faces no limitation on the
length of its sessions other than its members' own endurance. Except
for election years, the recent sessions of Congress have been almost
year-long. In their dealing with budget policy, many state legislatures
face difficult requirements that do not present themselves to Congress.
While Congress can decide about expenditures separately from revenues (with the federal government's borrowing power making up for
the deficit), the constitutions of several states require that expenditures not exceed projected revenues. In some states, additional restrictions also prevail. The legislatures of Maryland and West Virginia
may reduce the funds that the governor recommends for any agency,
but may increase only those recommended for the legislature or (in
West Virginia) the judiciary. In Nebraska, a simple majority may
reduce the governor's recommendations, but a three-fifths vote is
necessary to increase them. In Rhode Island, any increases voted over
the governor's recommendations must be covered by revenue estimates or existing surpluses or by additional financing enacted along
with the budget.

The large number of administrative systems in state governments
permits the use of comparative analysis to determine what effects
different components of the administrative system may have upon
each other. The literature is still limited, and the findings that are
available pertain to few aspects of administrative systems. There are
some findings, however, about control mechanisms that the governor
can exercise over administrative agencies and about the power which
these give him vis-a-vis government policies.

One study of state budgeting finds that the governor's control
over the appointment of agency heads, his own potential for tenure,

and his veto power have some bearing on his influence over appropriations. Where the governor has substantial powers of appointment, his own budget recommendations are more honored by the legislature than where there are many agencies headed by separately-elected executives. The governor's appointment-authority seems to give him some measure of control over the demands of the agency and its tactics in the legislature. When the agency is headed by the governor's man, it lacks a separate base of political power, and it seems less able to pursue funds beyond those provided in the governor's budget. The governor's potential for tenure also strengthens his position with the agencies and in the legislature. When he is unhindered by the state constitution or by statutes from succeeding himself in office, he offers the possibility of remaining for some time as a dispenser of patronage and a formulator of policy. Under these conditions, his budget is more likely to pass the legislature without substantial deletions or additions. The governor's veto-power seems to help him in dealing directly with agency requests. Where his veto power is strong (i.e., where he can veto individual items in a budget and where it takes a large majority in the legislature to override him), the governor is better able to hold down agency requests for budget expansion.[26] The simple existence of strong veto powers may warn assertive agencies that resistence to the governor's wishes may not save them from eventual control.

ADMINISTRATIVE ORGANIZATIONS OF LOCAL GOVERNMENTS AND THEIR CONTROL MECHANISMS

Local governments present even more diversity in their administrative systems than do state governments. In part, this reflects the great number of local governments, the diversity of their economic and social characteristics, and the diversity of their legal responsibilities. In 1966, there were approximately 81,000 "local governments" in the United States, and there were almost 3,200 municipalities with populations in excess of 5,000.[27] The diversity in the structures of local administrative systems also reflects the influence of the several intel-

[26] Ira Sharkansky, "Agency Requests, Gubernatorial Support, and Budget Success in State Legislatures," *American Political Science Review*, 62 (December, 1968), 1220–31.

[27] "Municipal" governments provide general government services to a city, town, or village; they are distinguished from "special-district" local governments which provide only a limited range of services, generally defined by their title (e.g., school or sewerage districts). Counties are the other principal type of local government.

lectual roots of administrative structure that we described above. The spokesmen for each of these roots express their desires with respect to local administrative organizations. Conflicts in local politics, as well as notions about proper organization, shape administrative structures. Also at work are the requirements of state laws and constitutions which make some options available to local governments within the state and bar other options from consideration. In Chapter 9 (pp. 258–62), we discuss several varieties of administrative units that provide services within metropolitan areas. Here we limit our attention to some prominent categories of executive and legislative forms within municipal governments. They are relevant to us for the kinds of controls they exercise over local administrators.

The form of municipal government that bears the closest resemblance to national and state governments includes a single elected executive and an elected legislature. Among these "mayor-council" cities, there is great variety in the powers that are assigned to the executive and to the legislature. However, executive and legislative bodies generally share control over the local administration. Department heads are typically appointed by the mayor or by commissions that are themselves appointed by the mayor. The mayor generally compiles the budget requests of the departments and submits his own recommendations to the council.

Two forms of local government are most interesting for their departure from the models set by the national and state governments. These are the council-manager government with an appointed professional executive and the commission form of government where a small group of elected officials serve both executive and legislative functions. Neither of these models are used as widely as the mayor-council format. However, manager and commission forms together account for about 48 percent of the cities of over 5,000 population.[28] Of the two forms, the council-manager form is more popular. It is found in about 40 percent of the cities of over 5,000 population and most often in cities of 25,000–250,000 population; over half of the cities in this class have appointed city managers. In the class of the largest cities, however (over 500,000 population), less than 20 percent have managers. The complexity of social and economic problems and the intensity of political demands in very large and heterogeneous cities may require a government that permits politicized demands to filter through the executive as well as the legislature. However, studies of manager and non-manager cities in the middle-population range find

---

[28] International City Managers Association, *Municipal Yearbook, 1966* (Chicago: International City Managers Association, 1966), p. 90.

little difference in the social or economic compositions of manager and non-manager cities.[29]

In most manager cities, the appointed executive is responsible for the selection of department heads, the preparation of the budget for submission to the council, and the general management of the administration. One appeal of the manager form of government is the opportunity for a city to hire a professionally-trained executive who is familiar with the technical problems of municipal services. At one time, the manager was considered neutral in matters of policy; he was limited to "administering" the policies of the council. In recent years, however, it is recognized that the acts of budget preparation and personnel selection are intimately involved with matters of policy. It is now generally recognized that the manager involves himself in policy both when he makes recommendations to the council and when he exercises the discretion that the council assigns to him. Successful managers must deal skillfully with the politicians in the city council and with the citizens' groups that urge policy changes on the city.

Some research finds some tendencies for manager-governed cities to differ from mayor-governed cities in the kinds of policies they enact. Large population groups seem to exercise less influence over policy decisions where there is a city manager. This kind of structure is neutral, by design, to the special demands of political parties or distinct population groups. In contrast, government based upon the direct election of the chief executive is designed to bestow power on those groups who can muster support at the polls.

There is also lower "expenditure effort" (expenditure as a percentage of personal income) in communities governed by a city manager than in communities governed by an elected mayor.[30] This has been interpreted to mean manager-governed structures occur in business-minded, conservative communities and that such structures work against high taxes and expenditures. Yet, a study of school-board expenditures finds the highest spending in communities governed by city-managers.[31] It is tempting to see some connection between city-manager governments and a policy emphasis on education. However, differences in research techniques limit any direct comparisons between the studies.

---

[29] Robert L. Lineberry and Edmund P. Fowler, "Reformism and Public Policies in American Cities," *American Political Science Review*, 61 (September, 1967), 701–16.

[30] Lineberry and Fowler, *ibid.*

[31] Thomas R. Dye, "Governmental Structure, Urban Environment, and Educational Policy," *Midwest Journal of Political Science*, 11 (August, 1967), 353–80.

A city-commission form of government consists of from three to seven commissioners, each of whom is popularly elected. One commissioner receives the title of mayor, but his duties are seldom more than ceremonial. The entire commission sits as the local legislature; and individual members serve also as the heads of major departments. This form of government is not widely used and seems to be declining in popularity. Less than 8 percent of cities of over 5,000 population have commission governments, and only one of the 27 cities of over 500,000 population has a commission government.

THE GROWTH OF ADMINISTRATIVE UNITS IN THE TWENTIETH CENTURY

We have seen that administrative structures are neither uniform nor static. They reflect the influences of four different intellectual roots and of demands for "special considerations" that are made in behalf of particular programs. Now we shall examine dramatic changes in the overall nature of administrative activities—as reflected by changes in their economic resources. Agencies have grown in magnitude, and new agencies have been created in response to increases in population, to new demands for public services, and to certain traumas that have generated widespread dependence on government services.

Before we can assess the growth of administrative units, we must agree on some rules of measurement. Several events have influenced the meaning of resources used by agencies and, thus, confound the inferences we can make. We measure the resources of administrative units by reference to government expenditures.[32] We cannot overlook the obvious facts that expenditures in raw dollars increase partly to provide fixed activities to an increasing population and partly because inflation diminishes the purchasing power of each dollar spent. By correcting expenditures for population increases and inflation, we avoid a gross exaggeration of growth in government bureaucracies. Between 1932 and 1962, uncorrected spending figures for the total of federal, state, and local governments increased by 1,240 percent: from $12.4 billion to $176.2 billion. During the same period, however, spending in *constant dollars* (at the 1954 level) *per capita* increased

---

[32] A relatively small proportion of government expenditures support the legislative, judicial, and executive branches of government. The 1969 federal budget showed $433 *million* in expenditures for the legislative and judicial branches and for the Executive Office of the president. The bulk of the remaining expenditures—$183 *billion*—were made by the administrative units.

TABLE 4–1
Expenditures of All American Governments, 1902–1962

	Total		Common-function	
	Total Expenditures Per Capita in Constant Dollars	As Percentage of GNP	Common-function Domestic Expenditures Per Capita in Constant Dollars	As Percentage of GNP
1962	$ 731.90	31.7%	$329.28	14.3%
1955	648.30	25.6	256.48	11.0
1953	701.49	30.1	235.21	10.1
1950	536.00	24.7	250.55	11.6
1944	1,253.02	52.0	211.47	8.8
1940	341.94	20.3	239.91	14.2
1936	297.09	20.3	233.52	15.9
1932	252.73	21.3	177.18	14.9
1927		11.7		8.2
1922		12.6		8.1
1913		8.0		5.7
1902		6.9		4.6

SOURCE: U.S. Bureau of the Census, *Historical Statistics on Governmental Finances and Employment, U.S. Census of Governments, 1962* (Washington, D.C.: U.S. Government Printing Office, 1964), Vol. VI, No. 4.

only 190 percent: from $252.73 to $731.90.[33] We can also distort the appearance of growth at the federal level by failing to take account of the tremendous increase in the nature of responsibilities that are peculiar to the federal government. If our goal is to understand the factors that affect the resources given to federal, state, or local administrative agencies to operate the services that they provide in common, we must exclude federal expenditures for defense, international affairs, space exploration, the postal service, and interest on the national debt. During the 1940–1962 period, spending for these five functions increased from 39 percent to 73 percent of the federal budget.

The figures shown in Tables 4–1, 4–2, and 4–3 permit several kinds of analysis. In order to identify changes in the proportion of resources assigned to administrative units at federal, state, or local levels of government, we can use the percentage of spending for

---

[33] This section relies on Ira Sharkansky, *The Politics of Taxing and Spending* (Indianapolis: Bobbs-Merrill, 1969), Chapter V.

common functions made by federal, state, and local governments. To identify changes in the distribution of resources to each of the major domestic services, we can use the percentages spent for education, highways, public welfare, health and hospitals, natural resources (agriculture, parks, conservation, recreation), public safety, and general government (the support of the legislature, executive, and judiciary, plus financial administration). To identify changes in the total resources made available to administrative units, we can use per capita expenditures in constant (1954) dollars.

Several patterns are evident in the records of administrative resources. First, total levels of expenditures have increased over the period from 1902–1962. The increase is much less, however, if we remove the activities of the federal government that are concerned largely with international and military activities. Second, the events of depression, war, and post-war reconversions seem to have triggered sharp spurts or lags in certain kinds of activities. Third, each of these major events had a different effect on the administrative systems of federal, state, and local government.

Total spending shows its greatest increases during the Depression, World War II, and the Korean Conflict.[34] Spending for domestic programs, however, remained stable or showed some actual decline during war years and increased again after the wars. The spending increases of the Depression were greatest during the 1934–1936 period. The data of Table 4–2 show that natural resources and public welfare accounted for much of this increase. During those years, federally aided programs were begun or enlarged for surplus commodity distribution, wildlife restoration, soil conservation, support for grazing lands, price parity, old age assistance, aid to families with dependent children, aid to the blind, and child welfare.

During the war years, there was a decline in resources for domestic activities, especially in state and local governments. The decrease reflected scarcities brought about by the military mobilization. Manpower, capital equipment, and materials became less available for civilian purposes and precluded many opportunities for government agencies to pursue their activities at previous levels. The domestic field that showed significant increases in resources during both wars was general government. This increased its share of total spending

---

[34] The years used to mark the beginning and end of the Depression, World War II, and the Korean Conflict are governed to some extent by the availability of data. The years of the Depression are considered to be 1932–1940; World War II (including the prewar mobilization) is 1940–1944; and the Korean Conflict is 1950–1953.

TABLE 4-2
All Governments' Common-function Expenditures by Percentage Allocated to Each Major Field, 1902–1962

	1962	1953	1950	1944	1940	1932	1922	1913	1902
Education	28.8%	27.4%	29.3%	15.1%	19.7%	26.6%	28.5%	25.3%	23.1%
Highways	13.3	13.7	11.8	6.5	15.2	20.2	21.6	18.2	15.7
Public welfare	6.5	8.0	9.0	6.2	9.2	5.1	2.1	2.5	3.7
Health and hospitals	10.1	11.4	10.3	5.8	6.3	9.2	10.5	9.1	10.2
Natural resources	16.4	13.8	16.1	15.4	19.5	5.4	3.7	4.4	22.5
Public safety	4.2	4.6	3.8	4.0	4.3	6.4	4.5	7.3	8.1
General government	2.8	5.1	4.7	5.9	5.1	6.9	7.3	11.1	15.7

SOURCE: U.S. Bureau of the Census, *Historical Statistics on Governmental Finances and Employment, U.S. Census of Governments, 1962* (Washington, D.C.: U.S. Government Printing Office, 1962), Vol. VI, No. 4.

from 5.1 to 5.9 percent during 1940–1944, and from 4.7 to 5.1 percent during 1950–1953. This suggests expansions in economic regulatory activities that accompanied mobilization. The sharp wartime declines in the percentage spent for public welfare and education reflected, in part, reduced demands for these services. Reductions in welfare payments occurred with increases in employment and wage levels. Reductions in education reflected wartime drains on teaching staffs and college enrollments and, perhaps, the feeling that investments in education must wait until hostilities end.

After the wars, the availability of manpower, capital equipment, and materials, plus the backlog of needs for repairs and new facilities, spurred increases in government spending and employment. States and localities increased tax rates in order to meet their needs, and the federal government responded with increased financial aid. State and local taxes increased from 5.6 to 9.4 percent of personal income during 1946–1962, and federal grants increased from 5.7 to 12.8 percent of state and local revenues. Significant new federal programs begun during the post-war years included aid for federally impacted school districts, national defense education, and interstate highways. Education and highways benefited most during the years immediately following the Second World War; both fields almost doubled their share of total spending during 1944–1950. By the 1960's, the baby crops of the 1940's and 1950's were putting pressure on a wide range of government services. They—and now their children—have required vastly increased activities in the fields of elementary, secondary, and higher education, hospitals, correctional institutions, recreational facilities, and highways.

The Depression, wars, and post-war reconversions had different effects on the administrative systems of federal, state, and local governments. Table 4–3 shows the division of resources (spending for common domestic functions) among the three levels of government at selected years during the 1902–1962 period. The resources of the federal government increased most dramatically during the Depression and during World War II. From 1932 to 1944, federal spending increased from 14 to 58 percent of the total expenditures. This change reflects a number of factors, including the relative isolation of the federal government from economic catastrophe, its capacity to obtain tight resources during periods of wartime scarcity, and its responsibility during wartime for many domestic programs that had a direct effect on the war effort. During the Depression, the federal government did not suffer—as did states and localities—from the dramatic diminution of the real property tax base. Moreover, the federal gov-

TABLE 4–3

All Governments' Common-function Expenditures by Percentage Spent* by Federal Government, States, and Localities, 1902–1962

	1962	1953	1950	1944	1940	1932	1922	1913	1902
Federal	33.8%	32.1%	38.0%	58.0%	41.8%	13.6%	15.2%	10.9%	9.9%
State	39.4	39.8	37.3	24.3	30.6	31.7	22.3	16.9	16.7
Local	50.2	50.5	44.9	33.4	45.4	66.5	69.6	76.8	78.7

SOURCE: U.S. Bureau of the Census, *Historical Statistics on Governmental Finances and Employment, U.S. Census of Governments, 1962* (Washington, D.C.: U.S. Government Printing Office, 1964), Vol. VI, No. 4.

* Percentages sum to more than 100 because intergovernmental expenditures are counted twice: once for the granting level and once for the level of final expenditure.

ernment had flexible borrowing powers that are denied the officials of most state and local governments by their own state constitutions. And compared to most state and local officials, federal officers may have been better prepared philosophically to fight the Depression with new programs and increased spending. During World War II, the federal government invested in a number of domestic programs that made a contribution to the war effort. One of these was the improvement of ports and canals. Between 1940 and 1944, federal expenditures for these facilities increased from $321 million to $4.5 billion annually. Since World War II, there has been a resurgence of state and local activities in the domestic sector. Between 1944 and 1962, the federal share of common-function spending declined from 58 to 34 percent, while the shares of both state and local governments increased.

During the Depression and World War II, the state governments showed greater stability than the local governments in maintaining their share of total domestic resources. This stability reflects the more flexible financial position of state governments. Both state and local governments entered the Depression as heavy reliers on the property tax. When the value of real property suffered greatly and curtailed its use as a generous producer of government revenue, many state governments shifted to other forms of taxation. Beginning with Mississippi, 23 states adopted the retail sales tax during the 1930's. Local governments, however, were limited by their state constitutions to the declining tax base of real property. Also, state governments enjoyed a wider taxing jurisdiction than did localities and could redistribute resources from "have" to "have-not" areas. Also, the state governments benefited more than did localities from the new federal programs of the 1930's. During 1932–1940, state receipts from federal aids increased from $267 million to $725 million, while those of the cities increased only from $10 million to $275 million.

At the present time, it is not possible to determine the full impact of the Viet Nam Conflict on the resources allotted to various federal, state, and local units. It appears, however, that this trauma will join the Depression, World War II, and the Korean Conflict in altering the distributions of resources to administrative agencies.

SUMMARY

The units within the conversion process fit no simple pattern. The basic model is the hierarchy, but there are so many qualifications of the hierarchy that it hardly qualifies as a common trait. Three other intellectual roots for the organization of administrative units raise conflicts with the hierarchical model and with each other: the concern for political accountability; the separation of powers and checks and balances; and the concern for professional competence. These show their influence in the numerous mechanisms that provide legislators and citizens with access to administrative decisions; in structures that thwart the "political" control of personnel-selection; and in the ambiguous borders between the control responsibilities of the executive, legislature, and judiciary. The hierarchy fails for reasons of managerial ineptness as well as for notions of organizational propriety. Hierarchies are not sensitive to the complex values and motivations of organizational members, to the likelihood of conflicts within organizations over matters of policy, or to the chief executive's inability to gather adequate information about the goals and resources that are relevant to policy decisions.

The principal units of administrative systems and of their executive, legislative, and judicial controllers illustrate the diverse theories and the many particular stimuli that motivate those who design administrative units. The national government includes numerous kinds of units on the periphery of the conversion process of its administrative system, including government corporations, federally aided corporations, government contractors, and such hybrids as the Office of Economic Opportunity, the Selective Service System, and the presidential commissions. The OEO represents a unit in the executive's "staff unit" (the Executive Office of the president) which operates like a service-providing "line" member of the administration. The Selective Service System shows how thoroughly it is possible to mix an agency of the federal government with strong components of state and local governments; and the presidential commissions show how a chief executive can put together representatives of several governmental and private institutions to handle a particular task that has a profound —but perhaps temporary—meaning for the nation.

The administrative control mechanisms of the national government also present great diversity. Principal control mechanisms in the executive branch are the White House Office, the Bureau of the Budget, and the Council of Economic Advisors. In the legislative branch are the legislative, appropriations, and special investigating committees, plus the General Accounting Office. In the judicial branch, there is the federal district court system, plus special courts for claims, customs, patents, and the military. Not clearly in any branch of government, but exercising a wide range of controls over the administration, is the Civil Service Commission.

In state and local governments, there are further varieties in the structures and procedures of administrative and administrative-control units. These illustrate, as in the case of the federal units, the numerous influences that are brought to bear on those who establish —and help to evolve—each unit. There is no central architect of public administration in the United States who operates with consistent standards. The building and changing of administrative organizations is a continuing process. Insofar as it reflects various demands and influences from clients or prospective clients and from those who design organizations, the process of organization-building is as much a part of politics as are other features of policy-making.

5

THE PERSONNEL
OF ADMINISTRATIVE AGENCIES

The focus of this chapter is the elemental actor in the administrative system—the administrator himself. In viewing the administrator, we look at those things which he brings to his job, including his social background, his education, and his values, attitudes, beliefs, and skills. We also examine the techniques that administrative agencies use to select their personnel and to deal with the tasks of training, promotion, and dismissal. A further consideration in this chapter is a personnel issue that has achieved the status of a major controversy, especially in local political arenas. This is the role of collective bargaining in public administration.

Not all agencies use sophisticated personnel procedures. Some agencies have devised programs to identify the traits they wish their personnel to possess, and they seek those traits in the employment market. From among their existing personnel, agencies select some persons for further training or promotion to leadership positions, and other persons for re-assignments or dismissal. Even the most sophisticated agencies may not find all the skilled personnel they desire, may not hire those who are available, or may not make the most efficient use of these skills. Administrative personnel are chosen only partly according to a well-reasoned design. To some extent, administrative agencies cannot control the skills, values, and attitudes that employees carry through the door.

RECRUITING, SELECTING, AND TRAINING
POLICY-MAKERS FOR ADMINISTRATIVE AGENCIES

Some of the most controversial issues in administrative organizations concern the methods used to select administrators. President

Andrew Jackson was the first to raise personnel policies to the status of a major reform issue. His own policies—especially as adopted by subsequent chief executives—became the targets of reformers in later generations. Some reformers have been concerned with personnel policies for their own sake, without reference to their influence on other features of the administrative system. Others have assumed that the nature of personnel—and the methods used to select them—influences the nature of services that are provided by government departments. Jackson himself sought to change the substance of government programs by changing procedures used to select administrators. He wanted personnel that were responsive to the elected chief executive and that permitted him to transform the public's mandate into government programs. Despite a reaction against the excesses of "Jacksonian" personnel techniques, many contemporary reformers have "returned" to the belief that the elected chief executive should exercise control over his subordinates. However, there are significant differences between the proposals of Andrew Jackson and those of present-day reformers. While Jackson—and even moreso some of his adopters—sought political control over the entire administrative corps, modern reformers concede the protections of the merit system for the vast majority of government employees. However, they would enhance the executive's control over those administrators in high-level policy-making positions. The executive would have an integrated policy-making team, with each member appointed on the basis of his willingness to accept the chief executive's leadership. Also, contemporary reformers see the personnel task as more complex than it was viewed in Jackson's day. It is not simply a matter of giving the power to hire and fire to the chief executive. There is a need to forecast personnel needs, to compete with private enterprise for the desired skills, to train new employees, to provide sufficient rewards, and to allocate personnel to the positions where they can make the greatest contribution to the administrative system. A study published by the Brookings Institution listed several components that must be included in an effective personnel program for high-level positions:

1. Analyze future needs for higher personnel and evaluate prospects of meeting such needs.
2. Compete successfully with other employers for superior personnel.
3. Make systematic, reliable, and valid evaluations of employees' performance and potential—as a basis for development and promotion.

4. Develop and train enough superior employees to fill most higher jobs—employees whose professional skills are excellent and up to date and whose perspectives are broad and mature.
5. Select the best candidates from a reasonably broad area of consideration for promotion or appointment to higher jobs—with reference to the particular needs of each job.
6. Provide advancement in compensation at a rate consistent with the employee's professional development and rates of advancement offered by competing employers.
7. Provide flexibility of assignment to meet needs of the program and also changing circumstances of the employee.
8. Compensate personnel at fair market value for their services.
9. Retain and use to fullest advantage those employees who make a valuable contribution to organization goals.
10. Motivate personnel to give a full measure of cooperative effort.
11. Shift substandard personnel to jobs they can do effectively or discharge them.[1]

Any evaluation of the personnel procedures that are employed by administrative agencies are complicated by differences between career and political appointees. Both categories include people who are at the highest levels in administrative units and who are involved in policy-making. However, the two groups differ in their overt alignment with political parties and involvement in election campaigns, as well as in the kinds of job protection they enjoy. Control over political appointees is generally given to popularly-elected executives, while control over the career service is typically held—or shared—by an institution protected from partisanship. The goals of the Brookings study are suitable for both career and political positions; but their detailed applications would vary. The procedures used for evaluating,

[1] David T. Stanley, *The Higher Civil Service* (Washington, D.C.: Brookings Institution, 1964), pp. 7–8. Copyright © 1964 by the Brookings Institution. The "GS" rating of a position refers to its level in the General Schedule classification. The higher the rating, the more status, "importance," and salary are assigned to a position. The specific meaning of the term "high-level administrator" varies with the studies that supplied the information used in this chapter. W. Lloyd Warner, *et al., The American Federal Executive* (New Haven, Conn.: Yale University Press, 1963), examines federal administrators at the levels of GS 14 and above. David T. Stanley, *The Higher Civil Service,* considers levels GS 15 through GS 18. Dean E. Mann, *The Assistant Secretaries: Problems and Processes of Appointment* (Washington, D.C.: Brookings Institution, 1965), considers departmental assistant secretaries, under secretaries, and their equivalent positions in the independent offices.

advancing, and retaining employees could include or exclude partisan criteria.

"NON-POLITICAL" PERSONNEL PROCEDURES IN THE NATIONAL ADMINISTRATION

The United States Civil Service Commission is the central personnel unit of the national government's administrative organization.[2] (Its activities are summarized in Chapter 4, pp. 102–3.) The primary concern of the Commission is lower-level positions. In the policy-making categories examined by the Brookings project, selection is primarily decentralized. The heads of departments and agencies have virtual control over the choice of their immediate subordinates. When looking for such personnel, they tend to promote individuals from within their own organizations or to solicit applications from other agencies of the federal government, from state or local administrations, or from private industry. The main sources are their own organizations or other units of the federal administration. Of the high-level administrators studied by the Brookings project, only 11 percent first entered the federal service at the level of GS 15 or above;[3] the large majority were appointed to these policy-level positions from subordinate places in the administration.

Two devices that federal agencies use to support and purchase work done by outside institutions permit the agencies to avoid many details of recruiting and selecting personnel; these two devices are grants-in-aid and federal contracts. By giving grants to state or local governments, federal agencies make an important contribution to the provision of certain public services, without having to worry about recruiting personnel who can do the work.[4] By giving contracts to universities or to private industry, federal agencies can likewise "pass-on" their personnel choices. Contracting is particularly attractive where high-priced skills are involved. The contracting party can pay salaries above the normal federal scales in order to obtain skilled individuals who would not otherwise be available.

The lack of central control over personnel procedures for policy-level jobs and the flexibility offered by grants and contracts have wide

---

[2] For background information on this subject, see Paul Van Riper, *History of the United States Civil Service* (Evanston, Ill.: Row, Peterson, 1958).

[3] Stanley, p. 95.

[4] State and local agencies that receive federal grants must use employment criteria subject to certain standards of the U.S. Civil Service Commission. The recruiting and selection of specific persons, however, is left to the recipient agency.

appeal in administrative agencies. One project of the Brookings Institution claimed there were no serious difficulties in competing for personnel with private industry.[5] It also criticized several proposals for centralizing personnel procedures for policy-level positions. Such a change would deprive agency heads of control over their subordinates and would weaken the concept of an agency "team" united by common program perspectives. Moreover, a central mechanism might move personnel from one agency to another to relieve their present supervisors of difficult employees. If agency administrators themselves keep control over high-level appointments, they can elevate the agency's own needs to a foremost position in the selection criteria.[6]

With respect to the *evaluation* of current employees and their further *training*, the Brookings study found civilian agencies are far below desired performance. Its standard of excellence is the military which assigns its officers to long periods of formal schooling and which makes periodic evaluations to decide about promotion or retirement. Civilian agencies have been slow in realizing the value of employee training paid for by the government. As recently as 1963, the training expenditures reported by the Civil Service Commission were only $35 million, or $14 per employee. In that year, only 24 employees from grades GS 15 and GS 16 were assigned to long-term (more than 120 days) training. Recently, there have been marked increases in employee training. Programs include Executive Seminar Centers and a newly opened Federal Executive Institute. The Institute adjoins the campus of the University of Virginia in Charlottesville and provides graduate-level courses to selected groups of upwardly mobile federal executives. Yet many civilian executives still have negative attitudes toward extensive training programs. Some agency heads feel that if they grant a leave for training they indicate over-staffing and loose opportunities to get additional personnel. Budget officers have cut agency funds on the grounds that training is a sign of overstaffing.[7] Individual employees feel they will lose their chance for promotion if they take training leave. To a large extent, the statement of President Andrew Jackson ("the duties of all public officers are . . . so plain and simple that men of intelligence may readily qualify themselves for their performance") prevails despite the technological transformations that have occurred in public administration. Some administrators and legislators oppose the use of any government money for training civilian employees.

---

[5] Stanley, p. 81.
[6] Stanley, p. 97.
[7] Stanley, pp. 86–88.

The magnitude of the selection and training problems for high-level personnel are made evident by the number of persons who might be involved. A federal "Task Force on Career Development" reported that the federal administration employed (in 1967) about 761,000 persons in professional, administrative, and technical occupations and that it would need an additional 225,000 in the following decade. Because of a gross turnover estimate of 675,000, it will be necessary to recruit and/or train about 900,000 such persons by the mid-1970's.[8] A special problem of this decade reflects the influx of young talent that occurred during the Depression. These people are now leaving the government through death or retirement. Problems of mass replacement are made difficult by the boom in the private economy and by the pale cast on the federal government by the war in Viet Nam. The economic boom means that talented people have high-priced non-governmental alternatives; and the War may be particularly discouraging to the kinds of young, bright idealists who went to Washington during the early years of the New Deal or during the Administration of John F. Kennedy.

In most matters of evaluation and retention, procedures favor the employee. After a person has survived his probationary period, it is difficult to identify unsuitable characteristics and dismiss him from the service. The procedures require formal charges and permit an appeal by the person being dismissed. The experience is said to upset other employees in an organization, to distress the leadership, to produce a general malaise, to increase voluntary resignations, and to reduce efficiency. "There are ways to do this, but they are expensive and they make us sick to our stomachs."[9] Some officials employ informal techniques to urge unwanted employees to leave. These include unpleasant assignments and social rejection. These techniques may serve their immediate purpose; however, they also reduce the morale of other employees who wonder if informal, unchallengeable procedures will someday be directed against themselves.

The lack of any systematic procedures for evaluating the work of civilian administrators is one of the factors that discourages any greater centralization of the personnel system. Without a sure-fire way for making evaluations in the Civil Service Commission, the task is left to the agency heads. Presumably, they have insight into their agencys' special requirements and perhaps have some knowledge of personalities that is helpful in identifying those employees to be promoted and

---

[8] Roger W. Jones, "Developments in Government Manpower: A Federal Perspective," *Public Administration Review,* 27 (June, 1967), 134–41.

[9] Stanley, p. 112.

those to be kept in menial tasks or even dismissed. However, the size of most federal agencies precludes any real control over personnel evaluation by the agency head. Moreover, the standards used to select employees for promotion are often indirect or even haphazard. Some of the haphazard standards include reports from clients, length of service, or performance on particular occasions that are noted by the press or by the employee's superiors. There are serious problems of sampling that make it unwise to generalize about a man's performance on the basis of individual observations. Length of service may testify to nothing more than the employee's success in not offending anyone; it says nothing about his positive contributions to the agency. Some indirect measures of performance include academic degrees and professional certification. These do show that an employee has certain academic experiences and has passed the screening procedures of a professional body. They also suggest general competence. However, some schools and professional organizations are more lax than others in granting their *imprimatur*. And even the most prestigious certificate may not indicate that an individual can perform the specific responsibilities that are assigned to him.[10]

COLLECTIVE BARGAINING IN THE PUBLIC SERVICE: CONFRONTATIONS WITH PERSONNEL ADMINISTRATION

An aspect of personnel policy that is an increasing problem for administrative agencies is their relations with the union-like organizations of their employees. The difficulties include: challenges of established anti-union or anti-strike statutes; political squeezes between the citizens and legislators who are outraged at the suspension of public services and the public employees who are outraged at their own lack of desirable salaries or working conditions; and moral confrontations between those who argue that government employees should have the same rights to organize and bargain collectively as do employees in the private sector and those who argue that the state's sovereignty cannot be compromised by granting public employees the right to thwart the policies of constitutional offices.[11]

A basic problem of both the employees who organize and of those administrators who must deal with them reflects the insensitivity of

---

[10] David T. Stanley, "Excellence in Public Service—How Do You Really Know?" *Public Administration Review*, 24 (September, 1964), 170–74.

[11] This section relies on Frederick C. Mosher, *Democracy and the Public Service* (New York: Oxford University Press, 1968), Chapter 6.

earlier civil service reformers to the collective demands of employees. The "merit system" and related mechanisms come down on the side of the individual rather than the group. Its features include open competitive examinations, criteria rewarding individual excellence, and employee classifications on the basis of objective analysis of performance. Against these principles, the demands of unions are in the tradition of a closed shop, of recruitment on the basis of union membership or occupational license, of promotion on the basis of seniority, and of negotiation of employee classifications and working conditions.

Along with the individualistic tradition of civil service reformers, there are some political theories that lead otherwise pro-labor politicians to oppose collective bargaining with public employees. "To the extent that [employees' organizations] can advance the interests of their members they deprive political representatives, who are responsible to the whole people, of power over public policy."[12] President Franklin Roosevelt wrote:

> [Collective bargaining] has its distinct and insurmountable limitations when applied to public personnel management. The very nature and purposes of government make it impossible for administrative officials to represent fully or to bind the employer in mutual discussions with government employee organizations.[13]

The unions of government workers, plus employees' organizations and professional associations that behave like unions, have not been confined by these principles or by the anti-strike laws which exist in most jurisdictions. Government unions, especially at state and local levels, are now the fastest growing sector of the union movement. The American Federation of State, County, and Municipal Employees multiplied its membership by three-and-one-half times between 1956 and 1966; and it could reach one million members by the mid-1970's. By 1964, about 60 percent of the employees of the Post Office, 33 percent of the blue-collar workers in other federal departments, and 14 percent of the white-collar employees were unionized. The figures on unionization of government employees are no smaller than comparable figures for white-collar or service industries in the private sector.

Along with growing size, there is also growing militancy among public-employee unions. Although most of them exist in jurisdictions that formally outlaw the strike for government employees, one study

---

[12] Mosher, p. 178.
[13] Mosher, p. 177.

recorded 38 strikes in 1962, 42 in 1965, and more than 150 in 1966.[14] In many actions, the leaders take care to avoid the term "strike." However, slowdowns or sick-leaves that occur in a cohesive manner during crucial periods of collective bargaining leave no doubt about their purpose. Some "strikes" take the form of strict enforcement of regulations that are otherwise slighted for purposes of convenience. Local policemen have enforced parking regulations with unusual thoroughness, sometimes against the vehicles of prominent citizens or of the policy-makers themselves. In the summer of 1968, the air traffic controllers of the Federal Aviation Agency expressed their displeasure by refusing any of the customary deviations from strict safety requirements. The resulting delays at the major airports led Congress and the Budget Bureau to release additional funds for recruiting and training new traffic controllers. One observer of the traffic-controllers' activities saw in it a strategy for the employees of other federal agencies:

> If it is obvious that airways traffic control cannot stand still until such time as war expenditures are reduced (enough to permit increased expenditures for air safety), it is equally obvious that official exhortations to make do with inadequate funding will not suffice for the Post Office, the National Park Service, the National Institutes of Health, or other agencies. The problem for these other agencies is to find ways to dramatize their plight.[15]

One of the features in many confrontations between public agencies and their employees is the nature of employees' goals. Often, they are not so interested in wages or fringe-benefits, but in the ways that services are administered. The air traffic controllers defended their demands for additional manpower in the name of improved air safety. Likewise, welfare workers and nurses have gone on strike (or taken equivalent actions) while demanding reduced case-loads in order to provide better service for their clients. And teachers have gone on strike to reduce the number of pupils in a classroom. During the fall of 1968, New York City teachers stayed out for 11 weeks over the decentralization of policy-making and over the school board's use of "non-professional" standards for assigning teachers.

The strike is not the only weapon of employees' organizations. Where government workers are numerically strong and are unified behind certain proposals, they can mount an awesome force in election campaigns. This force assures a receptive hearing many elected

---

[14] Mosher, p. 190.
[15] Karl M. Reppenthal, "No Money for Safe Landings," *The Nation*, August 26, 1968, pp. 142–44.

executives and legislators. Strikes, slowdowns, or sick-calls generally reflect the demands of certain labor categories who cannot mobilize the support of the whole government work force. Also, the unresponsive nature of many local legislatures may affect the greater tendency of local (rather than state or federal) employees to strike.[16]

PERSONNEL PROCEDURES FOR POLITICAL APPOINTEES IN THE NATIONAL ADMINISTRATION

The civil service reformers of the 19th century portrayed hordes of office-seekers descending on newly-elected presidents. In their cartoons, the chief executive was unable to attend to important business because of the job-applicants. Today this is a false image. The president searches for talent; and he may have to persuade his choices to leave well-established situations in business or in their profession. To his prospects he offers the opportunity to serve his administration, typically a substantial reduction in salary, and a substantial increase in their personal expenses.

Recent presidential candidates have postponed decisions on political appointments until after the election. Although this delay has disturbed some observers of the presidential transition, the campaign itself has consumed the most important resources of the candidate and his assistants. One of John Kennedy's aides said that "Kennedy wouldn't have won" if his staff had devoted any more attention to post-election matters.[17] Both Eisenhower and Kennedy detailed a group of advisors to concentrate on high-level personnel immediately after the election. The central figures in Eisenhower's group were Herbert Brownell and Lucius Clay. Brownell was experienced in Republican party politics as a former national party chairman and campaign manager for Thomas Dewey. Clay was a military associate of the president-elect, had been active in the 1952 political campaign, and was chairman of the board at Continental Can Company. The key people in Kennedy's personnel team (the "Talent Hunt") were his brother and campaign manager Robert Kennedy and his brother-in-law R. Sargent Shriver. Both the Eisenhower and Kennedy teams solicited names of prospective appointees from their contacts in politics, business, the professions, and universities; screened the qualifications of various prospects; cleared them with political leaders and professional or business associates; and made recommendations for each cabinet position. The Eisenhower and Kennedy teams differed in

---

[16] Mosher, p. 191.
[17] This section relies on Mann, pp. 72ff.

their styles. Eisenhower's resembled a smooth-running military staff, while Kennedy's was loosely-structured and took longer to make its decisions. Kennedy appointed his first cabinet secretary on December 1, which was the same date in 1952 when Eisenhower announced his final appointment.

There is no question about the direct involvement of the president-elect in the selection of cabinet secretaries and the heads of major independent offices. There have been differences, however, in their involvement in making appointments just below those levels. President Eisenhower left the selection of subordinate appointees to the new cabinet secretaries and agency heads. This was consistent with his policy of delegating decisions and permitting administrators to operate their own organizations. This policy disappointed some Republican Congressmen who could not get presidential intervention for the sake of a "deserving constituent." On some occasions, Eisenhower's staff urged a department to take "political considerations" into account; but the president-elect did not involve himself directly. Generally speaking, Kennedy exercised more control over subordinate appointments than did Eisenhower. Indeed, Kennedy's first announcement—made even before the announcement of a Secretary of State— was G. Mennan Williams as Assistant Secretary of State for African Affairs. This presidential concern may have won some credits among elites in the new African states, but it also signalled to the State Department that Kennedy would make decisions that formerly were delegated to the secretary. President-elect Kennedy appointed Chester Bowles as Under Secretary of State and Adlai Stevenson as Ambassador to the United Nations. Also, each of Kennedy's cabinet secretaries was assigned a member of the personnel team to review candidates available for subordinate appointments.

Recent presidents have used a combination of occupational competence and political acceptability as personnel criteria. The Kennedy team asked about a prospect's "judgment," "toughness," "integrity," "ability to work with others," "industry," "devotion to the principles of the president-elect," and whether his appointment would enhance the administration's prestige "nationally," "in his state," "in his community," or "in his professional group." With the press of time and many prospects to be reviewed, however, evaluations were simplified to "highly qualified," "qualified," or "some qualifications" with respect to competence; and "good Democrat," "political neutral," "Republican," or "politically disqualified" with respect to partisanship.[18]

---

[18] Mann, p. 73.

As presidents pass the period of inauguration, they change procedures for political appointments. Without the crush of numbers, they no longer require a special task force. Both Eisenhower and Kennedy assigned the review of later political appointees to the White House Office (see pp. 96–97). As the presidents themselves concentrate increasingly on substantive problems, their cabinet secretaries take a prominent role in personnel decisions, most of which involve the selection of replacements for subordinates who resign.

Congress also has a role in political appointments. The Constitution gives Congress the power to determine procedures for filling appointive positions. In some positions, Congress gives the appointment to the president alone. This is the case for the Director and Deputy Director of the Budget. Within some cabinet departments and independent offices, administrative assistant secretaries do not require senatorial confirmation. These are typically named by immediate superiors to serve as personal assistants. As of 1965, all department secretaries, under secretaries, and assistant secretaries, as well as ambassadors, the heads of most independent offices, and federal judges, were subject to senatorial confirmation.[19]

Most of the time, the Senate makes only perfunctory examinations of candidates. The individual is introduced to the Senate committee that has charge of legislation for his department. There is seldom any searching probe of his background or intentions and often no formal record of the committee meeting. His name may go before the Senate with no debate and be approved by unanimous consent.[20] Most of the time, senators grant the president considerable discretion over personnel. They seldom offer any public opposition to his appointments.[21]

When opposition to an appointment does come from the Senate, it can take several forms. It can be a serious effort to block an appointment or merely the attempt of one senator to record his own opposition. Some opposition may be designed to elicit policy committments from the nominee. Few candidates for political appointments actually are rejected by the Senate. Until 1965, only eight cabinet nominations had been rejected, and no nominations for assistant secretaries or under secretaries had been rejected since 1933. Yet this is not the full record. Some nominations are withdrawn by the president because he fears the embarrassment of a formal rejection; and some, presumably, are never formally submitted because key senators expressed intense opposition during a preliminary clearance.

[19] Mann, p. 35.
[20] Mann, pp. 135–52.
[21] Mann, p. 149.

THE SIGNIFICANCE OF ADMINISTRATORS' PERSONAL TRAITS IN ADMINISTRATIVE ORGANIZATIONS

It is impossible to say just how much the personal traits of administrators influence the activity of administrative agencies. At the present time, there simply is not enough information about the backgrounds, values, or skills of administrators to attempt the evaluation. Most of the information to be reported in this chapter concerns large groups of government employees. There is not enough data about the personnel of individual agencies to do a comparative analysis that would show the correspondence between administrators' traits and the policies of administrative agencies. Even our descriptive effort must be limited to the administrative agencies of the national government. The most valuable data focus on federal employees in high-level professional or technical positions or on those having policy-making responsibility. These personnel are the most likely to shape the decisions of their agencies.

The information available shows that administrators at policy-making levels differ from the general adult population in their social backgrounds and educational experiences. However, they do not differ markedly from individuals in positions of responsibility in other branches of government or in large business firms. Some studies indicate that among government administrators a *higher* proportion have advanced education and a *lesser* proportion come from upper-class families than do members of the legislative branch or executives of large private firms. Yet the differences are not great. In these and other traits, the high-level personnel of public agencies are more like their counterparts elsewhere in government or business, than any of these groups are like adults in the society as a whole. Generally speaking, responsible positions in many fields attract persons with more-than-average education and from upper-income families. There is no indication that the personal traits of government administrators are so different from those of other policy-makers that their presence is likely to distinguish the decisions of government agencies from other institutions.

The multiple influences on agency policies provide some competition for whatever influences may come from the personal traits of administrators. Moreover, control procedures found in many agencies reduce even further the influence that is open to personal traits. The personal attributes of administrators must "compete" for influence over policy with formal and informal communications from the legislative, executive, and judicial branches of government, from officials at other levels of the federal system, and from clients and other members of the public. Moreover, different aspects of the administrators' own characteristics may compete with one another for influence over their decisions. The "interests" identified with their family's social status, for example, may conflict with the professional orientation that they acquired as part of their formal training. Within one administrative unit, the personal interests of administrators may compete with one another and make it unlikely that any one's personal interest can shape the agency's decision. Most administrative agencies have procedures that guard against the overt influence of personal interests on official decisions. These include: multiple decision-makers within individual agencies; the separation of powers and checks and balances which surround an agency with several executive and legislative supervisors; and conflict-of-interest procedures that are used to screen out applicants who would have a substantial financial stake in the agency's policies.

It is still helpful to describe the personal traits of administrators, even though we can find little discernible impact of these traits on the outputs of administrative organizations. The composition of the public service has significance for questions of employment opportunities. To what extent do the children of different social classes or ethnic groups have equal opportunities to enter public employment and reach policy-making levels? In some groups that have been the target of severe discrimination in private industry, the government may be the most likely source of jobs that are commensurate with their skills and training. The opportunity for government employment is one of the major outputs that an administrative organization provides to some groups in the population. There are also significant questions about the public-mindedness and dedication of government employees. These require information about the personalities, values, and aspirations of administrators.

WHO ARE PUBLIC ADMINISTRATORS?

Compared to the population as a whole, high-level administrators[22] in the federal government come disproportionately from communities having large population, from families in the middle and upper ranges of occupational status, and from Protestant religious groups. This combination of traits suggests that high-level administra-

---

[22] See Note 1 above.

tors enjoyed a number of childhood benefits. These benefits increased the likelihood of cosmopolitan rather than parochial perspectives and made available attractive educational opportunities and career prospects in science, the professions, or management. The administrators' own educational experiences complement their middle- and upper-class backgrounds. Almost all of them graduated from college, and a sizable proportion have advanced degrees. A high percentage received their pre-collegiate education in private high schools and took their college degrees at the most prestigious colleges and graduate schools.[23]

Although the backgrounds of high-level administrators differ markedly from those of the "average citizen," they are not very different from the backgrounds of people in other positions of responsibility in government or private industry. Table 5–1 brings together data from several studies of elites' backgrounds. The data illustrate several conclusions about the social backgrounds of elites. All of the elites come from social groups that have had more advantages than the average citizen has had. Compared to the population as a whole, they have had significantly more education and are more likely to be Protestant. Other data show that they are more likely to come from executive-professional families than is the average citizen. The religious affiliation suggests that elites come from "old" families, rather than from "recent" immigrants from Ireland or southern and eastern Europe.

There are some differences in the traits of high-level government administrators in civilian posts and those of other elite groups. There is a higher incidence of Catholics among government administrators and a higher incidence of laborers' sons; this suggests the relative "openness" of the federal bureaucracy, as compared to private industry. The higher incidence of advanced education testifies to the skills found in the bureaucracy and suggests that many administrators overcame their family or cultural disadvantages by their own hard work in school.

The traits of people elevated to the highest positions in federal administrative agencies reflect to some extent the influence of the particular president who appointed them. Table 5–2 shows some information about the political appointees of recent presidents. There

---

[23] Warner, et al., Chapters 2–4; Mann, Chapters 2–3; and Stanley, The Higher Civil Service, Chapter 3. Also, for a study of the changing composition of the U.S. Foreign Service with respect to the undergraduate backgrounds of recruits, see Martin B. Hickman and Neil Hollander, "Undergraduate Origin as a Factor in Elite Recruitment and Mobility: The Foreign Service—A Case Study," Western Political Quarterly, 19 (June, 1966), 337–53.

TABLE 5-1
The Social Backgrounds of Elites in the 1960's

	Federal Political Executives	Top Federal Civil Servants	Business Executives	Congress		Military Leaders			General Public
				House	Senate	Army	Navy	Air Force	
Religion:									
Roman Catholic	19%	N.A.*	9%	12%	21%	11%	10%	16%	36%
Jewish	4	N.A.	5	1	3	—	—	—	5
Protestant and other	77	N.A.	87	87	77	89	90	84	56
Education:									
No college	2	4%	9	7	4	N.A.	N.A.	N.A.	83
Some college	5	13	16	14	13	N.A.	N.A.	N.A.	9
College degree	93	83	74	79	83	N.A.	N.A.	N.A.	8

SOURCES: David T. Stanley, et al., Men Who Govern (Washington, D.C.: The Brookings Institution, 1967), pp. 15–18; and Lloyd Warner, et al., The American Federal Executive (New Haven, Conn.: Yale University Press, 1963), pp. 29–36.

* NOTE: Because the table is compiled from different sources, it has been necessary to leave some cells with data missing. These are designated as N.A. (not ascertained).

TABLE 5–2
Traits of Federal Political Appointees, by Presidents Making Appointments

	Franklin Roosevelt	Harry Truman	Dwight Eisenhower	John Kennedy	Lyndon Johnson
Political party:					
Democrat	89%	84%	5%	81%	84%
Republican	10	13	76	9	8
Other or none	1	4	20	9	9
Occupational background:					
Was a prior occupant of federal appointive position	23	41	18	22	20
Education:					
Doctoral degree	11	8	9	18	19
Religion:					
Roman Catholic	18	20	14	26	33
Jewish	3	6	1	7	6
Protestant or other	79	74	85	67	61

SOURCE: David T. Stanley, et al., Men Who Govern (Washington, D.C.: The Brookings Institution, 1967), Chapters 2 and 3. Copyright © 1967 by The Brookings Institution.

are only marginal differences between the appointees, but those differences that do exist seem to reflect the political party of each president. President Eisenhower appointed a proportionately lesser number of Catholics and Jews than have recent Democratic presidents perhaps because there are fewer Catholics and Jews among Republicans than among Democrats. Among the Democratic presidents, the more-recent Kennedy and Johnson administrations appointed proportionately more Catholics and Jews than did the earlier Roosevelt and Truman administrations. This may reflect the increasing acculturation of Catholic and Jewish families and the greater likelihood that their children will have the social and educational advantages that help prepare them for high government positions. The lower incidence of appointments made from within the federal bureaucracy during the Eisenhower administration suggests both the distrust of bureaucrats thought to be loyal Democrats and the great numbers of out-of-power party members who wanted federal appointments after their victory. After 20 years without a presidential victory, there were many Republicans who considered themselves suited for a federal appointment. The higher incidence of persons with doctoral degrees among the appointees of the Kennedy and Johnson administrations may reflect a propensity to recruit from university faculties, as well as the increasing importance of administrative tasks that require technical expertise.

CAREER ROUTES AND SUCCESS IN ADMINISTRATIVE AGENCIES

An individual's career route is one background element that may affect his decisions as an administrator. His first job, the length of time spent in earlier occupations, and his pre-executive experiences within the administrative organization may shape the way he views his work. If large numbers of government administrators follow similar career paths and if these paths differ significantly from those followed by elites in the private sector, then the discrepancies in experiences might lead to perspectives—and perhaps behaviors—that are different from those found in large private organizations. Family background influences the nature of one's early career. Thus, family backgrounds may affect the behavior of administrative agencies through its prior influences on the early career choices of persons who become high-level administrators.[24]

Of all occupations, the professions most consistently supply individuals for high-level positions in the federal administration. Table 5–3 shows that 46 percent of the persons who were high-level administrators (GS 14 and higher) in 1959 started their careers in a profession and that over 40 percent were in professional classifications 15 years after starting their careers. Many of those who began their careers in the categories of laborer and white-collar moved into the professional category before reaching their present administrative positions. A breakdown of the professional category shows that about one-third are engineers and that another one-third are either lawyers or scientists. Other professionals are physicians, professors, accountants, and public school teachers.

There are some differences in career paths within the federal administration and between the federal administration and large private firms. Within the federal administration, political appointees are the most likely to come from the professions; foreign service officers mostly progress through administrative positions; and other non-political civil service administrators are about evenly divided between administrative and professional backgrounds. Of the political appointees, 59 percent had been in professions 15 years after beginning their careers; 40 percent of the civil service executives and only 20 percent of the foreign service executives were in professions at that point. Non-political civil service and foreign service personnel are more likely to work their way through the minor administrative positions in

---

[24] See Warner, *et al.*, Chapter 10.

TABLE 5–3
Career Sequence of 1959 High-level Civilian Federal Administrators

Occupation of Federal Executive	First Occupation	Five Years Later	Ten Years Later	Fifteen Years Later
Laborer	14%	6%	4%	2%
White-collar worker	25	17	8	3
Minor executive	5	17	28	26
Major executive	0*	2	7	21
All professions	46	46	45	42
Uniformed service	5	8	5	3
Business owner	1	1	1	1
Other occupations	4	3	2	2
Total	100%	100%	100%	100%
The professions in detail:				
Engineer	15%	16%	16%	14%
Lawyer	6	7	8	8
Medical	2	2	2	2
Professor	4	4	3	2
Public school teacher	6	2	1	0*
Scientist	5	7	8	8
Accountant	1	1	1	1
Management	1	2	2	2
Other professions	6	5	4	5

SOURCE: W. Lloyd Warner, et al., The American Federal Executive (New Haven, Conn.: Yale University Press, 1963), p. 150.
* Less than 0.5 percent.

government organizations or to transfer into government from managerial positions in the private sector. Only 24 percent of business leaders began their careers as professionals. In contrast to the 25 percent of government administrators who began in white-collar occupations (clerical and sales), 44 percent of business leaders began in such occupations. Business leaders enter management positions more rapidly than do their counterparts in government: after 15 years, 82 percent of business leaders were minor or major managers, while only 47 percent of government administrators were in such positions.

These findings have serious implications for the common stereotypes of government administrators as bureaucrats who glory in red tape and of business leaders as more flexible individualists. It is the business leader who follows the route of white-collar→minor manager→major manager through his business bureaucracies; while the government official—especially the political appointee—more often is educated in a professional or graduate school and then transfers into the government at a level where he enjoys prestige, discretion, and responsibility for policy decisions. If any class of leaders shows the behavioral affects of a bureaucratic career, it is more likely to be the businessman than his counterpart in government.

Within the federal government, career paths show the influence of the parents' social and economic characteristics. The data presented in Tables 5–4 and 5–5 concern the careers of persons who have reached high-level positions in the federal bureaucracy. Table 5–4 shows that children of laborers and farmers were likely to be in the lower echelons of the policy-making corps (GS 14 and GS 15), while the children of professionals and executives were likely to reach positions of GS 16 and above. Major executives' children who became high-level political appointees reached such positions 5 years earlier in their careers than did for the children of laborers. The data in Table 5–5 suggest that father's occupation is most relevant for one's first career opportunity. The children of laborers and white-collar employees were the least likely to begin their careers in the professions—the route which seems most propitious for subsequent career advancement. Over half of the children born into lower-status families began their careers as laborers or white-collar employees, while over half of those born into professional homes began their careers as professionals. The children of lower-status homes were less likely to reach as high positions in the government; and they usually took longer to reach their positions.

GOVERNMENT EMPLOYMENT OF THE SOCIALLY DISADVANTAGED

One of the questions that is properly asked about administrative agencies is: *To what extent do they include members of groups that are discriminated against in the private sector?* The answer to such a question has several implications. First, it indicates the commitment of administrative agencies to provide some opportunities to individuals who are socially disadvantaged. If this commitment is sizable, it can provide an important "output" of the administrative system: opportunities for employment and even influence over policy for those individuals who are shut out of many non-governmental opportunities. Second, the employment of the disadvantaged stands as one device that can provide members of these groups with the feeling that they can better develop their opportunities within the established order rather than by seeking drastic change. Thus, the employment policies of administrative organizations may lessen—or aggravate—whatever tendencies toward nihilism and violence may develop among disad-

TABLE 5-4

Occupations of Fathers of 1959 High-level Civilian Federal Administrators at Several GS Levels or Equivalent*

Executive's GS Level	Father's Occupation						
	Laborer	Farmer	Owner of Small Business	White-collar Worker	Professional Man	Business Executive or Owner of Medium or Large Business	Total
Above GS 18	11.1%	10.5%	9.5%	11.3%	33.3%	24.3%	100%
GS 16 to 18	14.8	14.0	13.2	12.9	23.1	22.0	100
GS 15	21.4	13.4	15.2	14.8	18.4	16.7	100
GS 14	23.8	17.2	14.8	14.6	15.7	14.0	100
Ratios† of Father's Occupations to Occupations of U.S. Adult Males in 1930							
Above GS 18	0.23	0.50	1.43	0.79	8.25	8.00	
GS 16 to 18	0.31	0.64	1.86	0.93	5.75	7.33	
GS 15	0.44	0.59	2.14	1.07	4.50	5.67	
GS 14	0.50	0.77	2.14	1.07	4.00	4.67	

SOURCE: W. Lloyd Warner, et al., The American Federal Executive (New Haven, Conn.: Yale University Press, 1963), p. 163.

* Salary grade levels for the services are equated by placing individuals in an equivalent rank within the General Schedule (GS) system.

† Percentage of civilian federal executives at salary grade level/percentage of U.S. adult males in occupational group = ratio.

TABLE 5-5
Fathers' Occupations and Career Patterns of High-level Civilian Federal Administrators

Occupation of Father	Occupation of Federal Executive						
	Laborer	White-collar Worker	Professional Man	Minor Executive	Major Executive	Other*	Total
First Occupation							
Laborer	23%	28%	37%	6%	0%	6%	100%
White-collar worker or minor executive	14	28	42	7	0†	9	100
Owner of small business	13	24	43	7	1	12	100
Farmer	12	19	48	5	0	16	100
Professional man	9	19	55	7	1	9	100
Major executive or owner of large business	8	22	43	14	1	12	100
Five Years Later							
Laborer	9	18	39	21	1	12	100
White-collar worker or minor executive	6	14	43	22	2	13	100
Owner of small business	5	10	51	21	1	12	100
Farmer	6	11	49	19	1	14	100
Professional man	3	7	57	20	2	11	100
Major executive or owner of large business	3	9	42	29	3	14	100
Ten Years Later							
Laborer	5	4	42	36	6	7	100
White-collar worker or minor executive	4	4	41	37	6	8	100
Owner of small business	3	4	49	31	6	8	100
Farmer	4	2	49	29	6	10	100

TABLE 5-5—Continued
Fathers' Occupations and Career Patterns of High-level Civilian Federal Administrators

Occupation of Father	Occupation of Federal Executive						
	Laborer	White-collar Worker	Professional Man	Minor Executive	Major Executive	Other*	Total
Professional man	2	2	52	29	7	8	100
Major executive or owner of large business	3	2	48	35	12	10	100
Fifteen Years Later							
Laborer	3	1	39	32	21	4	100
White-collar worker or minor executive	2	2	37	32	22	5	100
Owner of small business	2	1	45	26	21	5	100
Farmer	3	1	43	27	20	6	100
Professional man	1	1	48	26	18	6	100
Major executive or owner of large business	1	0†	36	28	27	8	100

SOURCE: W. Lloyd Warner, et al., The American Federal Executive (New Haven, Conn.: Yale University Press, 1963), p. 157.
* Includes military service, training program, and business owners.
† Less than 0.5 percent.

vantaged groups. Third, the employment of individuals from all groups suggests the efforts of government recruiters to search all potential labor markets. Where government employment is skewed against disadvantaged groups, large pools of manpower probably remain untapped. These pools may require "cultivation" with special educational and employment opportunities. If they remain unexploited, however, administrative agencies deprive themselves of important resources.

Negroes in Government

At the present time, the incidence of nonwhites in government employment is about the same as their proportion in the total population.[25] By this measure alone, nonwhites have "equal" access to administrative systems. Yet their skewed distribution among job categories testifies to continued disadvantages. Nonwhites are employed mostly in low-wage, low-status positions. They face overt discrimination in some agencies of the federal government and of numerous state and local governments.

An increasing number of middle- and upper-level positions in the federal administration are being filled by Negroes. During 1961–1965, Negroes filled 28 percent of the new positions. While there was an actual decrease in the Negroes at levels GS 1 through GS 4, there was an increase of 50 percent at the GS 5 through GS 11 levels, and a tripling at the GS 12 through GS 18 levels. Even after this progress, however, Negroes comprised only 1 percent of all those in the GS 12 through GS 18 positions and comprised over 32 percent of those in GS grades below the salary level of $5,000.[26] There is also the new problem of Negroes in middle- or upper-level positions who feel they are hired as symbols rather than as skilled professionals.

> Negroes all too often find that their newly created posts have no real duties. Often the accoutrements of office are obviously beyond the level of work demanded. The Negro bureaucrat at the upper reaches is often given extra status, a fancier desk, than he would receive on the merits of his position. The suspicion that he is there to perform the function of Art Buchwald's Negro PhD with an engineering background who speaks ten languages—to sit by the door to convince everyone of the egalitarian principles of the busi-

25 See Samuel Krislov, *The Negro in Federal Employment: The Quest for Equal Opportunity* (Minneapolis: University of Minnesota Press, 1967), p. 94. This section relies on Krislov, Chapters 5 and 7.

26 Krislov, p. 101.

ness office in which he is employed—haunts virtually every major Negro bureaucrat.[27]

The geographic distribution of Negroes in the federal service raises another question about their "progress." Is the increase in Negro employment more a function of residential concentration in Washington than a reflection of deliberate policy? During 1965, Negroes comprised about one-fourth of federal employees in the Washington area, but only one-eighth of *total* federal employment. Actually, a combination of population concentration and deliberate policy may explain the increased employment. Negroes have not moved to Washington by accident. A factor in their migration is the attraction of federal employment. All regions have shown some recent increases in Negro employment. Even Mississippi experienced a 450 percent increase in the number of Negro federal employees during 1964–1965. In that state, Negroes accounted for 9 percent of the federal employees in 1965. Although a sign of some recent progress in opportunities, this proportion was still much less than their percentage of the state population.[28]

Generally speaking, Negroes have found the most employment opportunities in those offices that have Negro clients and in new government agencies or programs. Negro representation is relatively high in welfare, housing, and urban affairs agencies[29] and in those units of the State Department dealing with African affairs.[30] A significant exception to the principle of Negro-clientele–Negro-employment opportunities occurs in the Department of Agriculture. The political impotence of the Negro clients (southern, rural Negroes) has limited the opportunities for Negro employees. As late as 1965, the U.S. Commission on Civil Rights reported:

> In some programs, effective service to Negroes has been made dependent upon the number of Negroes employed, on the untenable theory that Negro farmers should be served only by Negro staff.[31]

Even in recent years, some offices in the Department of Agriculture have not permitted Negro employees to serve white farmers, have isolated Negroes in separate offices and at segregated meetings, and have provided Negro staff members with less in-service training than that provided to whites. Where equal opportunity is provided in the

---

[27] Krislov, p. 100.
[28] Krislov, p. 104.
[29] Krislov, p. 127.
[30] Krislov, p. 134.
[31] Quoted in Krislov, p. 133.

Agriculture Department, it is likely to be in newer programs dealing with food inspection and consumer services.[32]

It is a mistake to ascribe the low incidence of Negroes in high-level jobs entirely to discriminatory policies. To be sure, some discrimination is probably at work. However, the low incidence of Negroes in responsible jobs is due partly to their lack of preparation. To reverse this situation, it may be necessary to affect major changes in the colleges and universities that train people for government employment and to affect some changes in the Negro subculture.

In 1966, the Chairman of the U.S. Civil Service Commission described some far-reaching goals of its equal opportunity program: "eradicating all vestiges of prejudices, a complete review of Federal employment practices, and heavy emphasis on training and development of employees."[33] Training and development of employees may be the most difficult goals; it may require more than the simple willingness of colleges and universities to admit qualified Negro applicants. Because of educational disadvantages that limit the skills of many Negro high school graduates, as well as the graduates of predominantly Negro colleges, it may be necessary to practice compensatory "discrimination" by soliciting applications from prospective Negro students and by providing special opportunities that will make up the deficiencies of earlier schooling. Not only will this require large sums of money, but it will also require educational institutions to move from their recently acquired concern for "equal opportunity" to a new willingness to provide "special opportunities." For those who must provide the funds for these programs (i.e., the government itself or private foundations), there is the question of which institutions should be aided. One sentiment is to "minimize . . . duplication and overlap and (seek) the gains due to having available the best minds and physical plant."[34] This would mean a concentration of resources at prestigious—largely white—institutions. Another feeling is to provide resources to the predominantly Negro institutions. They already serve the greatest concentration of black students; but many of them lack strong programs relevant to the needs of administrative agencies. Other barriers to equal employment opportunities may lie in the Negro community itself. Generations of discrimination have not prepared black families to place a high value on academic accomplishment. If programs are made available and recruiters are sent into the

[32] Krislov, pp. 132–33.
[33] Warren I. Cikins, "Graduate Education, Public Service, and the Negro," *Public Administration Review*, 26 (September, 1966), 183–91.
[34] Cikins, *ibid.*

black communities, the goals may still fail if potential students cannot take these new overtures as a sincere expression of the white man's interest in the black man's future.

Women in Government

The status and problems of women in administrative agencies are similar to those of Negroes. The exclusion of women from certain positions raises similar questions about discrimination and about the failure of administrative agencies to exploit potential resources. The number of women in white-collar federal positions is about the same as the proportion (49 percent) of women in the population.[35] As in the case of Negroes, the problem is not so much their number as their distribution. As of 1959, women were only 4 percent of the federal employees above the level of GS 12, and barely 1 percent above GS 15. Also like Negroes, women are employed disproportionately in certain kinds of jobs where the clientele would anticipate—and perhaps appreciate—them. They are concentrated in child welfare, public assistance, and vocational rehabilitation. About one-third of the women who had attained executive status in the federal government in 1959 were employed in the Departments of Labor and Health, Education, and Welfare.

Women who do reach policy-level positions in the bureaucracy have no obvious traits of family backgrounds that distinguish them from male colleagues. More than the average adult in our society, they come from middle- and upper-status families in medium or large cities; their fathers were professionals, executives, or white-collar employees; and they have college, plus some graduate education. In these traits, they resemble male administrators. Two other characteristics of women executives are more distinctive. First, women are slightly older than men at comparable positions. This may reflect discrimination in selection or promotion, the time that women must spend on other aspects of their social roles (e.g., raising a family), or several "false starts" before selecting the route of education and employment that is suitable. In any case, the greater age of women at comparable administrative levels indicates special difficulties that are not encountered by their male colleagues. Second, women executives are typically single. About two-thirds of the higher-level female administrators studied in 1959 were unmarried, compared to 5 percent of the men. The choice of career instead of family is one of several difficult choices that many women face.

---

[35] This section relies on Warner, et al., Chapter 11.

These 145 women who have become federal executives (as of 1959) bucked a system which began working against them when they were born, around 1910. They selected not to play the highly patterned woman's role in our society. They went to college, they elected to enter the professions; many of them made, what was for some of them, the hard choice of a career rather than marriage; some had the energy and intelligence to combine marriage and career. They had the determination to stay within their chosen way of life until they achieved positions of equal responsibility with men in government.[36]

VALUES, ASPIRATIONS, AND PERSONALITIES IN ADMINISTRATIVE AGENCIES

The backgrounds and educational experiences of high-level administrators suggest what kinds of family, educational, and career experiences provide the most likely routes to responsible positions in administrative agencies. From their backgrounds alone, we cannot infer that government administrators have any peculiar values, aspirations, or personality traits which set them apart from individuals in other large and complex institutions.

It is very difficult to obtain information about the values, aspirations, and personalities of government administrators. Detailed psychological research is time-consuming and expensive. However, a group of scholars headed by Professor Lloyd Warner conducted intensive interviews with a random sample of 257 civilian administrators in the federal government at the levels of GS 14 and above.[37] The interviews included Thematic Apperception Tests and lasted three to four hours. The sample is large enough to tell us something about the general tendencies in the federal bureaucracy. However, it does not have enough respondents in each occupational subgroup to permit analysis of categories within the federal service. Moreover, it includes no business executives who can serve as a standard of comparison with the government administrators.

The personal values, aspirations, and personalities of federal administrators—as reported by Professor Warner and his colleagues—suggest that they are men of large perspective. They see themselves as functioning within a complex and demanding set of institutions and as being responsible for programs with great social value. They view their authority as coming from outside of themselves. Authority is a source of support as well as instruction; they generally accept author-

---

[36] Warner, et al., p. 187.

[37] This section relies on Warner, et al., Chapters 12–14.

ity as legitimate, although sometimes resent intrusions on their own activity. By and large, they accept the restrictions of large organizations, and they accept the need for coordination and cooperation. They show the traits of group workers rather than individualists.

High-level administrators also tend to be men of lofty ideals. They aspire to community improvement more than to self-aggrandizement. Along with this idealism, government administrators also have strong needs for achievement. This combination of traits may add up to public-minded realism. Their need for achievement, as well as their appreciation for organizational constraints, may temper their idealism so that goals come within the range of feasibility. Perhaps because of this, their goals are usually expressed in concrete terms that are relevant to their field of specialization. Instead of abstract principles that do not lend themselves to clear definition or attainment, they desire improved services in education, health, welfare, transportation, or resource development.

Their values also reveal a great respect for the institutions of government and a strong motivation to serve the interests of the public. They appear more oriented to public service than to private gain.

> Plato's conception of the ideal ruling group was that of a class of men dedicated to the pursuit of wisdom and knowledge, with a taste for every type of knowledge. Such men, endowed with unquenchable curiosity, possessing courage and self-respect, sought after justice and truth. Not being concerned with the pursuit of wealth, nor allied with property, they could achieve objectivity. For them, to govern was a matter of duty and obligation—a sacred calling. They possessed the capacity for temperance, self-control, and a respect for authority. But above all they were dedicated to the pursuit of wisdom and ultimate truth.
>
> The ideology of federal executives comes very close to this ideal. The emphasis upon intelligence, intellectual values, and culture, the notion of restraint, the drive for self-respect and the respect of others, the concept of duty and obligation—all are strikingly reminiscent of the Platonic concept of the State. Even more significant is the emphasis in the federal executive ideology upon the search for justice and the fair resolution of problems. Fairness to others, concern for the public welfare, honesty, and "goodness" are characteristics held to be decisive.[38]

The data on high-level government administrators are not without contradictions. They show values and attitudes which appear

---

[38] Warner, *et al.*, pp. 235–36.

strange in combination with one another. Yet this is to be expected. Administrators in policy-making roles must live within the constraints of large organizations, of active clientele groups, and of legislators who may at any time insert their own desires into the considerations. Yet administrators also have powerful motivations and strong ideals of public service. It seems inevitable that many administrators will experience internal conflicts. Intensive interviews reveal not only an expressed ease about their dependence on a large system, but also a drive for independence and anxiety about the dependence that is necessary. Administrators both need and reject authority. Occasionally they show their rejection with expressions of resentment and ineffectual behavior.

> In situations in which he is working closely with others, he tends to be more at ease, to initiate more freely, to activate rather than be acted upon. This disposition to avoid "going it alone" is especially noted in areas calling for achievement that must be solely self-directed; here considerable anxiety arises.

> In general, the career civil service executive possesses psychological characteristics that may be described thus: he possesses lofty aspirations, the majority of which stem from external influences, from heroic figures or models, and from demands made upon him by the system and by his role as a career man. . . .

> Yet the career civil service executive frequently experiences feelings of inadequacy and lack of insight into the means to be used to realize his lofty aspirations. . . . [In some cases] he responds with feelings of hostility which in most instances take a hidden form such as resentment, or failing in tasks of "going it alone," or movement into fantasy and the realm of "magical" solutions.[39]

There is only limited evidence about the views of high-level administrators toward contemporary political issues. A study of political appointees of the Truman and Eisenhower administrations asked for their views about the proper role of government in the economy. The results suggest that ideological neanderthals are not well represented in such positions.[40] Of 53 individuals questioned, only 8 (15 percent) expressed classical *laissez faire* views about government

---

[39] Warner, *et al.*, pp. 194–96. Note that Warner's use of the term "executive" is equivalent to our term "high-level administrators."

[40] Alan H. Schechter, "The Influence of Public Service on Businessmen's Attitudes toward the Federal Government," *Public Administration Review*, 27 (December, 1967), 452–59. See also Marver H. Bernstein, *The Job of the Federal Executive* (Washington, D.C.: Brookings Institution, 1958), Chapter IX.

involvement in the economy. These felt that government should not regulate business or affect the business cycle; and they wanted to end social welfare programs. The remainder were divided between those (49 percent) who would have government engage in limited "framework setting" activities[41] and those (36 percent) who favored "limited positive government."[42] It is not surprising that almost all of the Truman appointees favored some government involvement, while Eisenhower's appointees (although mostly in favor of *some* government involvement) provided most of those respondents who would choose a minimal role for government.

SUMMARY

This chapter examines selected aspects of the procedures that administrative organizations use to select and assign their personnel and looks at the nature of the personnel themselves. The primary focus is career and political appointees at upper levels in the federal bureaucracy. It is people at these levels who are most likely to influence the nature of administrative decisions and, thereby, to affect interactions between their agencies and other actors in the administrative system.

There is a prevailing decentralization and a resulting lack of uniformity in the personnel procedures for high-level career positions. Most agency heads have the responsibility for filling positions immediately beneath them. They frequently promote people from within their own units. When they consider outsiders, they generally look to people they know in other agencies of the federal government, in state or local governments, or in private firms.

Procedures for upper-level political appointments are organized by each president to suit his view of a proper job. Recent presidents have relied on a screening team made up of individuals who are sensitive both to occupational competence and political acceptability. These procedures last only until the bulk of top appointments are filled. This is usually at the time of—or shortly after—the inauguration. After this, the president himself becomes preoccupied with the problems of program-development and implementation. His aides in

---

[41] They felt, for example, that government should engage in anti-cyclical policies only when needed and should regulate business only if extreme abuses of free competition occurred.

[42] They felt, for example, that government should engage in continuous efforts to ameliorate the business cycle, to regulate business, and to provide minimum social welfare programs.

the White House Office and the top administrators in each department handle the continuing problems of replacing those political appointees who leave office.

Studies of administrators' social backgrounds and educational and career experiences show marked differences between high-level government administrators and the "average citizen." Administrators are more likely to come from a middle- or large-size city, to have a father employed in middle- or upper-status occupations, and to affiliate with a Protestant religious group. The administrators are also more likely to complete four years of college and some post-graduate education and to begin their careers in one of the professions—most likely engineering, law, or science. Although high-level administrators differ greatly from the general public, they differ much less from other occupational groups which occupy positions of responsibility. In their social backgrounds and educational attainments, for example, government administrators show greater resemblance with groups of "business leaders" than do either of these groups show with the general public.

The occupational disadvantages of two social groups—Negroes and women—are evident in their distribution within administrative units. Both groups are represented disproportionately at the lower levels. Where they are in high-level positions, they are most likely in agencies that serve the specific interests of Negroes or women, respectively. In the case of Negroes, however, recent years have seen sizable increases in the number of employees placed in administrative positions, agencies, and geographic regions that had seen few Negro employees earlier.

There is very little information about the values, attitudes, and personalities of administrators. The information that is available ascribes to them a high regard for serving the public, an acceptance of the restraints that come along with large organizations and a pluralist political system, and an appreciation for the need to coordinate and cooperate with other administrators. There is a correspondence between this information about the federal employee and the public's image of the federal servant as described in the following chapter (see pp. 163–69). Federal administrators also have strong motivations to improve services within their fields of specialization. However, there are signs of conflict within administrators between the needs for achievement and the restraints felt from large organizations and the political process.

Several personnel issues generate political controversies. The control of appointments to government offices is a topic that has set Jacksonians—and now some neo-Jacksonians—against Civil Service reformers. There are sharp disagreements about the rights and prerogatives of government employees' unions and about the policies pursued by agencies to recruit members of minority ethnic groups.

Part Two

THE INPUTS OF THE
ADMINISTRATIVE SYSTEM

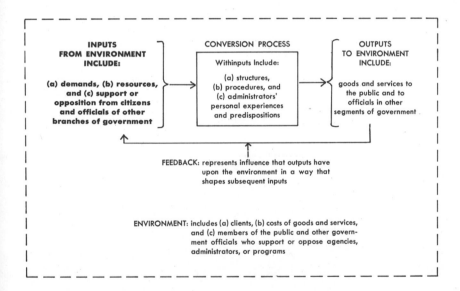

The inputs of the administrative system are the transmissions that come to the conversion process (i.e., administrative agencies) from actors in the environment. These actors include: clients of the agencies; government officials in the legislative and executive branches; administrators in other administrative agencies; political parties; interest groups; the mass media; and interested citizens. The inputs these actors provide to administrators include: demands for services; political support or opposition; and the resources of tax funds, legal authority, and citizens' willingness to accept employment in administrative agencies.

Chapters 6, 7, and 8 deal with various kinds of inputs. Chapter 6 examines the attitudes toward administrators that exist in the political cultures of the United States. These attitudes can make themselves felt in the political support that administrators receive from the public and from legislators and executives who are sensitive to the voters' wishes. Chapter 7 focuses directly on relationships between citizens and administrative agencies and on several institutions that contribute to those relationships, i.e., the mass media, public opinion polls, elections, interest groups, and political parties. Chapter 8 describes two branches of government which figure prominently as providers of demands and resources to administrative agencies: the legislature and the executive.

6

THE STATUS
OF PUBLIC ADMINISTRATION

"Political culture" includes the beliefs, attitudes, and values which affect public affairs. In this chapter, we are concerned with those aspects of the political culture which relate to administrative agencies.[1]

Political culture provides several kinds of inputs to administrative agencies. First, it nurtures those individuals who are eligible to join the bureaucracy. Thus, the attitudes about government bureaucracies that prevail in the culture can make public employment a generally desirable or undesirable career or—because of the attitudes in certain subcultures—can make it more desirable for some social groups than for others. Prevailing attitudes can pose serious problems for government recruiters, especially if the distribution of attitudes means that the skills most needed by government agencies are found among people who are the least-favorably disposed to join the agencies. Second, a political culture can influence the elites who allocate resources to administrative agencies. In the United States, elites include elected legislators and executives who make formal decisions about government programs, plus interest-group and party leaders, the corporate leaders who control the mass media, and private citizens who have the skills, money or time to involve themselves heavily in public affairs. The feelings of these groups can affect the legal authority and the funds which are given to government agencies.[2]

---

[1] See Samuel C. Patterson, "The Political Cultures of the American States," *Journal of Politics*, 30 (February, 1968), 187–209. This article is valuable in itself *and* for the extensive bibliography cited in it.

[2] It is not clear whether officials respond to their own judgments or to those of their constituents in making decisions; available research suggests that this

A search through the commentaries about public bureaucracies does not reveal any consistent set of beliefs, attitudes, or values. Administrative agencies are frequent targets for positive and negative comments. There is no homogeneous attitude about public employees or about the administrative departments of government. Although some statements suggest that there is a sizable reservoir of negative sentiment toward administrative processes, many people believe that public agencies should be given even greater responsibilities and resources than they have received so far.

Among the terms used to describe administrators are: unimaginative, hindering, protectionist, security-conscious, dull-witted, unfit for private employment, harsh, aggressive, empire-building, insensitive to popular values, and aloof. These terms have been used by elected officials and by candidates for office, as well as by political commentators and by private citizens asked for their views in opinion surveys. Yet other people in these same categories use contrasting terms about public employees: honest, able, well-trained, efficient, dependable, interested in serving the public, personable, and sensitive. Public administrators can see opportunities as well as problems in the political culture.

ASSESSMENTS OF ADMINISTRATIVE AGENCIES IN PAST POLITICAL LITERATURE

The early years of the American Republic passed without much commentary about administrative agencies. The concerns of political writers focused on other features of government, e.g., the division of powers between state and national governments and the powers of the executive, legislative, and judicial branches of government. The Constitution has little to say about administrative departments and agencies. Although it has influenced the evolution of administrative organizations in national and state governments, this is largely the result of the powers assigned to the president and to Congress and, thus, of their roles in administrative development.

The administration is mentioned several times in the *Federalist Papers,* but its position is distinctly subordinated to the constitutional offices. Hamilton mentions the administration more often than other

varies with the kind of decision to be made and with the degree of interest shown by constituents. See Warren E. Miller and Donald E. Stokes, "Constituency Influence in Congress," *American Political Science Review,* 57 (March, 1963), 45–56. Also see Charles Cnudde and Donald McCrone, "The Linkage between Constituency Attitudes and Congressional Voting Behavior," *American Political Science Review,* 60 (March, 1966), 66–72.

authors; and he gives it a secondary rank below the presidency. He argues that the president should control the appointments of administrators and should be responsible for their supervision. He defends a long term for the president, partly because it permits long terms for his subordinates. "There is an intimate connection between the duration of the executive magistrate (i.e., the president) in office and the stability of the system of administration."[3] While Hamilton acknowledges the importance of administration, he sees the presidency as of greater concern than the administration:

> . . . we cannot acquiesce in the political heresy of the poet who says:
>
>> For forms of government let fools contest—
>> That which is best administered is best—
>
> yet we may safely pronounce that the true test of a good government is its aptitude and tendency to produce a good administration.[4]

At the heart of this early fixation on the roles of the presidency and legislature was the relatively small role that administrators played. In the following passage, Hamilton makes his own estimate about the small numbers of people involved in administration and argues that they are not likely to show any major increase:

> It is evident that the principal departments of the administration under the present government are the same which will be required under the new. There are now a Secretary of War, a Secretary of Foreign Affairs, a Secretary for Domestic Affairs, a Board of Treasury, consisting of three persons, a treasurer, assistants, clerks, etc. These officers are indispensable under any system and will suffice under the new as well as the old. As to ambassadors and other ministers and agents in foreign countries, the proposed Constitution can make no other difference than to render their characters, where they reside, more respectable, and their services more useful. As to persons to be employed in the collection of the revenues, it is unquestionably true that these will form a very considerable addition to the number of federal officers; but it will not follow that this will occasion an increase of public expense. It will be in most cases nothing more than an exchange of State for national officers.[5]

Although Hamilton may have underestimated the size of the federal establishment for the purposes of his argument, he was not far from

---

[3] *The Federalist Papers* (New York: Mentor Books, 1961), Number 72.
[4] *The Federalist Papers*, Number 68.
[5] *The Federalist Papers*, Number 84.

the truth. By 1792 the federal service counted only 780 employees, plus some additional deputy postmasters; by 1801 there were only 2,120 civilians plus another 880 deputy postmasters. Few of these employees were engaged in anything more complicated than tax collecting, record keeping, and copying. The professionals consisted of some physicians and engineers employed by the military, plus surveyors and lawyers. The civil service was hardly the body of expertise that it has become; and there seemed little threat that it would challenge the constitutional branches as a maker of important decisions.[6]

Perhaps the earliest—and most profound—concern with the administrative system occurred during the presidency of Andrew Jackson. By 1830, the federal bureaucracy had grown to over 11,000 civilian employees and was populated largely by members of upper-class families who were appointed during the administrations of John Quincy Adams and James Monroe. To Jackson, the incumbents were aliens both in social class and in partisan loyalties. In his inaugural address and messages to Congress, President Jackson described the character of the administration as a hindrance to reform. Unless he removed large numbers of incumbents and replaced them with his own supporters, he could not count on the departments to carry out his programs. President Jackson felt that the responsibilities of public officials were "so plain and simple that men of intelligence may readily qualify themselves for their performance."[7] He had a dual justification for removing the appointees of his predecessor and replacing them with his own men: (1) the administration's policies should conform with those of elected officials; and (2) government jobs are simple enough to permit frequent turnover without significant loss in expertise.

Perhaps in response to Jackson's personnel policies, some observers noted a decline in the competence of public administrators. In the early 1830's Alexis de Tocqueville found, "so much distinguished talent among the citizens and so little among the heads of government." Also,

> It is a constant fact that at the present day the ablest men in the United States are rarely placed at the head of affairs; and it must be acknowledged that such has been the result in proportion as democracy has exceeded all its former limits.[8]

---

[6] See Leonard D. White, *The Federalist* (New York: Macmillan, 1948).

[7] From Jackson's *First Annual Message to Congress*, December 8, 1829.

[8] Quoted in Franklin P. Kilpatrick, *et al.*, *The Image of the Federal Service* (Washington, D.C.: Brookings Institution, 1964), p. 32.

"Jacksonian" personnel administration represents some procedures for appointing and dismissing employees on the basis of "political," rather than "technical" qualifications. It was—and is—practiced to varying degrees by many executives. It is identified with Jackson not because he was the first to sweep out existing employees when he came to office. Actually, he removed no larger a percentage of federal employees than did President Jefferson 20 years earlier.[9] However, Jackson provided the rationale for political removals and appointments and practiced the art in an overt manner. The public service may have reached its most political level at the time of the Civil War. President Lincoln used his powers of appointment and removal to select pro-Union administrators and to assure that government officers would use their powers in support of the Union. The civil service was not freed from political control after the Civil War. It experienced the clash of noble and ignoble values that typified Reconstruction.[10]

Throughout the period from President Jackson to President Arthur, there were several efforts to isolate government employment from the worst excesses of venality and partisanship. Reform at the national level took a major step forward with the Pendleton Act of 1883. Its major features were: a Civil Service Commission that would —with some political independence of the president—administer personnel policies; "merit" as a primary criteria for government employment; competitive examinations for the selection of employees; protection of "covered" employees from being coerced to support the campaigns of political parties; the immediate coverage of about 10 percent of federal employees; and authority given the president to expand the service covered by the Act by means of executive orders.

This is not the place to describe in detail the mechanisms of personnel administration as they evolved through frequent amendments of the Pendleton Act, or as they were adopted by many state and local governments (see pp. 119–25 and 128–30). Despite 140 years of talk and activity since Jackson's inaugural message, there are still disputes about administrative organization. By now, however, the administrators of many governments are sufficiently "professional" for most disputes to avoid extreme charges about patronage and venality. Some commentators describe public agencies in the most negative of terms; but others would expand the roles that administrators play in policy-making. Some would expand professionalism where a partisan

<hr/>

[9] Kilpatrick, *et al.*, p. 32; for a general history of the period, see White; plus, Paul Van Riper, *History of the United States Civil Service* (Evanston, Ill.; Row, Peterson, 1958), Chapters 2–3.

[10] Van Riper, Chapter 4.

service still exists; but some argue that merit protection has advanced too far. They find chief executives—especially the governors of certain "merit" states—unable to fill important positions with individuals who share their policy perspectives; like President Jackson, these executives feel they cannot control their administration without having more control over appointments.

CONTEMPORARY VIEWS OF PUBLIC ADMINISTRATION

It is not easy to report a fair representation of the views toward public administration that are expressed by contemporary observers. Politicians range from outright condemnations of "bureaucrats" and "red tape," to praise for the administrative units that operate their favorite programs. Among political scientists, there is a mixture of respect and reservation about the activities of administrators. Two political scientists who reflect this mixture in their own writings are Norton Long and Emmette Redford.

Professor Norton Long provides some of the most articulate and comprehensive arguments that commend administrative agencies and urge increases in their responsibilities. As a counter to those who view the administrative organization as unimaginative, protectionist, or insensitive to popular values, Long's writings merit attention. He argues against the notion that the bureaucracy must be controlled constantly in order to curb its lust for power.[11] He feels that bureaucracies add to constitutionalism by representing interests that are not otherwise heard in the legislative and executive branches.

According to Long, the bureaucracy's involvement in the policy-making process is inescapable. The bureaucracy contains the highest concentration of information about existing programs; this includes information about the operation of current projects and about the unmet needs that are not being served. Most proposals that are considered each year by Congress and the presidency come from the administrative departments. The administration's expertise makes it representative of interests that do not have adequate spokesmen in the legislature. The departments contain the talents of science, professions, and institutions of learning; more than in the legislature, the values that are identified with these institutions are likely to be voiced in the administration. The departments contain people who are trained to think in terms of general principles and of the implications

[11] Norton E. Long, "Bureaucracy and Constitutionalism," *American Political Science Review*, 46 (September, 1952), 808–18.

of policy for those principles, as well as containing people who would pursue the immediate benefits that are sought by clientele groups. Moreover, the bureaucracy is likely to contain persons coming from a wider range of social and economic backgrounds than is the case in congressional committees. To the extent that these backgrounds are indicative of values, they insure that the bureaucracy will make its proposals only after extensive deliberation. Because of both wider expertise and more diverse values, the nature of decision-making in the bureaucracy is likely to be more thorough and more responsive to social needs than it is the legislative process.

> The bureaucracy is in policy, and major policy, to stay; in fact . . . the bureaucracy is likely, day in and day out, to be our main source of policy initiative. The role of the legislature and of the political executive may come to consist largely of encouraging, discouraging and passing on policy which wells up from the agencies of administration. All of this is because the bureaucracy is not just an instrument to carry out a will formed by the elected Congress and President. It is itself a medium for registering the diverse wills that make up the people's will and for transmuting them into responsible proposals for public policy. . . .
> The theory of our constitution needs to recognize and understand the working and potential of our great fourth branch of government (the bureaucracy), taking a rightful place beside President, Congress, and Courts.[12]

Long is not so pleased with the administrative procedures that he would accept these unchanged. The administrators' potential for representing diverse interests in their deliberations does not guarantee that all such interests have access to those who make crucial decisions. Long feels that agencies need additional mechanisms to gather more information about the public's needs for services and to assure that they consider an adequate number of alternatives before embarking on new policies.

> . . . The advisability of building constitutionalizing elements into the bureaucracy [is] of prime importance. . . . A loyal opposition in the upper levels of the bureaucracy could serve a function well nigh as socially useful as that performed by the loyal opposition in Parliament. We have only begun to think of how best to staff and organize administration if a major part of its job is to propose policy alternatives —alternatives that have run the gauntlet of facts, analysis,

---

[12] Long, *ibid.*

and competing social values built into the administrative process.[13]

Emmette Redford is concerned with the responsiveness of the "administrative state" to the norms of democratic procedures. He sees American society inexorably enmeshed in administrative processes, whether they be with the public agencies of government or the private organizations of big business, labor unions, schools, or charitable foundations. Yet the administrative state can operate in a way to respect the primary democratic morality. Redford summarizes this morality as concern for individual men in the criteria used in making decisions; as an effort to assign each man's needs equal weight in policy deliberations; and as an effort to make as broad as feasible the opportunities for men to participate in the decisions that affect them.[14] Redford identifies several features that administrative units should have in order to respect the democratic morality. Then he gives the administrative organization of the national government high marks with respect to them. The crucial features include:

1. Sufficient fragmentation of administrative decision-making so that a limited group of individuals does not have the sole authority to make the important decisions for any sector of policy;
2. Wide access to policy-making machinery by citizens who can act through the election of legislators and a chief executive, who can make individual requests of administrators, or who can exert concerted action through group protests or civil disobedience;
3. Adequate control of administrative units by "overhead" institutions that represent the electorate;
4. The interaction of individuals with different perspectives (of social class or professional training) within the arenas in which important decisions are made; and
5. Efforts to keep the personal interests of employees out of policy-making, perhaps by enforcing conflict-of-interest regulations or by a program of professional training that socializes decision-makers into universalist (as opposed to particularist) norms.[15]

---

[13] Norton E. Long, "Public Policy and Administration: The Goals of Rationality and Responsibility," *Public Administration Review*, 14 (1954), 22–41.
[14] Emmette S. Redford, *Democracy in the Administrative State* (New York: Oxford University Press, 1969), p. 6.
[15] Redford, Chapter II.

Like Long, Redford has high respect for individual administrators, but is not content to permit administrators to operate their own agencies without some assurance of external and/or internal controls. Redford would probably be less willing than Long to rely on internal administrative controls. A major weakness that Redford finds in his study of national administration occurs outside the administration itself—in the structure of Congress. He feels that the latter's leadership is inadequately responsive to the demands of the broad national constituency. This problem results from the congressional seniority system which puts into positions of importance, vis-à-vis the administration, legislators who are not subject to a wide range of policy demands from their own constituents. Because of this inadequacy in Congress, Redford finds that a great burden of administrative control is left with the president. Yet this individual—even with the assistance provided by the Executive Office—is overloaded and unable to carry the burden of transmuting citizen demands into administrative policies.

THE PUBLIC'S VIEW OF PUBLIC ADMINISTRATION

The sophisticated views of political commentators testify only to the availability of certain ideas in the intellectual marketplace. The favorable sentiments of Norton Long and Emmette Redford do not by themselves indicate that large numbers of people are willing to accept the role of administrators in policy-making, or would limit administrators' actions by the control procedures recommended by Long and Redford. Yet the presence of their thought in a culture that has ridiculed its "bureaucrats" suggests the ambiguous posture of the culture.

Some valuable information about the public's opinions of administrators comes from a survey sponsored by the Brookings Institution which dealt with views toward administrators of the national government. The product of its survey—*The Image of the Federal Service* by Franklin P. Kilpatrick, Milton C. Cummings, Jr., and M. Kent Jennings—reports the attitudes of more than 5,000 people chosen to represent a cross-section of the employed population outside of the federal government, federal civilian employees themselves, students and teachers in high school and college, plus several groups of business and government executives, natural scientists, social scientists, and engineers.[16]

---

[16] This study focuses primarily on the public's view of federal administrative jobs and jobholders. In this section we extrapolate at times from its findings to other features of the public's view about administrative agencies.

The Brookings study shows no clear set of attitudes held by any large majorities in the population. There is a large reservoir of favorable sentiment toward administrators, but this support is not so widespread or unqualified that the administration can expect unlimited grants of resources. There is a higher regard for some attributes of administrative units than for others. Unfortunately, individuals in upper-status occupations (who are most important as potential recruits or political allies) show the least favorable sentiments toward the administration.

People reveal their sentiments most clearly when asked to compare the public service with some counterpart in their surroundings. In this way, they are least likely to confuse their description by using a wide variety of "unanchored" standards. If people report that some feature of administration is "better" or "worse" than a comparable institution in the private sector, we can see where administration stands in their evaluations. The most useful data in the Brookings survey shows evaluations of top-level people in the federal service in comparison with top-level people in private business. Table 6–1 shows the different ratings given on 10-point high-low scales of several traits. Positive scores indicate higher ratings for the federal service—and by how much on the 10-point scale—and negative scores show lower ratings for the federal service.

The general employed public and almost all of the occupational and educational groups within it rank top-level public employees higher than their counterparts in business on the traits of *honesty* and *interest in serving the public*. However, federal employees score less favorably than the businessmen on having the *respect* of respondents, a *drive to get ahead,* and *ability*. These figures are consistent with other information from the same survey. When the respondents were asked in open-ended questions to describe the federal service, the largest number of them (28 percent) listed attributes that could be labelled "good personal character." These traits included honesty, high integrity, ethical standards, moral fiber. In contrast, only 13 percent ascribed similar traits to the employees of large business firms. However, the trait of security-consciousness was also assigned to public employees. Of the respondents, 13 percent described the federal employees as having strong personal security motivations (e.g., placing personal security above advancement), while only 2 percent listed this trait for the employees of large businesses.

People with high levels of educational attainment and skills most needed by government are likely to have less respect for federal than for business administrators and are likely to give the federal adminis-

TABLE 6–1

Evaluations of Top-level People in the Federal Service and in Private Business*

Types of Respondents	Average Number Answering	Honesty	Interest in Serving the Public	How Well Respected They Are	Ability	Drive to Get Ahead
General employed public	(1,093)	+.6	+.4	−.2	−.4	−1.0
By educational level						
High school not completed	(308)	+.5	+.3	+.1	0.0	−.6
High school completed	(495)	+.7	+.4	−.2	−.3	−1.0
Some college	(124)	+.4	+.6	−.4	−.6	−1.4
College graduate	(137)	+.5	+.4	−.9	−1.1	−1.9
Students						
High school students	(356)	+1.0	+1.3	−.1	−.1	−.8
College seniors	(401)	+1.0	+1.5	−.6	−.5	−1.8
Graduate students	(379)	+1.0	+1.5	−.9	−.9	−1.6
Groups in education						
High school teachers	(277)	+.6	+1.0	−.4	−.6	−1.3
College teachers	(464)	+.9	+1.4	−.7	−.4	−1.8
Natural scientists	(118)	+.8	+1.8	−.4	−.5	−1.6
Social scientists	(103)	+.9	+1.9	−.9	−.3	−1.6
Engineers	(87)	+.6	+1.2	−.6	−.7	−1.6
Groups in business						
Executives	(273)	+.1	+.1	−1.1	−1.2	−2.1
Natural scientists	(84)	+.4	+1.3	−.4	−1.0	−2.0
Social scientists	(70)	+.5	+.8	−.9	−.9	−2.2
Engineers	(88)	−.1	+.1	−1.0	−1.3	−1.8

SOURCE: Franklin P. Kilpatrick, et al., The Image of the Federal Service (Washington, D.C.: The Brookings Institution, 1964), p. 222. Copyright © 1964 by The Brookings Institution.

* Differences between ratings made on the ten-point, high-low scale. Plus scores indicate that federal service people are rated higher, negative scores show they are rated lower.

trators low marks on ability and drive to get ahead. This is particularly true for respondents who are employed in private industry as executives, scientists, and engineers. Respondents who teach science and engineering in colleges are somewhat more generous in their evaluations of federal administrators. It is probably not surprising that executives, scientists, and engineers who already work for government give higher grades to the federal service than do their counterparts in the private sector. But even these government employees rank top-level business leaders higher than government employees on public respect, ability, and drive.[17]

Although private employees are viewed more favorably than government employees on the traits of respect, ability and drive, this finding should not be taken as a sharply negative evaluation of the public bureaucracy. Table 6–2 shows where the respondents ranked federal employees on the 10-point scale on each of the traits. On each trait, the general public ranked the federal service in the upper one-third of the range. In only two cases did subgroups of the general population score the federal service below 5.0: business scientists and engineers gave low marks to federal employees in their "drive to get ahead." The lack of ambition—and the related trait of security-consciousness—is a component of the public's feeling toward administrators. However, this trait may not reflect a strong condemnation of administrators. When this finding is viewed along with the assessments of honesty, interest in serving the public, and ability, the assessment of low personal ambition suggests that many people respect the administrators without suspecting them of power-mania. The public might approve increased resources for the administrative agencies without fearing that administrators will use the resources in an unrestrained manner.

One of the most important resources that citizens can grant to government is their own talent. To the extent that people will consider a government job for themselves, they show a support for administrative units that may include a willingness to grant other resources, e.g., tax money and legal authority. Several questions on the Brookings survey assess the willingness of people to consider employment with

---

[17] These findings are consistent with those observed in other studies of public opinions about government employees or government employment. See Leonard D. White, *The Prestige Value of Public Employment in Chicago* (Chicago: University of Chicago Press, 1929); and White's *Further Contributions on the Prestige Value of Public Employment* (Chicago: University of Chicago Press, 1932); and Morris Janowitz, Deil Wright, and William Delaney, *Public Administration and the Public* (Ann Arbor: University of Michigan Institute of Public Administration, 1958).

TABLE 6–2

Evaluations of General Federal Employees on Five Characteristics*

Types of Respondents	Average Number Answering	Honesty	Interest in Serving the Public	How Well Respected They Are	Ability	Drive to Get Ahead
General employed public	(1,093)	7.6	6.8	7.0	6.9	6.6
By educational level						
High school not completed	(308)	7.7	7.1	7.4	7.3	7.1
High school completed	(495)	7.6	6.9	7.1	7.1	6.7
Some college	(124)	7.5	6.3	6.6	6.4	6.1
College graduate	(137)	7.4	5.9	6.2	6.0	5.6
Students						
High school students	(356)	7.7	7.1	7.0	7.2	6.7
College seniors	(401)	7.1	5.9	5.8	6.1	5.6
Graduate students	(379)	7.1	5.7	5.5	5.9	5.3
Groups in education						
High School teachers	(277)	7.5	6.4	6.6	6.5	6.1
College teachers	(464)	7.5	6.2	6.0	6.2	5.7
Natural scientists	(118)	7.7	6.2	6.0	6.2	5.5
Social scientists	(103)	7.5	6.1	5.7	6.1	5.8
Engineers	(87)	7.4	6.0	5.9	5.8	5.5
Groups in business						
Executives	(273)	7.7	5.9	6.0	5.9	5.4
Natural scientists	(84)	7.5	6.1	5.9	5.9	5.2
Social scientists	(70)	7.5	5.5	5.5	5.6	4.6
Engineers	(88)	7.6	5.4	5.6	5.7	4.9

SOURCE: Franklin P. Kilpatrick, et al., The Image of the Federal Service (Washington, D.C.: The Brookings Institution, 1964), p. 219. Copyright © 1964 by The Brookings Institution.

* Mean ratings on the ten-point high-low scale; the higher the score, the higher the employees are rated on the characteristic.

the federal government as compared to comparable positions in the private sector.

There is a substantial reservoir of sentiment that favors the government as an employer, but not among many skilled and educated persons that government agencies most want to attract. However, there is some evidence that the *most* talented individuals are the most inclined to accept federal employment. Table 6–3 shows the relative

TABLE 6–3
Students' Grade Averages, Related to Occupational Appeal of the Federal Government vs. Large Private Business

| Grade Averages | Average Number Answering | Appeal of Working for | | Difference: "Federal" Minus "Business" |
		Large Private Business Firm	Federal Government	
High School Juniors and Seniors				
A	(51)	5.3	5.9	+0.6
B	(142)	5.7	5.6	−0.1
C and below	(160)	5.6	5.4	−0.2
College Seniors				
A	(88)	4.7	5.0	+0.3
B	(202)	4.8	5.3	+0.5
C and below	(106)	6.0	4.9	−1.1
Graduate Students				
A	(154)	4.6	4.9	+0.3
B and below	(205)	5.2	5.1	−0.1

SOURCE: Franklin P. Kilpatrick, et al., The Image of the Federal Service (Washington, D.C.: The Brookings Institution, 1964), p. 107. Copyright © 1964 by The Brookings Institution.

appeal of federal and private employment among several educational groups. The most encouraging sign—from the government's point of view—is the greater appeal of government service for high school, college, and graduate students with the highest academic grades.

What features of government employment are the major attractions and drawbacks? Again, the opinions are consistent with other tendencies already reported. People are most likely to cite security and fringe benefits as the attractions of government employment, while the lack of self-determination, "bureaucracy," and "red-tape" are the greatest deterrents.[18] People who prize ambition and drive are more

---

[18] Kilpatrick, et al., p. 120.

attracted to private than to public employment. Those with higher incomes are most likely to be disturbed by problems of self-determination in government, while those with low incomes are most attracted by the security, fringe benefits, and working conditions in government.[19] Even among those with the highest incomes, however, it is only a substantial minority (35 and 27 percent) who cited lack of self-determination and bureaucracy or red-tape as undesirable features of federal employment. Federal recruiters may have to work harder in convincing well-trained individuals to consider government jobs; but the level of anti-government sentiment is not pervasive among them.

POLITICAL CULTURES AND ADMINISTRATIVE ORGANIZATIONS IN STATES AND REGIONS

The opinion poll sponsored by the Brookings Institution sought the public's assessment of the national government's administration. A few polls have asked about the public's regard for the administrators of state or local governments. Because these have been taken in scattered communities or college populations, they offer no information about the *general public's* regard for state or local administrators. Studies made among college and high school students in Maryland and Georgia agree in finding higher regard for *federal* than for local administrators. However, the Maryland study found higher regard for *federal* than for state administrators, while the Georgia study found higher regard for *state* than for federal administrators. Although the results are not conclusive, they suggest the influence of "states' rights" sentiments may affect attitudes toward state administrative units as one moves deeper into the South.[20] Professor Daniel J. Elazar has identified the prevailing political culture in 228 separate areas of the 48 mainland states; his work is speculative, but provides some insight into the support offered to the administrative units of different state and local governments.[21]

Elazar identifies three principal types of political culture: Moralism, Individualism, and Traditionalism. As he describes them, they form a linear scale on several traits. Two of these traits are relevant

---

[19] Kilpatrick, *et al.,* p. 122.

[20] The Maryland study is reported in H. George Frederickson, "Understanding Attitudes toward Public Employment," *Public Administration Review,* 27 (December, 1967), 411–20; the Georgia study is reported in Frank K. Gibson and George A. James, "Student Attitudes toward Government Employees and Employment," *Public Administration Review,* 27 (December, 1967), 429–35.

[21] Daniel J. Elazar, *American Federalism: A View from the States* (New York: Crowell, 1966).

for the kinds of supports that an administrative organization requires from its environment. In its orientation toward *bureaucracy*, the Moralist culture values extensive, well-paid, and professional administrative corps at all levels of government. The Individualist views government bureaucracy as a fetter on private affairs, but also as a resource that public officials can use to further their own goals; some Individualists support political machines that carve up public resources and distribute them as payments to individuals.[22] The Traditionalist is most opposed to the growth of bureaucracy as a restraint on the traditional political elite. Thus, a Moralistic culture should coexist with a large and well-paid administration, while an Individualistic and Traditionalistic cultures should have smaller and less-well-paid administrative staffs.

On another dimension that is relevant to administrative units, the Moralist welcomes public services for the good of the commonwealth; the Individualist would minimize public services to permit a balance of satisfactions from activities in the private and public sectors; and the Traditionalist would oppose all government activities except those necessary to maintain the existing power structure. Thus, the Moralistic culture should coincide with high levels of taxation and government expenditure and with generous levels of public service. Individualistic and Traditionalistic cultures should score low on taxes, expenditures, and services. Based on several years of observation and on research in state histories and newspapers, Elazar maps the cultures that prevail throughout the continental United States. Figure 6–1 shows his designations.

While Elazar's designations of political culture cannot—by the nature of his research techniques—be considered the final word on the subject, they do highlight some prominent regional differences that have long been observed, plus some intraregional variations that suggest the ambiguous nature of political cultures in many areas. The South is the most Traditionalistic section of the country, but it has a Moralistic component in the Appalachian region and has Individualistic regions in the Southwest and Border states. Moralism is prominent in New England and in a number of Middle Western states that experienced populist or progressive movements. Individualism is not prominent throughout any large section of the country; it is present as a secondary culture in many areas and appears dominant only in Nevada and Wyoming.

---

[22] See Edward Banfield and James Q. Wilson, *City Politics* (Cambridge, Mass.: Harvard University Press, 1963), Chapters 9 and 13, for a discussion of "private regardingness."

FIGURE 6–1

The Distribution of Political Cultures within the United States

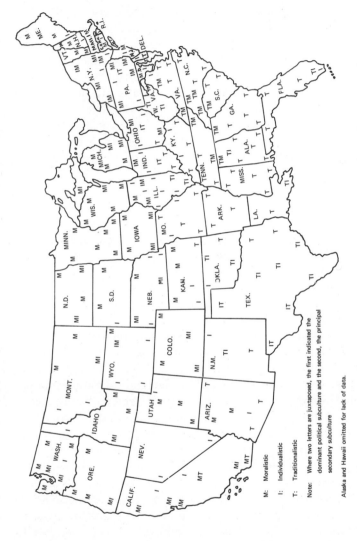

M: Moralistic

I: Individualistic

T: Traditionalistic

Note: Where two letters are juxtaposed, the first indicated the
       dominant political subculture and the second, the principal
       secondary subculture

Alaska and Hawaii omitted for lack of data.

SOURCE: Daniel J. Elazar, American Federalism: A View from the States (New York: Crowell, 1966), p. 97.

State scores on several measures pertaining to administrative units and their outputs correspond closely with the traits expected on the basis of Elazar's cultural designations. These dimensions of political culture seem to have some importance for administration.[23] The states that place high on the Moralistic end of the scale (and therefore low on Traditionalism) tend to show large numbers of state and local government employees relative to population, high average salaries for government employees, and a high incidence of government employees who are covered by subsidized health and hospital insurance. These states also show high tax payments relative to personal income, high government expenditures per capita, and high scores on several measures of educational services, public assistance programs, and highway services. Moreover, these findings are not simply the product of social or economic features of the states; they hold up even after statistical tests "control" for the incidence of urbanism and personal income in each state.

SUMMARY

This chapter is the first in a group that deals with inputs to administrative units. The focus is on political culture and, in particular, on the attitudes held about public bureaucracies. These attitudes may affect the willingness of citizens to seek government enployment and the willingness of elected officials to provide funds or legal authority to administrative agencies.

Prevailing attitudes are not the only factors which influence the resources allocated to administrative units. Elected legislators and chief executives respond to numerous other stimuli; they can overlook, modify, or help to shape public demands. Political cultures in the United States do not contain a single set of attitudes about public administration. There is much ambiguity and no widespread sentiment toward administrators which is clearly favorable or unfavorable. While some sharp sentiments may exist with respect to individual programs or agencies, the attitudes toward administration as a whole are generally mixed, moderate, and permissive. This is evident both from sophisticated commentaries about government administrators and from opinion surveys that measure the public's sentiments toward administration. Because of this ambiguity, the political culture is not likely to restrict the actions of elected officials toward the administration. The data in this chapter suggest that elected officials have

---

[23] Ira Sharkansky, "The Utility of Elazar's Political Culture: A Research Note," *Polity,* 2 (Fall, 1969), 66–83.

considerable "freedom" from public opinion when they allocate resources to the administrators.

Most people rank federal employees higher than business employees on the traits of honesty and interest in serving the public; but they rank business employees higher on the traits of personal drive, ability, and respect by the public. Perhaps it is most significant that people generally rank *both* federal employees and business employees in the middle ranges on a 10-point scale. There is some tendency for occupational groups that are most needed by the government to rank government service below business, but even here the data are not uniform. A large number of people in the desired occupations rank government employees higher than business employees, and there is a slight tendency for the most talented high school, college, and graduate students to give government employees higher scores than business employees. While the public's attitudes do not simplify the task of the government recruiter, neither should they discourage him. Many people having the skills needed by government are favorably inclined to the prospect of government services; and the attitudes unfavorable to government are not so intense—or so widely held—as to make it difficult for legislators or chief executives to allocate generous resources to administration. Yet sentiments toward administrators are not so clearly favorable that individual politicians cannot benefit from an occasional foray against the "bureaucrats."

7

CITIZEN DEMANDS
AND ADMINISTRATIVE AGENCIES

This chapter focuses on relationships between citizens and administrative agencies and on several institutions that are said to be transmission belts between them: the mass media, public opinion polls, elections, political parties, and interest groups.

INDIVIDUAL CITIZENS AS PROVIDERS OF INPUTS TO ADMINISTRATIVE AGENCIES

In discussing the roles that individual citizens play as input-providers vis-a-vis administrative systems, it is necessary to distinguish between general tendencies and special cases. Some private citizens are prominent in providing the stimuli that cause administrative agencies to formulate policies and make certain decisions. Moreover, the citizenry as a collective body is valued highly by many administrators. We saw in Chapter 5 that administrators express their sensitivity to public needs. An individual may receive a courteous hearing on a matter that affects him personally and may affect an administrator's decision about his own case. Chapter 6 shows that many citizens—when responding to public opinion surveys—give high marks to administrators for the traits of honesty and public-mindedness. When it comes to citizen influence over the major policies that are formulated or implemented by administrative agencies, the evidence is mixed. Moreover, the evidence does not apply directly to matters of administration. Most of the data come from studies that focus on other aspects of the political process, e.g., studies of popular attitudes and behaviors during election campaigns or in reference to policies being considered by the legislative branch.

174

There are some data which suggest that citizens are largely ignorant of policy matters. They are not familiar with the concepts that are central to policy debates, and they hold views about policies which appear "inconsistent" or "unreasonable." Although these findings do not by themselves signify a lack of knowledge about *administrative* activities, they do suggest that most citizens are unaware of the most prominent controversies about policy. A group of surveys taken during the 1943–1950 period showed that 84 percent of a sample did not understand the concept of "featherbedding";[1] 51 percent did not know the meaning of "balancing the budget"; 46 percent did not understand *any* of the terms "monopoly," "antitrust suit," "interlocking directorate," or "Sherman Act"; and about 75 percent did not know the meaning of "free enterprise."[2] To answer any of these questions correctly it was not necessary to provide the pollsters with a learned treatise. Any indication of familiarity was satisfactory. The findings of inconsistency in policy opinions have shown up in several polls. A survey made in 1956, for example, discovered that *supporters* of welfare programs were more likely to *oppose a tax* that would pay for these programs than were the people who opposed welfare programs. Also, those who were *most in favor of a tax cut* were also more likely to *support* programs that would guarantee employment, low-cost medical care, and federal aid to education.[3] The apparent irony is that many people oppose the taxes that seem necessary to pay for their desires. In contrast to these findings that demonstrate a lack of familiarity with matters of policy, there are some additional data that suggest that citizens are selective in their attention to policy. On matters of personal concern, they show awareness of issues and state preferences that are consistent with their economic self-interest. Even in the case of the "inconsistent" views about welfare programs and tax cuts that we just reported, the economic characteristics of people with these views suggest that they may be answering in a reasonable, well-informed fashion. People who express support of lower taxes and improved services tend to have low incomes. They favor services that would help them (education, job-security, and welfare), while they

---

[1] Although this term may be unfamiliar to the present generation of undergraduates, it was very salient in an era when government policies toward labor-management conflict was a prominent controversy. "Featherbedding" refers to the practice of requiring more workers on a job than is actually necessary. This data comes from V. O. Key, Jr., *Public Opinion and American Democracy* (New York: Knopf, 1961), p. 183.

[2] Robert E. Lane and David O. Sears, *Public Opinion* (Englewood Cliffs, N.J.: Prentice-Hall, 1964), p. 61.

[3] Key, p. 167.

oppose any increase in their taxes. Perhaps they expect other income groups to pay for the programs. This is not an unreasonable desire, insofar as the tax systems of most state and local governments are regressive and presently take a larger percentage-bite out of low incomes than out of high incomes.[4]

Other opinion surveys support the conclusion that people understand the implications of policies that have important *personal consequences*. One such poll was made in Wisconsin during a political campaign when gubernatorial candidates were debating tax policy. Low-income people were clearly more hostile to a general sales tax "on everything you buy" than were upper-income people. As expected, increased education added to the tendency of persons to answer in a fashion consistent with their economic self-interest. The well-educated poor were the most hostile to this proposal that threatened to tax the commodities (especially food) that account for most of their spending. These same low-income people were most likely to switch their support to alternative proposals that were less threatening to their pocketbooks—namely, a sales tax, with food and clothing exempted, plus an increase in the (progressive) state income tax and a reduction in the (regressive) local property tax.[5] This tax package would increase the tax burdens of upper-income persons, but reduce those of lower-income citizens. Other research complements these findings by showing that people who feel most involved in an issue are likely to demonstrate the most accurate information about it.[6]

There may be special significance in this juxtaposition of widespread ignorance about public policies, but "reasonable" responses to questions that are personally significant. Under ordinary conditions, most citizens ignore policy activity. When an issue arises with importance for their own lives, however, they may acquire accurate information and perhaps involve themselves in policy-making. They may vote according to candidates' positions on the key issues, join an interest group that pressures elected officials and administrative agencies, or take part in overt demonstrations against administrative units. The Viet Nam war has motivated many otherwise-passive citizens to demonstrate their opposition to conscription and other military

---

[4] Ira Sharkansky, *The Politics of Taxing and Spending* (Indianapolis: Bobbs-Merrill, 1969), Chapter II.

[5] Sharkansky, Chapter II. A "progressive" tax is one that imposes increasingly higher percentage demands on higher incomes; a "regressive" tax, in contrast, imposes its highest percentage demands on lower-income people.

[6] Key, p. 190. Also see V. O. Key, Jr., *The Responsible Electorate* (Cambridge, Mass.: Belknap Press of Harvard University Press, 1966); and James L. Sundquist, *Politics and Policy: The Eisenhower, Kennedy and Johnson Years* (Washington, D.C.: Brookings Institution, 1968), especially Chapter X.

policies and to disrupt the proceedings of government agencies. Like-wise, policies in the field of public assistance have motivated welfare recipients who are normally apolitical to support the policies that affect them directly or even to engage in violent actions against the property or personnel of welfare agencies.

THE MASS MEDIA AS INTERMEDIARIES BETWEEN CITIZENS AND ADMINISTRATORS

The mass media can add to the information that citizens have about public affairs and can enhance their influence on administrative agencies. The mass media—including newspapers, popular journals, radio, and television—function as transmission belts between people and administrative units. The media also have their own influence on administrators. First, they provide information about public affairs. Second, they help shape the agenda of public debate by emphasizing some issues and making them more important than others. Third, they originate some issues by "campaigns" against social problems, the failures of government programs, or the malfeasance of certain officials. The operators of newspapers and broadcasting networks liken themselves to other "muckrakers" who have been responsible for major innovations in public policies.[7] However, it is not clear how often the media influence policy. The events surrounding one televi-sion documentary illustrate the analytic problems involved in attribut-ing policy influence to the mass media.

In the May, 1968, CBS broadcast "Hunger in America," it illus-trated in powerful detail the horrors of starving children and the inadequacies of existing government programs. The television program had an immediate affect on some administrators, if only to force some defensive public statements. The Secretary of Agriculture identified some factual errors in the telecast and condemned it as "a biased, one-sided, dishonest presentation of a serious national problem."[8] Over the succeeding months, the federal government took several steps to increase the flow of food to the poor.

It is not possible to identify the specific impact of "Hunger in

---

[7] Classic examples of "muckraking" literature include: Upton Sinclair's *The Jungle*, which aided the campaign to begin the regulation of food processing by the federal government; Michael Harrington's *The Other America*, which in-formed and aroused readers about the condition below the "poverty line" in the United States and helped in the development of the programs of the Office of Economic Opportunity; and Ralph Nader's *Unsafe at Any Speed*, which provided much of the evidence—and passion—for the federal auto safety regulations.

[8] Elizabeth B. Drew, "Going Hungry in America," *Atlantic* (December, 1968), pp. 53–61.

America." Coming as it did in the midst of numerous other expressions about the same social problem, it probably added some pressure to Congress, to the president, and to the Department of Agriculture. Yet, the media joined a gang-attack that was already underway. In the preceding year, a private foundation sponsored a survey by several prominent physicians and local practitioners in the "Delta" counties of northwestern Mississippi. Their report to the Senate Subcommittee on Employment, Manpower, and Poverty then provoked other prominent groups and individuals. The subcommittee attracted a great deal of press coverage, partly because Robert F. Kennedy was a member of the subcommittee and (at the time) a potential candidate for the presidency. The food problem was made a target of the "Poor People's Campaign," which itself was stimulated by public reaction to the assassination of Dr. Martin Luther King. Labor unions also joined the issue. The Citizens' Crusade against Poverty (with support from the United Auto Workers) published a critical assessment of the federal government's food programs: "Hunger, U.S.A." Undoubtedly, the media increased popular interest in the food problem; their contribution was to popularize an issue that had been raised by others. The media also illuminated some administrative and legislative arrangements that limited the effectiveness of Agriculture Department's policies. Food programs were developed to relieve the surplus problems of farmers as well as the hunger of poor people; administrators and legislators who were directly involved seemed more oriented to agricultural than to social considerations. Part of the hassle that CBS entered was between House and Senate Agriculture Committees which included Mississippians Jamie Whitten and James Eastland (frequently accused of being short on social conscience) and the Senate Labor and Public Welfare Subcommittee on Employment, Manpower, and Poverty, chaired by Joseph S. Clark and including Robert F. Kennedy.

Several factors limit the influence of the media over either the public or administrative agencies.[9] These include people's lack of reliance on the media as their sources of political information, the lack of attention to public affairs that is evident in many of the mass media, and the media's lack of ability to force their political interpretations on citizens who are inclined in other directions.

The media do not have a captive audience of vulnerable personalities. Instead, citizens are involved in a network of relationships with one another which provide their own kinds of information. For many people, political discussions with compatible friends, family members,

---

[9] This section relies heavily on Key, *Public Opinion*, Chapters 14–15.

or co-workers are viewed as more reliable sources of political information than can be found in the media. Many individuals distrust the political messages that are included in the media which they otherwise enjoy, and they erect "defense mechanisms" against undesirable information. The phenomenon of "selective perception" leads individuals to overlook items of "fact" or "opinion" that challenge their own views.

From many newspapers or broadcasting stations, there is little *useful* information about administrative agencies or other aspects of politics. Most of the media are organized for commercial rather than political purposes. Local newpsapers or television stations carry wire-service copy on national or international news, usually in small proportion to the space (or time) devoted to sports, advertising or recreational material. Local political news is likely to be thin, perhaps because the manager wishes to avoid sensitive issues or lacks a news-gathering staff. Under these conditions, news about administrative agencies may be especially limited. Without the excitement guaranteed by election campaigns or the involvement of prominent personalities, the media are not likely to view administrative events as "newsworthy." Even news that is concerned with personnel appointments to major offices or changes in regulatory policies is likely to receive little coverage in local newspapers or television stations. If citizens wish to make intelligent assessments of administrative affairs, they may have to get their information from other sources.

PUBLIC OPINION POLLS AS INTERMEDIARIES BETWEEN CITIZENS AND ADMINISTRATORS

The public opinion poll is another institution that transmits citizens' opinions to administrative units. Polls are taken on a variety of subjects, e.g., support for political candidates and incumbent office-holders, plus various approaches to public policy. There seems to be no lack of information about the public's approval or disapproval of personalities and programs. However, the quantity of poll results does not assure public influence over administrative units or over other branches of government. Most of the time, opinion polls do not tell officials what the public is thinking about the problems they face. It is rare that an issue presents clear and simple alternatives that lend themselves to polling. The questions on most polls are too general to help the policy-maker. Opposition to an increase in taxes, for example, does not signify that the public will oppose an increase of a certain percentage—as applied to people with certain kinds of income—if the increase in revenues will be used to support certain kinds of public services. The public's support for a certain politician does not identify which of his programs is receiving support. Moreover, most surveys do not indicate how seriously people stand by their opinions. Many respondents may have thought for the first—and last—time about an issue when the pollster asked his question. Administrators must keep these limitations in mind when they ponder the implications of public opinion surveys for their agency's program. Most of the time administrators seek new programs—or try to maintain or enlarge existing programs—without any certain measure of the public's opinions. The information that administrators do have about public opinions comes only partly from polls. Other sources are informal solicitations of agency clients or casual reading of editorials.

ELECTIONS AS INTERMEDIARIES BETWEEN CITIZENS AND ADMINISTRATORS

Elections are frequently cited as the principal device for citizens to enforce their will upon public officials. The chief executives and members of the legislatures at all levels of government in the United States are subject to periodic election. Even those localities that employ a city manager as their chief executive officer make him the subordinate of an elected council. In state governments, election extends to the heads of major administrative units. Presumably, elected officials control administrative agencies and employ their control to produce the kinds of policies desired by the electorate. Yet the character of elections—as well as the imperfect mechanisms that elected officials use to control administrators—limits the usefulness of elections as a means of control over administrative agencies. In most cases, a voter cannot signal his support or opposition for a government program by the way he casts his vote. He is effectively limited to voting for a person, but without indicating to that person which policies he wishes to support.

Part of the voter's problem lies in the political parties. As we see below, they are not so tightly organized that they can discipline individual candidates to support a party program. Thus, a voter cannot be sure by a candidate's party label alone which kinds of policies he will support once in office. A second limitation on the election's utility lies in the complexity of the campaigns that are run by individual candidates. Each candidate typically supports more than one program. We can see the difficulty if we imagine even a simple campaign where two candidates oppose one another on only three issues. The presidential campaign of 1964 provides a convenient example. It was an unusually clear campaign in terms of the policy choices given to the voters. Among the issues expressed in the campaign, the voters could choose, for example, between Johnson and Goldwater on the issues of civil rights, of the war in Viet Nam, and of welfare policies. Most observers agree that Johnson took more "liberal" positions than his opponent on civil rights and welfare issues, and that he took a more "restrained" position with respect to extending the war in Viet Nam. The problem in interpreting an election comes when the pundits must determine which policies were supported by the majority that voted for the winning candidate. Despite the clarity of Johnson's victory in 1964, the election results alone do not indicate which positions the electorate supported. It is possible that only a *minority* of Johnson's supporters agreed with his civil rights platform. Most citizens could have agreed with Goldwater on this—or any other—issue, but voted for Johnson because they felt that he took the better position on the one issue (e.g., the war) they felt to be more important. When dealing with a presidential election, we usually have a large volume of poll results that we can compare with the election-outcome in order to gain some insight into the voters' policy preferences. However, these are not available for most state or local elections; the victorious candidate can read into his victory any combination of policy preferences, and his opponent cannot present substantial evidence to the contrary.

Even where election results can be compared with opinion surveys, they may result in little citizen control over the policies of the winning candidate. The statements of the campaign may not stay relevant beyond the first crisis that the new government enters. Again, the Johnson-Goldwater campaign provides an example. Although Johnson indicated his own opposition to expanded American participation in Viet Nam, conditions after the election allowed him to claim a release from his campaign statements. Although some voters felt the President had gone beyond his "mandate," others felt the conditions justified the subsequent war policies. Moreover, there were no control mechanisms to keep the President and his administrative subordinates from pursuing policies that ran counter to their campaign "promises."[10]

---

[10] See Robert A. Dahl, *A Preface to Democratic Theory* (Chicago: University of Chicago Press, 1956), p. 127. There is some evidence that a candidate's policy position can attract for him the support of marginal voters (i.e., those who shift from one party to another) in sufficient numbers to give him victory. (See Sundquist, especially Chapter X.) However, this does not counter the argument

INTEREST GROUPS AS INTERMEDIARIES BETWEEN CITIZENS AND ADMINISTRATORS

Much of the literature about interest groups (sometimes called lobbies or pressure groups) concerns their relations with legislatures. However, interest groups also concern themselves with administrative agencies. Even if a group is successful in the legislature, this does not guarantee that agencies will provide the services that it desires.

Several factors make the administrative system an arena for interest-group activity separate from the legislature. These include discretion that is provided by the legislature to administrators; contingencies that were not foreseen by the legislature, but provide administrators with some additional discretion; and the difference between legislative and administrative procedures that might upset the hierarchy of influence among interest groups that had prevailed in the legislature.

Most agencies operate with substantial grants of discretion that are included within their basic legislation or that are assumed by the administrators because conditions arise that were not foreseen by the legislature. Legislatures do not expect to provide for all possible situations by their statutes, and they permit administrators to operate within broad standards. The basic statutes establishing the National Aeronautics and Space Administration (NASA), for example, provides:

1. Research for the solution of problems of flight within and outside the earth's atmosphere, and develop, construct, test, and operate aeronautical and space vehicles;
2. Conduct activities required for the exploration of space with manned and unmanned vehicles;
3. Arrange for the most effective utilization of the scientific and engineering resources of the United States and for cooperation by the United States with other nations engaged in aeronautical and space activities for peaceful purposes;
4. Provide for the widest practicable and appropriate dissemination of information concerning NASA's activities and their results.[11]

---

presented in this section that election results alone (i.e., without carefully analyzed public opinion or preference polls) cannot indicate the policy preferences of the electorate.

[11] *U.S. Government Organization Manual, 1965–66* (Washington, D.C.: U.S. Government Printing Office, 1965), p. 462.

The administrators of NASA read this in a way to permit significant programs that are, at most, tangential to the exploration of space. They have subsidized research to measure changes in the quality of life-styles in the United States[12] and have supported university curricula to train public administrators as well as natural scientists and engineers. NASA distributed $128 million in fiscal 1966 to more than 200 institutions of higher education in all 50 states.

The values and atitudes of administrators can shape the ways in which agency powers are employed, and these values may differ from those that prevailed in the legislature. Because of this, the constellation of groups that influence the legislature may not control an administrative unit. Studies of regulatory commissions suggest that consumer groups may win strong statutory controls over business firms. Yet business firms gain enough influence in the administration to weaken the regulation that actually occurs.[13]

Many—perhaps most—agencies welcome the appearance of groups that represent their clientele or other interested segments of the population. Sometimes out of respect for the democratic norms of popular access and sometimes because legislation requires it, administrators establish formal procedures for interests to express their preferences. These procedures include: opportunities to petition the agency; opportunities to explain one's desires at an informal conference or a formal hearing; and the advanced notice of impending changes in policy with provision for interested parties to express their grievances. Some agencies establish advisory bodies selected to represent various segments of their clientele and invite them to assess agency policies on a continuing basis. Some procedures are more elaborate than others and provide more certain opportunities for affected interests to impress their desires upon administrators. One author has written that interest groups are offered the most generous opportunities to express themselves where the following conditions prevail:

1. Where a large number of people or a great magnitude of resources will be affected by the administrators policy;
2. Where the administrators can delay the implementation of their policy without causing substantial harm;

---

[12] See, for example, Raymond Bauer, ed., *Social Indicators* (Cambridge, Mass.: M.I.T. Press, 1966).

[13] Murray Edelman, *The Symbolic Uses of Politics* (Urbana: University of Illinois Press, 1964), especially Chapter 2; also see Marvin Bernstein, *Regulating Business by Independent Commissions* (Princeton, N.J.: Princeton University Press, 1955).

3. Where interests are given the status of legal recognition, i.e., where provisions in a statute require the consultation of certain groups; and
4. Where the impending policy decision will have the effect of finally disposing of an issue, without affected parties having the opportunity to prevent the loss or recoup their losses at a later hearing.[14]

Administrators' Pursuit of Interest-group Allies

Administrators do not always wait passively for interest-group allies:

A first and fundamental source of power for administrative agencies in American society is their ability to attract outside support. Strength in a constituency is no less an asset for an American administrator than it is for a politician, and some agencies have succeeded in building outside support as formidable as that of any political organization.[15]

Administrative agencies use several techniques to develop a constituency. They keep the mass media informed about their activities that have widespread public interest, and they maintain frequent contacts with the interest groups that are directly affected by their programs.

An allied interest group can help an agency in several ways. First, the group can take a position on an issue which coincides with a position held by administrators, but which the administrators cannot take publicly because it would offend their chief executive or important members of the legislature. Second, interest groups can support an agency's requests for funds or statutory authority with the executive and the legislature or can help the agency resist undesirable directives from the executive or the legislature. An interest group can make an argument and build public support for a position that cannot be articulated by an administrator who is currently the target of executive or legislative hostility.

Some agencies are so well endowed with the support of interest groups and private citizens that they seem virtually impervious to direction from the executive and legislative branches. The Federal Bureau of Investigation has a great reservoir of good will among associations of local police departments (whose members are trained at F.B.I. academies and whose analyses are done in F.B.I. laborato-

---

[14] William W. Boyer, *Bureaucracy on Trial: Policy-making by Government Agencies* (Indianapolis: Bobbs-Merrill, 1964), pp. 79–80.

[15] Francis E. Rourke, *Bureaucracy, Politics and Public Policy* (Boston: Little, Brown, 1969), p. 11; this section relies on Rourke, Chapter II.

ries) and among many private citizens (long-accustomed to watching the F.B.I. get its man on television shows which are put together with agency cooperation). One sign of the power of the F.B.I. is the tenure of its director, J. Edgar Hoover. He has held that post since the Coolidge administration, and recent presidents have kept him in office long beyond the "mandatory" retirement age for federal personnel.

Agencies also run a risk when they acquire close relations with interest groups. In exchange for political support, a group might win control of an agency program. The agricultural education programs of some state universities seem tailored to the demands of certain groups that are important in state politics. These may be thought of as "loss leaders," i.e., programs than an agency is willing to lose to the effective control of a farm group in order to receive the legislative support of that farm group for the university's total program.[16] One study of the early years of the Tennessee Valley Authority found close alliances between the TVA and certain groups in its region and found what appears to have been an effective veto by the interest groups over agency programs.[17]

Some alliances between administrative agencies, interest groups, and other organs of government are so strong that they are labeled "subgovernments." This term is applied to the military-industrial complex: a network of military and civilian personnel in the Department of Defense, defense contractors and the interest groups that represent them, and congressmen. They are allied partly by the economic incentives of defense contracts which appeal to industry and to the members of Congress whose districts will benefit from employment and capital expenditures and partly by the incentives of improving the military posture of the United States. Some commentators accuse this conglomerate of applying irresistible pressure on the president and Congress for increased expenditures on military hardware. These pressures have implications not only for the size of the military budget and the economic transactions that it can trigger, but also the flexibility of United States foreign policy. It is said that the State Department is hard-pressed to negotiate for arms control with the Soviet Union when the incentives are so great for a continued arms buildup. It is difficult to assess the accuracy of these allegations. However, the mutual economic-political incentives in arms-escalation has bothered officials at the highest levels of government. One of the surprising features of President Eisenhower's farewell address was his warning of the "ac-

---

[16] Rourke, p. 22.
[17] See Philip Selznick, *TVA and the Grass Roots* (Berkeley: University of California Press, 1949).

quisition of unwarranted influence . . . by the military-industrial complex."[18] In writing about the development of an anti-ballistic missile, one commentator perceived the following combination of economic and political motivations:

> Modern defense technology becomes its own master and makes its own decisions. In the case of Nike-X, the Defense Department spent $4 billion in research and development. Such a massive effort implicated a significant sector of the U.S. scientific, technological and industrial community. Long before the missile system reached any degree of technical ripeness, military and political pressures mounted to yank it from the development stage and to put it into production. When Nike-X gave hope of success, the politics of defense took over. . . . [T]he Republican National Committee issued a 55-page report on the missile defense question, titled: "Is LBJ Right?—Russia Deploys Anti-Missile Network—U.S. Refuses To Keep Pace."
>
> Had the Administration failed to deploy Nike-X, it would have been vulnerable to a 1968 campaign attack on a defense issue. Moreover, it would have to contend with Democratic legislators who have championed missile defense. Then too, the prospect of layoffs in the aerospace industry was not pleasant, especially coming on the heels of further cutbacks in the space program. In short, President Johnson must have felt the bite of the words that President Eisenhower used in his farewell address. . . .
>
> This year politicians will be able to take something back home to their constituents, thanks to Sentinel. There's something for almost everyone in the manufacture and deployment of the missile defense system. Less than a month after the Sentinel decision, Senator Mike Mansfield was able to announce at Great Falls, Montana, that a Perimeter Acquisition Radar (PAR) installation would be made north of that city. "When completed, this installation will probably have a contingent of up to 600 people permanently stationed or employed," the Senate majority leader said.[19]

Government Interest Groups

One kind of interest group that may have special advantages in the administrative system is the professional association that represents administrators themselves. It seems most likely to understand the policy-making process and most likely to have information about

[18] Douglass Cater, *Power in Washington* (New York: Vintage Books, 1964), Chapter II.

[19] Ralph E. Lapp, "Secretary McNamara's Incredible Last Stand," *The New Republic,* February 17, 1968, pp. 20–22. Reprinted by permission of *The New Republic,* © 1968, Harrison-Blaine of New Jersey, Inc.

concrete policies that match that of the policy-makers themselves. However the administrators' professional association may fall short of its potential because of its members' own inhibitions. If they feel that "political action" is outside the bounds of professional norms, then their organization may exercise no substantial influence over policy.

A study of the Oregon Education Association describes several features that limit the potential of an interest group composed of government employees. One problem lies in the non-political nature of most members' goals. Most join for the purpose of improving their own teaching and advancing their profession. Others join because they are "expected" to join and feel pressure from local school officials. It is only a small minority who join for political reasons, i.e., to support a group that will lobby for salary increases and improved working conditions.[20] With these different motivations among the members, it is difficult for the organization to maximize its resources for political activity. Another limitation comes from the mixture of teachers, principals, and superintendents in the same organization. Insofar as much of the teachers' political efforts might be directed against the principals and superintendents (or against an alliance of these and school boards), the mixed composition of the association severely limits its political usefulness. Finally, a large number of teachers do not feel they should engage in political activity. The notion that "teaching is above politics" or that lobbying is "unprofessional" limits the pressure that can be mobilized. The apolitical norms of the teaching profession are most inhibiting with respect to the teachers' use of the classroom as a political platform. By supporting "professional norms" (which include—for some people—political neutrality), the association may actually *depress* the political involvement of members who would otherwise be more active. Teachers who are active in the Oregon Education Association *are less expressive* about politics than teachers who are not active members.

> It appears that the ideology of the organization as it is perceived by the active members is one of caution. . . . The more experienced teachers are less [politically] expressive [than the less experienced teachers, and] those who are active in the organization are considerably less expressive than those who are not active in the organization. The educational association does not generate the same political interest among its members that other kinds of organizations do. The organization doesn't instruct its members to keep their mouths shut, but it is apparent that the official ideology of

[20] Harmon Zeigler, *The Political Life of American Teachers* (Englewood Cliffs, N.J.: Prentice-Hall, 1967), pp. 57–59.

the organization, as it is perceived by those who are in a position to understand it best, is acceptance of things more or less as they are.[21]

Many government personnel feel that it is quite proper to lobby their interests in the arenas where important decisions are made. The unions of government employees are certainly in this category (see pp. 125–28). Policy-making officials also have their interest groups. The National League of Cities and the U.S. Conference of Mayors represents urban governments before state and federal legislatures and administrative agencies. They frequently support new legislation that would establish—or enlarge—grants-in-aid, and they testify before appropriations subcommittees to support funding for existing programs. An offshoot of the U.S. Conference of Mayors provides special help to municipal legal officers. The National Institute of Municipal Law Officers (NIMLO) provides "the strength flowing from joint support of many municipalities where the protest of a single municipality would be ineffective." Among its services, NIMLO helps draft local ordinances and then helps defend the ordinances against court challenges.[22] There are also separate organizations for social workers, public health physicians, highway administrators, state departments of agriculture, and public safety officials. Although local and state boards of education may protest their own employees' involvement in "lobbying," school boards themselves (along with educational associations and teachers' unions) are represented in state capitols and Washington.

Individual states and municipalities maintain their own representatives in Washington, as well as support the variety of groups that represent their separate departments. The state governments that maintained separate offices in Washington during 1967 included: California, Florida, Illinois, Indiana, Maryland, Massachusetts, New York, Ohio, Pennsylvania, Texas, and West Virginia. In the same year, the cities of New York, Los Angeles, San Francisco, Boston, Dallas, New Orleans, San Diego, and Seattle also had their own Washington offices.[23]

The federal agencies should not be slighted in any description of government lobbying. Their principal targets are the committees that handle their legislation and appropriations. Although the U.S. Con-

---

[21] Zeigler, p. 110.

[22] Clement E. Vose, "Interest Groups, Judicial Review, and Local Government," *Western Political Quarterly*, 19 (March, 1966), 85–100.

[23] *Legislators and the Lobbyists* (Washington: Congressional Quarterly Service, 1968), pp. 63–64.

gress has objected and even outlawed the expenditure of public money for lobbying activities, an aide of President Johnson noted that there were about 40 "Congressional relations people" in "key roles" in the departments and agencies. They carry their unit's message directly to important legislators and enlist additional support from non-governmental interest groups. A study of the legislation dealing with the Model Cities program in 1967 found the following in support of the administration's position: U.S. Conference of Mayors, National League of Cities, AFL-CIO, National Governors Conference, American Institute of Architects, Mortgage Bankers Association; spokesmen for local civic groups, banks, and construction firms; and the heads of some prestigious corporations (General Electric, Westinghouse Electric, Detroit Edison, Allied Chemical, Chicago and Northwestern Railroad, Goodyear Tire and Rubber, Kaiser Industries, Continental Illinois National Bank and Trust Company, Chase Manhattan Bank, Neiman-Marcus Company).[24]

Limitations on the Influence of Interest Groups

Any effort to assess the role that interest groups play in administrative systems must reckon with several factors that limit their influence. Groups take advantage of numerous opportunities to express their demands to administrators. However, administrators themselves seem to dominate the relationships. The status of interest groups is ambiguous. Intermingled in their reputation is the image of the selfish lobbyist who would gratify his own group's interest at the expense of the public. There have been episodes of deceit on the part of interest groups, heavily-financed campaigns designed to defeat politicians who had opposed group demands, and overt attempts to bribe government officials. Policy-makers are sensitive to these aspects of interest-group tradition. If a government official perceives "undesirable pressures," he may terminate the access which a group has enjoyed and frustrate a campaign to influence policy.

Lobbyists themselves admit their secondary status in relations with government officials. In response to a question about the influence of various participants in policy-making, more than one-half of 114 lobbyists surveyed named the president or administrators as the most important actors, about 20 percent named the voters as most important, 10 percent named Congress, and only one of the respondents gave the lobbyists first rank.[25]

---

[24] *Legislators and the Lobbyists*, pp. 65–72.
[25] Lester W. Milbrath, *The Washington Lobbyists* (Chicago: Rand McNally, 1963), pp. 351–52.

POLITICAL PARTIES AS INTERMEDIARIES BETWEEN CITIZENS AND ADMINISTRATORS

Political parties also transmit information between citizens and policy-makers. However, a major factor that inhibits party participation in the policy decisions of administrative agencies is the lack of mechanisms to discipline their members on policy issues or to guarantee party unity in the legislature.

American parties lack several devices that parties in other countries use to enforce concerted action. There is no central control of financing or nominations, and there are no other incentives strong enough to assure that state and local organizations will support the positions of national party leaders.[26]

The decentralized structure of American parties is largely responsible for their lack of policy-discipline. Party candidates or incumbents owe their obligations to a variety of state and local parties, each of which has its own constituency of voters' attitudes, beliefs, and policy preferences. Nominations and financial support for state, local, and congressional campaigns come from these state or local organizations, which may be nothing more than personal organizations focused on the career of one politician. The nomination and much of the money for presidential campaigns also depend on decisions that are made in these state and local parties. There is no cadre of national officers who control political resources necessary to state organizations and who might issue policy directives to prospective party nominees. National party leaders lack any formal control over state or local nominations, and they lack financial sanction over most state organizations. There is more money transferred from state and local groups to the National Party Committees than is transferred outward from the center.[27] Some congressmen and governors campaign openly in opposition to the presidential nominee of their own party. At one time this was solely a Democratic problem, with liberal presidential nominees expecting to write-off the support of southerners. But the 1964 presidential campaign saw Republican Governors Nelson Rockefeller and George Romney, Senator Jacob Javits, and New York's Mayor John Lindsay refusing to endorse the candidacy of Barry Goldwater. Party leaders view their ideological diversity as an asset and perpetuate it by trying to cast a broad appeal with ambiguous platforms.

---

[26] See James MacGregor Burns, *The Deadlock of Democracy: Four-Party Politics in America* (Englewood Cliffs, N.J.: Spectrum Books, 1963).

[27] Alexander Heard, *The Costs of Democracy: Financing American Political Campaigns* (Garden City, N.Y.: Anchor Books, 1962), pp. 255ff.

Partly because of their ideological diversity, American parties are most likely to be governed by pragmatic office-seekers who put a premium on flexibility and on the capacity to make such adjustments in their policy positions as are necessary for electoral success. The parties are unlikely to develop strong, permanent staffs that would desire—or be able—to maintain a coherent set of principles on matters of public policy.[28]

Despite the barriers to strong political parties, elected chief executives assume the roles of party leaders and use existing party loyalties to help build a coherent program for the agencies to administer. When such executives make appointments to high-level positions within their administration, they typically appoint members of their own party. At the national level, 89 percent of Franklin Roosevelt's appointments to executive administrative positions were made from among Democrats; 84 percent of President Truman's appointments were Democrats; 76 percent of President Eisenhower's appointments were Republicans; 81 percent of President Kennedy's appointees were Democrats; and 84 percent of President Johnson's early appointments were Democrats.[29] In many state and local governments, the elected chief executive has an opportunity to fill not only some high-level positions, but also a large number of middle- and low-range positions with people who demonstrate at least a minimum of party loyalty.

The practice of appointing fellow partisans to administrative jobs has a long history in the United States and is justified with claims that it improves the government as well as the party. Presumably, a chief executive is more able to count on cooperation from his subordinates if they are linked to him with party ties. Fellow partisans are more likely to share his policy orientation and to help compile a record of administrative accomplishments that will appeal to the voters at the next election.

The appointive power that remains in the hands of chief executives is only a vestige of what they formerly had. Several changes in government programs and the public's regard for partisanship have limited the executive's freedom. Non-partisan criteria are now required for over 90 percent of the civilian positions in the federal government and for many positions in state and local governments.[30]

---

[28] Ira Sharkansky, *The Routines of Politics* (New York: Van Nostrand-Reinhold, 1970), Chapter VII.

[29] David T. Stanley, *et al., Men Who Govern: A Biographical Profile of Federal Political Executives* (Washington, D.C.: Brookings Institution, 1967), p. 24.

[30] O. Glenn Stahl, *Public Personnel Administration* (New York: Harper & Row, 1962), pp. 41ff.

For a number of positions, it is necessary for the chief executive to balance the several positions in boards or commissions with appointees of different parties. Government services are increasingly technical and require professional expertise in many administrative positions. A chief executive must often weigh professional competence above partisanship in selecting department heads even when the law permits him to use partisan criteria. In many instances, the only partisan standard that is feasible holds that the "right man" not be uncompromising in his support for the opposition. A man who is politically neutral or is even a bland member of the opposition party may be selected over a fellow partisan if the position calls for special competence. Sometimes a chief executive feels constrained to "balance" his administration when there is no legal requirement for this. President-elect Eisenhower seemed intent on appointing a Democrat as Secretary of Labor in 1952; and Nixon announced ahead of time in 1968 that his Ambassador to the United Nations would be a Democrat.

The Machine as the Archetype of Party Government

The machine is one kind of political party with strong discipline and a tradition of using its control of elective offices to staff and control administrative agencies. However, "machines have always been something of a genetic 'sport' among American political parties."[31] They were never "typical" of party organizations, and now they seem to be declining in number.

Several resources seem necessary for a party to operate as a well-disciplined machine. These include a large number of voters who desire tangible rewards that have low "unit-costs," such as jobs, food, help in finding a place to live, assistance in time of trouble with the police, welfare payments, or assistance in completing the forms necessary for welfare assistance. The voters who support a machine have only a secondary interest in the values of middle-class reformers: proper forms of government; efficiency in conducting public business; professional administration; and fair election procedures.[32] A machine also needs resources to "pay off" its voters and its ward and precinct organizers. These rewards include money, government jobs, and nominations for elected positions. Machines offer protection to bootlegging, gambling, narcotics, or prostitution. They also receive "kickbacks"

---

[31] See Frank J. Sorauf, *Party Politics in America* (Boston: Little, Brown, 1968), p. 58.

[32] Edward C. Banfield and James Q. Wilson, *City Politics* (Cambridge, Mass.: Harvard University Press, 1963), Chapter 9.

from contractors and public utilities that do business with the government or need a franchise in order to serve the public.

The machines earned their reputation for graft and corruption partly because of charges that they "fix" elections, partly because of the protection they provide to criminal elements, and partly because of the favoritism in the provision of benefits to certain groups and individuals. Some machine politicians claim there is a difference between "honest graft" and "dirty graft." While both are illegal activities, some are less undesirable than others. Honest graft involves the use of information and power to profit the machine in ways that do not offend the morals of most voters. It consists of knowing where roads, bridges, or public buildings are to be constructed, buying the land before that information is made public, and then selling it for a large profit. It also includes selecting a site for public construction near land already owned by friends of the machine and thereby enhancing the value of adjacent properties. Kickbacks from firms chosen to undertake public construction are also included in honest graft. If a profit were to be made anyway, then why shouldn't part of it go to the machine? Admittedly, the border between "honest" and "dirty" graft is hard to define. Contractors probably make the entire community pay for the kickback to the machine. Instead of taking the kickback out of their own profit, they would increase the total cost of the project or would lower expenses by using inferior materials or workmanship. Also, the whole community must pay for the increased land prices caused by the advanced purchase of land to be bought by the government. And if sites for public facilities are chosen for the profit of the machine rather than on service-related criteria, then the clients of the perspective facility suffer undue inconvenience.

Graft that is outright "dirty" involves the protection of criminal activities that offend large segments of the public. Here, too, there may be problems defining the borders of dirty graft. A numbers or bookmaking syndicate that satisfied the public's needs for gambling without rigging the odds too much or without investing its profits in local narcotics or prostitution might be considered "honest graft" in some communities. Substantiated charges of involvement in prostitution, however, have aroused otherwise queiscent voters and shaken some of the strongest machines. "Machines and their leaders could afford to ignore charges of being crooks, but not charges of being pimps."[33]

---

[33] D. W. Brogan, *Politics in America* (New York: Harper, 1954), Chapter IV, especially p. 147.

From the perspective of one who appreciates a well-run organization, the political machine is a marvel to behold. The party organization is virtually the government. Its candidates are elected to be chief executive and a majority of the city council, and it appoints the chiefs and subordinates in administrative organizations. Its diverse segments are united by a common loyalty to the success of the machine's candidates at the next election, and all can be counted on to mobilize the voters support. Between elections, the ward and precinct units serve the voters with personal favors. If the mayor or the machine boss (who may not be the same individual) wishes to change certain policies, he gets the cooperation of his majority on the council and his lieutenants in the administration with a speed and harmony that is unknown where political conditions show the plurality and confusion that is more typical of democracy.[34]

The demise of big-city machines is a product of several factors. Some are local in nature, and some reflect basic changes in American politics and economics. The Depression was a major blow to most machines. Immediately, it created a magnitude of poverty and personal distress much too-large for the machine's resources of food baskets, jobs, and rent money. In the long run, the Depression led to federally organized, financed, and supervised old-age insurance, unemployment compensation, and public assistance. These provided a level and consistency of benefits that no machine could match and took over a principal device that machines had used to attract large blocs of voters. While the machines were losing their welfare role, local governments also began to provide a range of services requiring the employment of skilled technicians and professionals. City hospitals, universities, and welfare organizations, plus an increased concern for excellence in the public schools, raised demands for highly trained employees who could not be recruited from ward and precinct workers.[35] Civil service reforms also took hold at the local level and increasingly required that middle- and low-level jobs be filled without regard to partisanship. Today there remain few big-city or state parties that merit the designation "machine." To be sure, some local and state parties unite many individuals in their support for certain candidates or policies. But the interlocking machine, with its "boss," mass electorate, control of the administrative apparatus, and tangible

---

[34] Robert K. Merton, *Social Theory and Social Structure* (Glencoe, Ill.: Free Press, 1957).

[35] However, the custodial positions at municipal hospitals and universities may still provide some job resources for local machines.

benefits for voters and precinct workers, is more a feature of American history than a contemporary reality.

ADMINISTRATIVE AGENCIES AS COLLECTORS OF INFORMATION

Government agencies are not merely the recipients of information about their environment. Beside their role as the receivers of demands from citizens, from lobbyists, and from the spokesmen of political parties, agencies also seek their own information. A prominent example is the *Report* of the National Advisory Commission on Civil Disorders. The Commission is one of those groups described in Chapter 4 as an "administrative hybrid." It was appointed by the president and included members of the legislative branch, state and local chief executives and administrators, and representatives of private industry. It was not an agency in the usual sense of that term. It carried out in a prominent way the tasks of information-collection and formulation of proposals that frequently occur in administrative agencies. The prominence of the problems in this case seemed to require the special attention of the president and a commission of prestigious individuals. In response to the riots in Newark and Detroit during 1967, this body tried to answer the questions: What happened? Why did it happen? What can be done to prevent it from happening again? The Commission's *Report* has several implications for the relationship between the public and policy-makers in administrative agencies and in other branches of government. First, it represents a major effort to understand conditions in black ghettos. The Commission found:

- Pervasive discrimination and segregation.
- Frustrated hopes raised by the legislative and judicial victories of the civil rights movement, but not realized for most individual blacks.
- A climate that tends toward approval and encouragement of violence—created by white terrorism directed against nonviolent protest, and by the defiance of law and federal authority by state and local officials resisting desegregation.
- Frustrations of powerlessness that lead some Negroes to the conviction that there is no effective alternative to violence as a means of redressing grievances.
- A new mood of racial pride.
- Hostility and cynicism directed toward the police.[36]

[36] *Report* of the National Advisory Commission on Civil Disorders (New York: Bantam Books, 1968), pp. 10–11. See also pp. 94–95 for a discussion of prestigious commissions as "administrative hybrids."

Second, the *Report* stands as an effort to affect the opinions of both white and black Americans. Its style is calculated to shock many whites into a feeling of guilt and responsibility for the plight of blacks and to generate conditions that will permit passage of ameliorating social legislation:

> Race prejudice has shaped our history decisively; it now threatens to affect our future. . . . White racism is essentially responsible for the explosive mixture which has been accumulating in our cities since the end of World War II.[37]

For blacks, the *Report* may stand as partial conciliation for wrongs previously committed and as an attempt to alleviate some of their most serious social problems. Among its proposals were:

- Bring the institutions of local government closer to the people they serve by establishing neighborhood outlets for local, state, and federal administrative and public service agencies.
- Expand opportunities for ghetto residents to participate in the formulation of public policy and the implementation of programs affecting them. . . .
- Review police operations in the ghetto . . . and eliminate abrasive practices.
- Recruit more Negroes into the regular police force, and review promotion policies to ensure fair promotion for Negro officers.[38]

The "public opinion environment" that surrounds each administrative unit is actually quite diffuse and presents several alternatives to the administrators. Some administrators "tune" to a conception of the "general public," while others concern themselves with particular groups. In each case, there are additional choices to make. As noted in the discussion of the Agriculture Department's food programs (see pp. 177–78), there may be several general interests and different particular groups that can be served by an agency. Some times it is not possible to serve them all. When the Interstate Commerce Commission permits a larger size trailer truck to operate on the highways, for example, it may help the truckers; but it may hurt the railroads by adding to the truckers' competitive advantage in the transportation industry and may also inconvenience—or endanger—the drivers of automobiles. Only a minority of administrative units make major investments in gathering information about the public. One study

---

[37] *Report,* p. 10.
[38] *Report,* pp. 16–17.

found that 60 percent of upper-level administrators in a sample rely on newspaper comment, letters of complaint, and clients' grievances.[39] In the haphazard way that many units gather their information, their image of the world may be shaped by which administrator receives a particular bit of information and by the nature of his responsibility for policy-making.

The nature of an administrator's job may have something to do with the way he gathers information about the public. One study categorizes the personnel in administrative agencies as "politicos," "professionals," and "administrators." "Politicos" make policy, defend the agency against the outside world, and are responsible to its external pressures; in this position, they are most likely to see a variety of interests that are relevant to the agency and to consider the broadest needs of the constituencies in making their decisions. A "professional" is a person with technical or scientific training who is typically in contact with only a portion of his agency's work and is likely to view its clients' needs as those of the particluar groups he encounters. "Administrators" have the most confined training and work-assignments. They supervise subunits within an organization and manage specific projects. With less of a cosmopolitan training than "professionals" and with more restricted responsibilities than "politicos," the "administrators" are inclined to take the most narrow view of the interests that are served by an agency's programs.[40]

SUMMARY

This chapter focuses on relationships between citizens and administrative units and on the roles of the mass media, public opinion polls, elections, interest groups, and political parties as intermediaries between them. Because of shortcomings in their interest and information, most individuals require some organized intermediary between themselves and the conversion process of the administrative system. On occasion, the mass media have added significantly to the public's information about a social problem or a public policy and have generated strong pressure on policy-makers. However, the media suffer from some of the same problems as individuals. They have other functions that distract them from the role of political-intermediary. Commercial and recreational functions consume many resources which might otherwise be employed in politics. Also, citizens "protect"

[39] Robert S. Friedman, *et al.*, "Administrative Agencies and the Publics They Serve," *Public Administration Review*, 26 (September, 1966), 192–204.
[40] Friedman, *et al.*

themselves from mass media just as they protect themselves from other involvements in politics. Many people do not consume the political news and editorials which the media provide. Because of selective perception, some fail to see items that would challenge their own views.

Public opinion polls also serve as intermediaries between citizens and administrators. However, the polls typically do not indicate that the public has taken a clear position on one side or another of an issue. Moreover, the questions asked on most polls are not precise enough to inform the policy-maker about the feeling of the public on the specific issue that he faces. Such an issue may not be support or opposition to an entire program, but rather support or opposition for certain aspects of a program. The polls also fail to indicate how seriously individuals take the positions that they announce. In many cases, respondents may think of an issue for the first—and last—time when they are approached by the interviewer. Polls that show support or opposition to a candidate—or an incumbent—do not provide the specific information needed by a policy-maker. Individuals can be reacting to any of several positions that the politician has taken; generalized support or opposition does not signify support or opposition for any of his policies. The same difficulty limits the electoral process as an intermediary between citizens and government policy-making. Elections do let the people decide about certain personnel. However, they do not show which of several campaign statements about policy actually won popular support.

Interest groups seldom appear to be dominant in the administrative system. The status of lobbying is ambiguous, and many officials take a guarded position in their dealings with interest groups. Officials in all branches of government receive a variety of demands, and they have some preferences of their own. Thus, interest groups cannot write their wishes on a clean slate; they must compete with directives that come to administrators from the legislature and the chief executive, from other administrative units, from officials at other governmental levels, and from the personal and professional values of the administrators themselves.

Political parties concentrate on winning elective offices and filling appointed positions, rather than on realizing policy desires. Their self-limitation reflects, in part, their inability to control party voters, candidates, or office holders. There is little to assure a party leadership that its members—even within the leadership cadre—are united on important policy issues. A political machine is a party organization that combines a disciplined control of executive, legislative, and administrative units, typically in city governments. However, the machine is a rare and declining feature of American politics. Its demise reflects several social and political changes that have withdrawn the types of resources that the classic machine needed. The development of merit systems and the spread of public services requiring technical and professional personnel removed the machine's control over government jobs that could reward large numbers of precinct workers and voters. And as the federal government provided massive cash doles for the needy, for job placement and job training, for unemployment compensation, for retirement programs, and for low-cost public housing, the machines lost control over welfare benefits.

Administrative agencies are not passive in their relations with citizens. They actively seek the support of interest groups; lobby in behalf of their own programs with the legislative and executive branches; and collect reams of information about social and economic conditions and about the problems that might be alleviated by public services. Thus, some of the "inputs" that seem to come from the environment of the administrative system are actually solicited and nurtured by the administrators who are, ostensibly, their targets.

8

EXECUTIVES, LEGISLATORS, AND ADMINISTRATORS

The executive and legislative branches are a major source of inputs to administrative agencies. They transmit demands and resources which take the form of statutes, executive orders, Committee *Reports*, and informal communications. These transmissions authorize or instruct administrative units to engage in certain activities, to hire personnel, and to pay their bills. These demands and resources from executive and legislative branches are not simply inputs to administrative agencies. Many get their start in the administration and are sent from there (as outputs) to the legislature and the executive for consideration. Among these outputs that go from administrative agencies to the executive and the legislative branches are proposals for new legislation, for personnel standards, and for budgets. Here our concern is with inputs to administrative units; in Chapter 10, we shall return to administrative relations with the legislative and executive branches and consider as administrative outputs the transmissions that stimulate subsequent inputs from the other branches.

It is no simple task to describe relationships among executives, legislators, and administrators. Their activities reflect the formal directives of the Constitution and of statutes, plus a variety of informal arrangements that have evolved over the years. There are some general tendencies, but numerous variations. Some variations reflect institutional peculiarities of the federal government or individual state or local governments. Other variations reflect the nature of the issue, the actors' view of the issue, and the intensity of their feelings.

There is general consensus about one feature of relationships between administrative agencies and the legislative and executive branches: they have changed markedly since the nation's founding. The administrator should no longer be considered the insignificant subordinate of the legislative and executive. The changes that have occured since 1789 are a profound example of relationships within the administrative system changing in response to environmental changes.

When the framers of the Constitution wrote their document, they concentrated on the legislative and executive branches and paid little attention to what was then a small cadre of administrators. The government they described resembles contemporary institutions only in their gross outlines. The magnitude and nature of government has changed dramatically. The federal administration has increased from a staff of 780 civilian employees in 1789 to a staff of 2.7 million in 1969. At the end of the 18th century, the principal activities were the post office, revenue collection, diplomacy, and a rudimentary armed service. Now there is space exploration, the administration of numerous health and welfare services, vast conservation and recreational programs, research and development in the natural and social sciences, the development of air, sea, and land facilities for transportation and communication, and global military responsibilities. State and local governments have accepted major responsibilities in education, transportation, recreation, health, and welfare which were inconceivable in the 18th century. One significance of this growth lies in the problems they raise for the chief executive and the legislature. The scope of activities has far outreached the capacity of these elected officials to initiate policy; it may even outreach their capacity to be thorough in their supervision and control of policy-makers in the administration! However, the legislative and executive branches still have some impressive powers of their own. And they still have the choice as to where and when to employ their powers.

LEGISLATIVE WEAKNESS IN RELATIONS WITH ADMINISTRATIVE AGENCIES

The major problems that the legislature faces are the fragmentation of its energies and a lack of information about policy issues. Fragmentation is a general term that covers a number of difficulties: the diffusion of legislative resources into two houses which—in a formal sense—duplicates each other's responsibilities; the diffusion of the members' interests between policy-making and a number of other responsibilities; and their failure to accept the discipline of any integrating mechanisms (e.g., a political party) which might coordinate them. The information that the legislature gathers is impressive in its own right, but is "lacking" in comparison to what is assembled by the administrative agencies and to what seems necessary for the control of administration.

Aside from formulating policy or supervising ongoing programs, legislators must also accomodate constituents who wish assistance in dealing with administrative agencies. This typically requires individual legislators and their staff assistants to tend to a much broader field than any of them can master. Constituents seek government jobs and contracts; assistance in qualifying for routine services; or help in appealing their cases after being denied their first application. State legislators, for example, deal with constituents who are denied admission to the state university or mental hospital or who are denied release from the same mental hospital or a parole from the penitentiary. Legislators also service local governments. Congressmen arrange appointments for local officials with federal granting agencies and often lend their physical presence to the meetings. At the state level, legislators introduce "local bills" to the legislature, testify in behalf of their community's needs, and steer the bills through committee. Where the state government controls many functions in the local community, legislators are kept busy as the delegates from city hall and the county courthouse. Legislators must also attend to their own political careers. Many of their service activities have political payoffs. Whenever a legislator assists a constituent or a local government, he can expect some good will in return. Other duties are more directly linked with re-election. They include speaking engagements and tours of the constituency. Legislators feel a continuing need for exposure— an opportunity to express their views or to solicit funds for the next campaign.

While legislators dissipate their resources to a number of distinct activities, administrators concentrate theirs by specializing in the affairs of a single agency—or more likely a single program. For many administrators, specialization begins in college or in graduate school and continues through their career. Few legislators have the knowledge to match the full range of their responsibilities. Most are content to serve a "generalist" function in supervising "specialists" in the administrative organization. It is related to the "representative" nature of legislators that they are somewhat like the rest of us in lacking the specialized knowledge that can be found in administrative agencies. Yet legislators are also limited in what they can do for us by not having a complete understanding of their decisions.

The informational dependence of legislatures reveals itself in the procedures used to elicit the views of administrators on proposed bills. Many bills originate in the department that will be given responsibility for administering the program. A legislator typically refers his own ideas to the administration for evaluation and modification. One study of legislative-administrative relationships in the City of Los Angeles found that 25 percent of the bills considered by the council originated in the city departments, and almost all of the others were referred by legislators to the relevant departments for their comments. Lobbyists recognize the importance of the administrator's review: "If the administrators oppose us, we're sunk." "We find the Council checks with the departments on our requests and lets itself be governed by what they say." Almost all of the bills opposed by administrative agencies were defeated in the city council.[1]

SOURCES OF LEGISLATIVE STRENGTH IN RELATIONS WITH ADMINISTRATIVE AGENCIES

The legislature is not without resources to supervise or control administrative agencies. In Congress, committees, seniority, and staff assistants provide some opportunities for legislators to acquire information about administrative activities. Committees provide opportunities for specialization paralleled to the specialization of administrative units. A committee's jurisdiction usually includes a number of administrative units that pursue a related set of programs. The privileges of seniority protect a member's seat on his committee and allow him to accumulate information over the years. Congressional committees also have professional staff assistants who gather information for the members, conduct formal hearings, draft legislation, and write committee *Reports*. State legislatures are not as well-equipped. Many legislatures lack seniority guarantees. As a result, members are shifted from one committee to another and lose the benefits of information gained in past sessions. In some states, even the chairmen of committees do not have continuing rights to their committee assignments. The lack of seniority-guarantees in many state legislatures reflects the unattractive nature of the seats and the high turnover. The staff assistance and future political opportunities for legislators in many states are also markedly inferior to those of congressmen. In some states, the legislators have no office or secretary of their own. Without seniority or other features that allow the members to increase their expertise, state legislatures are likely to depend heavily on policy recommendations that come from administrative agencies.

Even when they are dependent on administrators' information,

---

[1] Harry W. Reynolds, Jr., "The Career Public Service and Statute Lawmaking in Los Angeles," *Western Political Quarterly*, 28 (September, 1965), 621–39.

legislators can assert a strong negative role in policy-making. And although they may not develop fully-mature proposals with their own resources, they do prompt administrators to innovate. When the legislature refuses to accept an administrator's proposal for new authority or for a certain level of expenditure, the administrator may be powerless. He *can* appeal the decision of the legislature. A successful appeal, however, may require sufficient time for a change in the policial environment that occasioned the first decision of the legislature. Some administrators evade the legislature. They cite an existing statute to justify new activities, or they transfer funds from one activity to support an activity that had not received an adequate budget on its own merits. Such evasions are often contrary to law or at least to prevailing norms that define "proper" relations between the administration and the legislature, and most administrators seem unwilling to use these methods. If discovered, an administrator might be subject to public rebuke and face the loss of legislative support in the future. If an administrator loses his rapport with the chairman and members of key legislative committees, he may lose standing with superiors in the administration and in the executive branch.[2]

The importance of the legislature in policy-making is shown by the resources that administrators use to persuade its members. If the legislature were a rubber-stamp for the recommendations for the administration, then government agencies would not lobby so heavily. The study of the Los Angeles City Council—which found heavy legislative reliance on the recommendations of the administration—also described a number of tactics that administrators use to strengthen their own recommendations. These include:

1. Personal visits with individual council members;
2. A continuing release of written material on the bills of interest to the administration;
3. The use of newspapers, the Mayor's office, interest groups, and prestigious private citizens to communicate circumspectly to the council; and
4. The careful timing of certain major proposals according to crises in the community that might emphasize their worth.[3]

There has been some effort to measure the resources spent by the federal administration in congressional lobbying. During the fiscal

[2] Ira Sharkansky, "Four Agencies and An Appropriations Subcommittee: A Comparative Study of Budget Strategies," *Midwest Journal of Political Science,* 9 (August, 1965), 254–81.
[3] Reynolds, pp. 621–39.

year 1963, 500 employees (at a cost of $5.4 million) were engaged in full-time congressional liaison. Countless other employees spent part of their time preparing information for Congress or responding to the requests of congressmen for information.[4]

A legislature can exercise some control because administrators fear the legislature's ultimate negative decision and because administrators try to anticipate and accomodate the wishes of the legislators. No administrator knows when a legislative committee will begin a prolonged inquiry into his affairs and decide to concentrate its energies on controlling his agency. Some administrative units receive exhaustive reviews. Their experience warns other units of what might happen. A study of relations between the National Aeronautics and Space Administration (NASA) and Congress found 5,371 pages of published testimony concerning the agency's budget for fiscal 1964, resulting in a budget cut of $600 million. "A thorough reading of the hearings, reports, and floor debates . . . indicates that the agency was not being given just an across-the-board cut. Rather, it was being explicitly told to absorb the cut by dropping, postponing, diminishing, or not expanding various activities or construction projects." During the 1959–1963 period, NASA was called before 12 different committees and many more subcommittees. Beside the appropriations committees in the House and Senate, they included the space, government operations, and armed services committees in both houses, plus the Senate Small Business Committee, Senate Judiciary Committee, the Senate Committee on Foreign Relations, and the Joint Committee on Atomic Energy.[5]

EXECUTIVE WEAKNESS IN RELATIONS WITH ADMINISTRATIVE AGENCIES

The president has nominal control over most administrative units of the federal government; but a number of formal exceptions, plus some political deficiencies, combine to weaken his influence over policy-making. The formal exceptions limit his powers of appointment. Members of independent regulatory commissions, for example, have fixed terms, and the president may find his removal powers

---

[4] G. Russell Pipe, "Congressional Liaison: The Executive Branch Consolidates Its Relations with Congress," *Public Administration Review,* 26 (March, 1966), 14–24.

[5] Thomas P. Jahnige, "The Congressional Committee System and the Oversight Process: Congress and NASA," *Western Political Quarterly,* 21 (June, 1968), 227–239.

limited by the need to cite certain causes for each dismissal (see pp. 88–90). He also must share most appointments with the Senate. Generally, this is a nominal requirement, but Senate opposition has led him to withdraw some major nominations. The greatest formal inhibition on the president lies in his need to share the roles of policy-initiation and supervision with the legislature. An uncooperative committee in either house can keep a president's bill from being considered on the floor.[6] A committee can also support an administrator who would challenge the chief executive.

The president's need to share policy-making with the legislature is only one part of a more general problem: his need to take account of several constituencies when making decisions. It is part of the president's power that he affects many different interests by his decisions. One study has identified five constituencies that the president leads: the legislature, the administration, his political party, citizens of the United States and the organizations that represent them, and foreign governments.[7] Another study of the presidency identifies ten roles which he plays: chief of state, chief executive, chief diplomat, commander-in-chief, chief legislator, chief of party, chief moral leader, chief keeper of domestic peace and tranquillity, chief guardian of the economy, and leader of an international coalition.[8] Each of these constituencies and roles represents a portion of the president's status. But each, too, represents the diverse sets of interests he must take into consideration when making any important decisions. A decision made in his role as chief legislator, for example, must not clash so much with the desires of constituents in the administration that he will lose the support of the administrators on another occasion. The president is hemmed in by his own vast power. Because so many of his decisions affect different constituencies, he is typically constrained from several sides at once. He is not without power to manipulate within these confines; but his power is tenuous and dependent on his ability to *persuade* the members of different constituencies that his decisions have some benefits and only minimal costs for their own interests.

---

[6] Procedures exist for "calling" a bill from a committee, but they are difficult and are seldom employed. See Malcolm E. Jewell and Samuel C. Patterson, *The Legislative Process in the United States* (New York: Random House, 1966), p. 260.

[7] Richard Neustadt, *Presidential Power: The Politics of Leadership* (New York: Wiley, 1960), p. 7.

[8] Clinton Rossiter, *The American Presidency* (New York: Signet, 1966), Chapter 1.

Constituent relations are relations of dependence. Everyone with any share in governing this country will belong to one (or two, or three) of his "constituencies." Since everyone depends on him, why is he not assured of everyone's support? The answer is that no one else sits where he sits, or sees quite as he sees; no one else feels the full weight of his obligations. Those obligations are a tribute to his unique place in our political system. But just because it is unique, they fall on him alone. *The same conditions that promote his leadership in form preclude a guarantee of leadership in fact.* No man or group at either end of Pennsylvania Avenue shares his peculiar status in our government and politics. That is why his services are in demand. By the same token, though, the obligation of all other men are different from his own. His Cabinet officers have departmental duties and constituents. His legislative leaders head *congressional* parties, one in either House. His national party organization stands apart from his official family. His political allies in the States need not face Washington, or one another. The private groups that seek him out are not compelled to govern. And friends abroad are not compelled to run in our elections. Lacking his position and prerogatives, these men cannot regard his obligations as their own. They have their jobs to do; none is the same as his. As they perceive their duty, they may find it right to follow him, in fact, or they may not.[9]

State governors seem to have even more problems than the president in controlling their administrations. Almost all the governors face severe formal limitations on their powers of appointment. The heads of many departments are named by direct election. Most states have separate elections for the attorney general, treasurer, secretary of state, auditor, and superintendent of public instruction.[10] Appointments of other department heads are made by boards or commissions over whom the governor has only limited control.

If the proposals of the executive threaten the established activities of administrative agencies, he may be drawn into a squabble that drains away his public standing. Administrators can openly dispute the executive's position or can supply information to interest groups or legislators who oppose the executive. At times like this, the executive's best weapon may be his informal power to persuade the policy-makers within the administrative organization. Aiding his power of persuasion in his prominent public position, his claim to represent "all of the

[9] Neustadt, pp. 7–8.
[10] Joseph A. Schlesinger, "The Politics of the Executive," in Herbert Jacob and Kenneth N. Vines, eds., *Politics in the American States* (Boston: Little, Brown, 1965), pp. 207–38.

people," and the technical arguments that are provided by his aides. Yet the weaknesses of persuasive power are the time that it consumes and the publicity it may give to the executive's problems. Executives have won confrontations with administrators, but the time and political costs involved may lead them to concede all but his most-vital concerns to the administration.[11]

The lofty position of the chief executive helps to isolate him from many administrative arenas where important decisions are made. The chief executive may have direct access to his department heads, but the operating bureaus are submerged within the departments. Unless the chief executive is willing to break through the hierarchical lines on his organization chart, he is separated from most policy-makers in the administration. One study of presidential relations with bureau chiefs estimated that 125 separate bureaus make essential decisions in the administrative organization of the national government. "The bureaus are, in fact, the bureaucracy. . . . In non-foreign affairs and non-military programs, they are the units of government closest to the citizen and also to Congress." A study of 20 bureaus found that their chief administrative officers had served a total of 170 years as bureau heads, but had met a total of only 79 times with the president. This averages to one meeting every two years for each bureau head. If meetings with the Internal Revenue Commissioner were excluded (25 visits in about 4 years), the average falls to one meeting every three years. These meetings include ceremonial and social functions as well as policy sessions. Seven of the 20 bureau heads had no contacts with the president except for social or ceremonial occasions; and 2 had no contacts with the president at all.[12]

SOURCES OF EXECUTIVE STRENGTH IN RELATIONS WITH ADMINISTRATIVE AGENCIES

Despite the handicaps, chief executives (state governors as well as the president) have certain policy-resources that the legislature lacks. The executive branch is organized in a fashion that is at least nominally hierarchical (see pp. 79–85). The single executive can probably make decisions with greater speed and with greater certainty that colleagues will cooperate than can any single legislator. The staff agencies of the executive provide him with a level of information

---

[11] See Neustadt's book for the best-known general discussion of this point.
[12] David S. Brown, "The President and the Bureaus: Time for a Renewal of Relationship?" *Public Administration Review*, 26 (September, 1966), 174–82.

superior to that which is directly available to the legislators (see pp. 96–98). His status as the chief executive helps recruit additional civilian advisors on matters of special concern. The chief executive can also attract the mass media—and through them, the public—in ways that are not possible for individual legislators.

The chief executive may dominate policy-making if he chooses to concentrate his resources of unity, information, and prestige. The outside borders of his control are defined by the "program" on which he chooses to concentrate his resources. Outside this scope, an executive may be heavily dependent on the proposals of administrative units. The notion of "program" is flexible. Administrative proposals may work their way into the executive's program or may be considered by the legislature with the passive consent of the executive. Even within the scope of his own program, however, the executive may leave the details of planning, bill-drafting, and implementation to the administration.

VARIATIONS IN RELATIONS AMONG THE EXECUTIVE AND LEGISLATIVE BRANCHES AND ADMINISTRATIVE AGENCIES

In the previous sections of this chapter, we have identified the features of the legislative or executive branches that may weaken or strengthen them in relations with administrative agencies. It is more difficult to generalize about the success of individual legislators and executives in their dealings with administrators. Some factors that seem important are: the intensity with which each actor views his position; the support he has from other officials, interest groups, or prominent citizens; and the alliances that are formed against his position.

Not all interactions between the administrative units and the legislative or executive branches are occasions for conflict. Many are informal occasions for helping one another in the common pursuit of improving public service. One study of relations between the House and Senate Committees on Small Business and the Small Business Administration (SBA) found:

> . . . the relations since 1961 have been characterized as a "love feast." In that year, President Kennedy named John Horne as head of the agency. According to a number of observers, Horne was one of the most popular administrators on Capitol Hill. They also suggested that relationships between the agency and the Committees since then have been

not so much the committees' overseeing the agency but rather one of "mutual backscratching."[13]

The small-business committees have "run interference" for the SBA with other committees in Congress and have helped to increase the statutory authority, as well as the funds, of the agency. The committees have also urged the executive superiors of the SBA to pay more attention to the agency's requests. Here is a case where a legislative "overseer" has dealt with the executive in order to help out an administrative agency.

Party Influence on Administrative–Legislative–Executive Relations

From one period of time to another, the positions of administrators, legislators, or executives can change because of the party composition in the executive and legislative branches. One study of budgeting in Congress found that normal procedures were *least* viable following major party changes in the presidency or Congress. During the 80th Congress (1949–1950), the newly-elected Republican majority made especially large cuts in the budgets submitted by President Truman. In the early Eisenhower years of 1953–1955 and in the Kennedy years of 1962–1963, there were also a large number of abnormal decisions. Perhaps congressmen saw the White House developing numerous innovative proposals and felt it necessary to involve themselves heavily in control procedures.[14]

Changes in the Status of Administrators

An increase in the status of military policies after 1945 provoked marked change in the relation of certain administrators (i.e., the professional military officers) with policy-makers in the legislative and executive branches. In previous postwar situations, the services demobilized to small cadres of officers and enlisted men and were typically starved for appropriations. In the years following World War I, spending for military *and* international activities dipped below the sums spent on the U.S. Post Office! After earlier wars, congressional involvement in military affairs was limited to matters of supply and logistics: How much was to be spent to support the armed services

---

[13] Dale Vinyard, "The Congressional Committees on Small Business: Pattern of Legislative Committee–Executive Agency Relations," *Western Political Quarterly*, 21 (September, 1968), 391–99.

[14] Otto A. Davis, M.A.H. Dempster, and Aaron Wildavsky, "A Theory of the Budgetary Process," *American Political Science Review*, 60 (September, 1966), 529–47.

and which military bases would remain in operation? Throughout the late 1940's and after the Korean conflict, however, the military and international budgets alone consumed upwards of 47 percent of federal expenditures. As the post-World-War-II military remained a significant consumer of federal revenue and became a central figure in the country's new prominence in international politics, Congress maintained an interest in military policy. There also developed serious conflicts between military officers and civilians in the Defense Department and White House. Perhaps due to the influence of newly acquired responsibilities, a sense of professionalism became more viable within the military and generated disputes with civilian administrators who had formal responsibilities for making policy. The result was a legislature interested in policy questions and a cadre of military administrators willing—if not anxious—to provide the legislators with alternative proposals to those offered by the civilian executive. Congressmen said they could discharge their constitutional responsibilities only if they could compare the "military" recommendations of the joint chiefs of staff with the recommendations of the president that were "compounded of a number of extramilitary considerations."[15] To facilitate its access to the military's recommendations, Congress wrote a clause in the National Security Act of 1949 which permitted a member of the joint chiefs of staff to present to Congress "on his own initiative, after first informing the Secretary of Defense, any recommendation relating to the Department of Defense that he may deem proper."[16]

The postwar opportunities for military officers to influence major policy decisions have also presented some difficult choices to these personnel:

> The annual psychic crisis of the Chiefs of Staff before the congressional appropriations committees is a new but apparently enduring phenomenon in American government. If the military chief accepts and defends the President's policies, he is subordinating his own professional judgment, denying to Congress the advice to which it is constitutionally entitled, and becoming the political defender of an administration policy. If the military chief expresses his professional opinions to Congress, he is publicly criticizing his Commander in Chief and furnishing useful ammunition to his political enemies. There is no easy way out of this dilemma. Military leaders in the postwar period varied in their behavior from more or less active campaigning against presidential policies

---

[15] Samuel P. Huntington, *The Soldier and the States: The Theory and Politics of Civil-Military Relations* (New York: Vintage Books, 1964), p. 415.
[16] Huntington, p. 416.

. . . to the defense of presidential policies which ran counter to their professional judgment.[17]

Changes in the Leadership of Administrative Agencies

It is not only military officers who have to make difficult personal judgments about their relations with legislative and executive "superiors." As noted above, both the legislature and the chief executive have grave limitations on their policy roles. Administrators are often left to define their own codes of behavior. The period of transition between one chief executive and another seems most likely to provide such choices to administrators. The loyalties formed under one executive may clash with the postures taken by a new superior. The moral questions raised by such occurrences are made difficult partly because there are so many options and partly because there is only a vague threat of punishment. It is hard to identify, and perhaps harder to punish, an administrator who deviates from the accepted options.

> What is a bureau chief to do under such circumstances? Where does his first loyalty lie? To his program principles? To the Secretary? To his clientele and "his" congressional committees? How far can he adapt himself to political redirection without seeming to knuckle under to a serious perversion of the program? Should he adapt himself, resign, or fight a rearguard action? Such moral dilemmas are political variations on the theme of *The Caine Mutiny*—less dramatic and less publicized but with somewhat similar ingredients. But mutiny on a ship in war-time is a henious crime, while the penalty for limited mutiny in a government agency is vague and rarely severe. The chances of unpunished success are all too great.[18]

A Cost-benefit Analysis of Legislative "Oversight"

In many areas of policy, the legislative, executive, or administrative personnel have an opportunity to involve themselves in basic decisions, but choose to abstain on account of the "costs" involved. Some costs occur because participants must focus their resources on a limited set of issues and must deprive themselves of opportunities presented by other topics. Other costs occur because an actor does not wish to "poison" his other relations with a protagonist. Legislators may avoid giving offense to a chief executive or to administrators, for example, in order to win their support on some other project that is more highly valued. One study of legislative "oversight" (i.e., supervi-

---

[17] Huntington, p. 417.
[18] Rufus E. Miles, Jr., "Administrative Adaptability to Political Change," *Public Administration Review*, 25 (September, 1965), 221–25.

sion) of agency programs concluded that the following types of conditions were likely to have a favorable ratio of benefits to costs and to affect legislative involvement in policy-making. When these conditions are present, a legislative committee is likely to make a formal investigation of agency activities:[19]

1. When the leadership of the majority party believes it can cause sufficient embarrassment, with accompanying profit for itself, to a past or current opposition chief executive who is held responsible for the performance of his agency appointees.
2. When the committee leadership or powerful committee members believe that constituent or group interests important to them cannot be satisfied by informal personal intercessions between legislators and agencies.
3. When legislators perceive that the chief executive will try to diminish their normal opportunities for influencing agency policy.
4. When, periodically, interest builds in the legislature for revising the basic policies under which the agency operates, committee oversight tends to occur as a byproduct.
5. When committee leaders become convinced that interests to which they are opposed will substantially advance their own purposes by exposing dramatic evidence of agency failure, the committee may move first to neutralize or minimize these gains by initiating its own inquiry.

The Formal Powers of the Legislative and Executive Branches

The nature of one's formal powers can also affect legislative or executive involvement in an administrative system. The legislature and chief executive in some governments have more formal authority than in others. Among the state governments, for example, there is considerable variation in the power of the governors to appoint the heads of major departments, to veto legislation, to succeed themselves in office, and to formulate the administration's budget.[20] Where the chief executive is relatively weak on these dimensions, the legislature may be relatively successful in having its policies implemented by administrative organizations. There is some evidence to support this

---

[19] Seymour Scher, "Conditions for Legislative Control," *Journal of Politics*, 25 (August, 1963), 526–51; these propositions are extrapolated here beyond the context of Scher's study of congressional-committee–regulatory-commission relations.

[20] See Schlesinger.

hypothesis. A survey of agency heads in 50 states showed that the governor was perceived to exercise the greatest control over agency affairs (as compared with the legislature) where his formal powers were strongest. His power of appointment seems particularly important. Among those agency heads who were popularly elected, only 9 percent felt that the governor exercised greater policy control than the legislature. Among those who were appointed by the governor alone —without the consent of a commission or the legislature—57 percent felt that he exercised more control over policy than the legislature.[21] However, formal authority does not always provide what it seems. The "item veto" has been heralded as a device to permit the chief executive greater control over the expenditures of administrative agencies. It is used, presumably, to veto discrete items of an appropriations act; the executive can deny the funds for certain programs, without having to threaten many other programs by vetoing a whole appropriations bill. The governors of 41 states now have the item veto; and it is mentioned in the remaining states as a device to increase the governor's control over the administration. Yet state legislatures have learned to protect favored programs against the threat of an item veto. A study of the item veto in Arizona found that it was used only 11 times since 1912 and not at all in the most recent 16 years. When the legislature senses that a certain item may draw a veto from the governor, it typically lumps it with items the governor is likely to approve. It thereby structures the "item" so the governor cannot veto it, even though he opposes parts of it.[22]

There is no simple answer to these questions: What are the "typical" relations among administrators and legislative and executive branches? What conditions will provoke the legislative or executive branch to play an assertive role in policy-making? When conflict arises within the administrative system, there is no clear indication as to who will prevail. The literature is replete with statements of general tendency. Some scholars have also probed the relative involvement of the legislature or the executive under each of certain conditions. However, their conditions do not exhaust the range of contingencies that face policy-makers, and their research methods have not been adequate to quiet skeptical social scientists. It is necessary to admit that

[21] Deil Wright, "Executive Leadership in State Administration," *Midwest Journal of Political Science*, 11 (February, 1967), 1–26.
[22] Roy D. Morey, "The Executive Veto in Arizona: Its Use and Limitations," *Western Political Quarterly*, 19 (September, 1966), 504–15.

there is much that is not known about the scope of administrators' autonomy or about the influence of legislators or executives in policy-making.

BUDGET RELATIONS AMONG LEGISLATORS, EXECUTIVES, AND ADMINISTRATORS

Budgeting involves legislators, executives, and administrators in their most regular and continuous relations. Budgeting is a cyclical process that repeats itself once annually (or once every two years in the case of state governments that use a biennial budget period). Members of the legislative appropriations committees, the chief executive and his central budget office, and spokesmen for the administrative agencies deal with one another both formally in budget proceedings and informally as they seek clearance when conditions require deviations from the existing budget. In many cases, budget interactions involve the same personalities for many years at a time. This occurs when the legislature respects seniority and guarantees a member's seat on the appropriations committee and when a central budget office is staffed with professionals who survive turnover in the office of the chief executive. Budgeting differs from the sporadic kinds of legislative-executive-administrative interactions that occur when a controversial issue generates momentary interest in the legislative or executive branches. Moreover, the medium of exchange that is involved in budgeting facilitates the description and analysis of general patterns and deviant behaviors. By focusing on the decisions made in the executive and legislative branches about the budget requests of administrative agencies, it is possible to discern which actors seem to prevail in the outcomes.

The Chronology of Budgeting

The budget calendar of the federal government provides a convenient device to identify the principal administrative, executive, and legislative actors in budgeting and to note some important features of their interactions. Although the details of the calendar vary in state and local governments, some general features tend to be constant. There are the initiation of requests by administrators, subsequent reviews by upper levels of the administration and of the executive budget staff, and final review in the legislature.

The major elements of the federal budgeting process consume 28 months. Program planning for fiscal year 1972, for example, begins in

March of 1970.[23] The length of time is significant in itself. It under-scores both the number of actors who involve themselves in the budgeting process and the importance of giving each one a chance to ask questions and to make evaluations. The time involved in budgeting also has its costs. The months of lead-time between planning and expenditures requires considerable re-planning during each budget cycle. And when a new president is elected to office, much of the budgetary process for the *coming* fiscal year is already complete. By the time of his inauguration in January, the outgoing president has already submitted a budget to Congress that will provide funds extending 18 months into the new administration. The graphic presentation of the budgeting-spending processes that is included in Figures 8–1, 8–2, and 8–3 is divided into three segments: the *Formulation of the Executive Budget; Congressional Action:* and *Execution of the Enacted Budget.*

Formulation in the Executive

The decisions in the *formulation* period begin with agency programming which then provides the basis for making its financial estimates. The agency defends its own estimates in the departmental budget office. (In this budgeting section, the term "agency" refers to an operating subunit of a major federal administrative department.) The departmental budget office (whose activities are shown merged with the "agency" in Figure 8–1) plays an intermediate role between the operating agencies and the Budget Bureau. The hearings of the department budget office provide the agency with its only opportunity to defend its *own* requests. After the department budget office makes a recommendation to the Budget Bureau, the agency budget office is then obligated to defend the department's recommendation. Typically, this recommendation is lower than the agency's request. The agency gets an opportunity to defend the budget that the department has recommended for it before the examiners of the Budget Bureau. At the next opportunity the agency has to defend its budget (before an appropriations subcommittee in the House of Representatives), it is obligated to support the recommendation (usually reduced further) made for it by the Bureau of the Budget.

The formal rules obligate the agencies to accept the successive recommendations of the department budget office and the Bureau of the Budget. However, there are certain opportunities to evade these

---

[23] Fiscal year 1972 runs from July 1, 1971, to June 30, 1972. This section draws on Ira Sharkansky, *The Politics of Taxing and Spending* (Indianapolis: Bobbs-Merrill, 1969), Chapter III.

rules. Agencies vary in their assertiveness, with some being more prepared than others to exploit their opportunities for self-expression. For those who are willing, it is possible to mobilize support at the presidential level while the agency's budget is still within the formulation period; and later it is possible to mobilize the support of interest groups or legislators in the appropriations subcommittees.

Although the president does not play a continuing role in the formulation of agency budgets, he does have an opportunity to review the decisions made by the Budget Bureau and to hear appeals from the agencies. With more than one hundred agencies and a total budget of almost $200 billion, it is obvious that the president cannot give equal (or in many cases any) attention to all who would desire additional funds. One of the devices that agencies may employ to attract the president's attention is the influential individual or organization. Most agencies have a coterie of clientele groups, and some have developed efficient media of communications that inform the groups when the agency is threatened with an insufficient budget. In certain agencies, however, there is a feeling of impropriety about interest groups. According to this view, each of the agencies is part of the "president's team" that is governed by the Bureau of the Budget. To seek a redress of the Bureau's recommendations would be to work against the team.

Congressional Action

The budgets of cabinet departments and independent offices are assigned to specialized Subcommittees of the House of Representatives Appropriations Committees. The House examines budgets before the Senate does, owing to custom and to an interpretation of a constitutional provision that gives the House precedence in money bills. When the agency budgets are in the congressional stage, there are opportunities for assertive agencies to indicate their true desires. Although it is against the regulations for agencies to ask Congress for funds that have not been recommended by the Budget Bureau, it is proper for agencies to respond accurately when a legislator asks them about their "real needs." An agency that wishes a larger budget than recommended may plant a question with a cooperative legislator— perhaps through the intermediary of a friendly interest group.

When the appropriations subcommittees examine agency budgets, they seem to be most thorough in their investigation of the assertive agencies. In dealing with these agencies, the subcommittee members ask more questions during the hearings; they are more likely to demand that the agencies justify certain portions of their request;

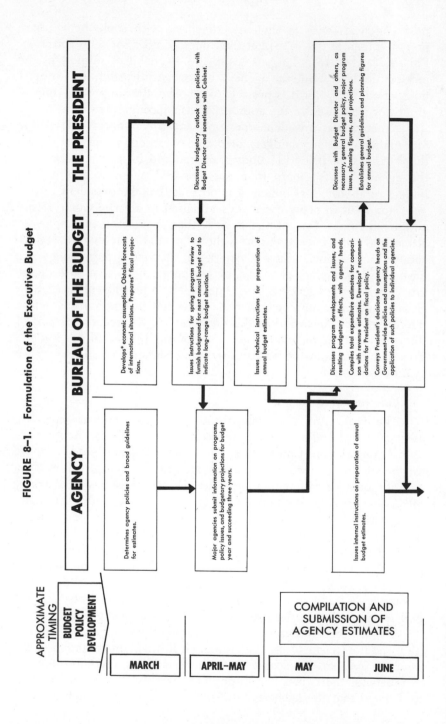

FIGURE 8–1. Formulation of the Executive Budget

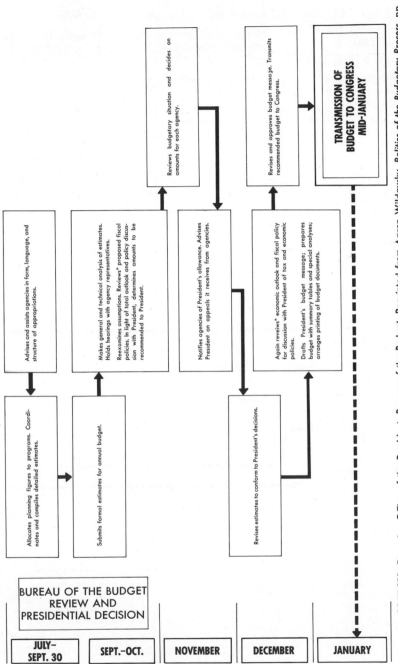

BUREAU OF THE BUDGET
REVIEW AND
PRESIDENTIAL DECISION

| JULY–SEPT. 30 | SEPT.–OCT. | NOVEMBER | DECEMBER | JANUARY |

Advises and assists agencies in form, language, and structure of appropriations.

Allocates planning figures to programs. Coordinates and compiles detailed estimates.

Submits formal estimates for annual budget.

Makes general and technical analysis of estimates. Holds hearings with agency representatives.

Reexamines assumptions. Reviews* proposed fiscal policies. In light of total outlook and policy discussion with President, determines amounts to be recommended to President.

Reviews budgetary situation and decides on amounts for each agency.

Notifies agencies of President's allowance. Advises President on appeals it receives from agencies.

Revises estimates to conform to President's decisions.

Again reviews* economic outlook and fiscal policy for discussion with President of tax and economic policies.

Drafts President's budget message; prepares budget with summary tables and special analyses; arranges printing of budget documents.

Revises and approves budget message. Transmits recommended budget to Congress.

TRANSMISSION OF
BUDGET TO CONGRESS
MID-JANUARY

SOURCES: Executive Office of the President, Bureau of the Budget. Reprinted from Aaron Wildavsky, *Politics of the Budgetary Process*, pp. 194–95, by permission of the publisher. Copyright © 1964, by Little, Brown and Company.
* In cooperation with the Treasury Department and Council of Economic Advisers.

220

FIGURE 8–2. Congressional Actions on Appropriations, January–July*

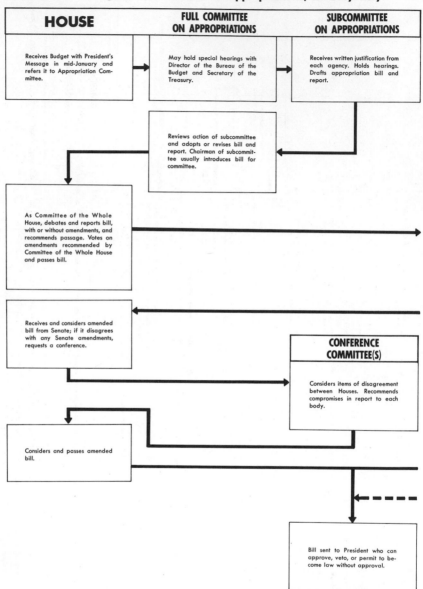

FIGURE 8–2—Continued

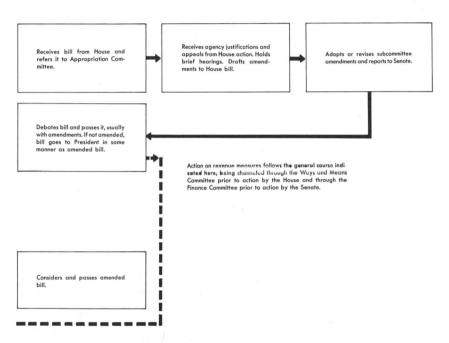

SENATE	SUBCOMMITTEE ON APPROPRIATIONS	FULL COMMITTEE ON APPROPRIATIONS
Receives budget with President's Message in mid-January and refers it to Appropriation Committee.		

NOTE: Senate hearings are sometimes held before House completes action.

Receives bill from House and refers it to Appropriation Committee.	Receives agency justifications and appeals from House action. Holds brief hearings. Drafts amendments to House bill.	Adopts or revises subcommittee amendments and reports to Senate.
Debates bill and passes it, usually with amendments. If not amended, bill goes to President in same manner as amended bill.		

Action on revenue measures follows the general course indicated here, being channeled through the Ways and Means Committee prior to action by the House and through the Finance Committee prior to action by the Senate.

Considers and passes amended bill.

Bureau of the Budget prepares Midyear Review, a summary of Congressional determinations and revised budget outlook for new fiscal year.

SOURCES: Executive Office of the President, Bureau of the Budget. Reprinted from Aaron Wildavsky, *Politics of the Budgetary Process*, pp. 196–97, by permission of the publisher. Copyright © 1964, by Little, Brown and Company.

* If action is not completed by June 30, enacts continuing resolution.

they are more likely to ask the department secretary and his budget officer about the agency's budget; and they are most likely to reduce the agency's request and add special restrictions to the agency's use of its funds in the committee *Report* or in the appropriations act. Thus, the assertive agencies get some rough treatment from Congress. But over the long run, the assertive agencies may increase their budgets more than timid agencies do. The treatment of assertive agencies may fail to cancel the impact of their more aggressive requests and tactics. While the agencies that ask for the largest increases and pursue their goals most aggressively may suffer the largest cuts, they may also have the largest increases remaining after the fray.[24]

Budget Execution

It is actually the Bureau of the Budget that has the last say about an agency's expenditure. Figure 8–3 shows that the Bureau makes apportionments of the funds voted by Congress. The Bureau cannot increase an agency's appropriation above the congressional figure; but it can reduce the agency's appropriation either to reserve funds for contingencies, to save money as part of a general economy drive or to hold the agency at a certain level of program development. Thus, the Budget Bureau can enforce on an assertive agency the budget recommendations that it made initially to Congress.

Nature of Budget Decisions in the Executive and Legislative Branches

Incrementalism is the prime feature of budget decisions in both federal and state governments. Its principal rule is: previous decisions are generally legitimate; concentrate investigations on the increments of growth that are requested.[25]

The use of incremental budgeting in the federal government is evident in the participants' fixation on the "base" of expenditures established by earlier decisions. Agency personnel are concerned with the percentage of increase over their existing budget that they should request for the coming year; reviewers in the departmental budget offices and in the Bureau of the Budget calculate their actions in terms of percentage cuts to be imposed on the agencies' requests. Members of the House of Representatives discuss their own percentage

---

[24] Ira Sharkansky, "An Appropriations Subcommittee and Its Client Agencies: A Comparative Study of Supervision and Control," *American Political Science Review*, 59 (September, 1965), 622–28.

[25] This section draws on Ira Sharkansky, *The Routines of Politics* (New York: Van Nostrand-Reinhold, 1970), Chapter IV.

changes in the president's budget. Senators talk about the percentage changes they will make in the House decision.[26]

A continuing controversy in incremental budgeting concerns the size of the increment. It is routine that calculations begin from the base of a previous budgetary decision; but it is less regular that the size of the increment is stable from one period of time to another or from one actor to another within a year's budget cycle. As might be expected, the spenders typically request larger increments than budget-reviewers will grant. A study of federal agencies during 1947–1962 provides some information about the increments that were voted.[27] Twenty-four agencies made annual requests that averaged at least 10 percent above previous appropriations; 11 made annual requests that averaged at least 20 percent above their previous appropriations; and the annual requests of two agencies averaged at least 75 percent above earlier funds. The appropriations committee in the House of Representatives permitted annual growth rates in excess of 10 percent for only 12 of the agencies and an annual growth rate in excess of 20 percent for only one of them.[28] The appropriations committee in the Senate typically serves as a court of appeals to the House decisions. The Senate concentrates on the grievances that agencies hold after their House experience, and it typically adds to the House grant. The House appropriation is the "base" from which the Senate works, and the increment between the House and Senate figure is usually small. For only 10 of the 36 agencies in the study did the Senate provide an average of 5 percent more of its request than did the House, and for only 2 of the agencies was the Senate's generosity as much as 10 percent above the House.[29]

State governments provide a useful laboratory for the observation and analysis of incremental budgeting. Their many agencies and diverse economic, social, and political environments provide opportunities for several variants of incremental budgeting to show themselves; and the multiplicity of conditions provides the opportunity to see what types of situations give rise to which varieties of incrementalism.

As in federal budgeting, the common ingredient of incremental-

[26] Aaron Wildavsky, *The Politics of the Budgetary Process* (Boston: Little, Brown, 1964), especially Chapter 3.

[27] Richard F. Fenno, Jr., *The Power of the Purse: Appropriations Politics in Congress* (Boston: Little, Brown, 1966).

[28] Fenno, Chapter 8.

[29] Fenno, Chapter 11.

FIGURE 8–3. Execution of Enacted Budget

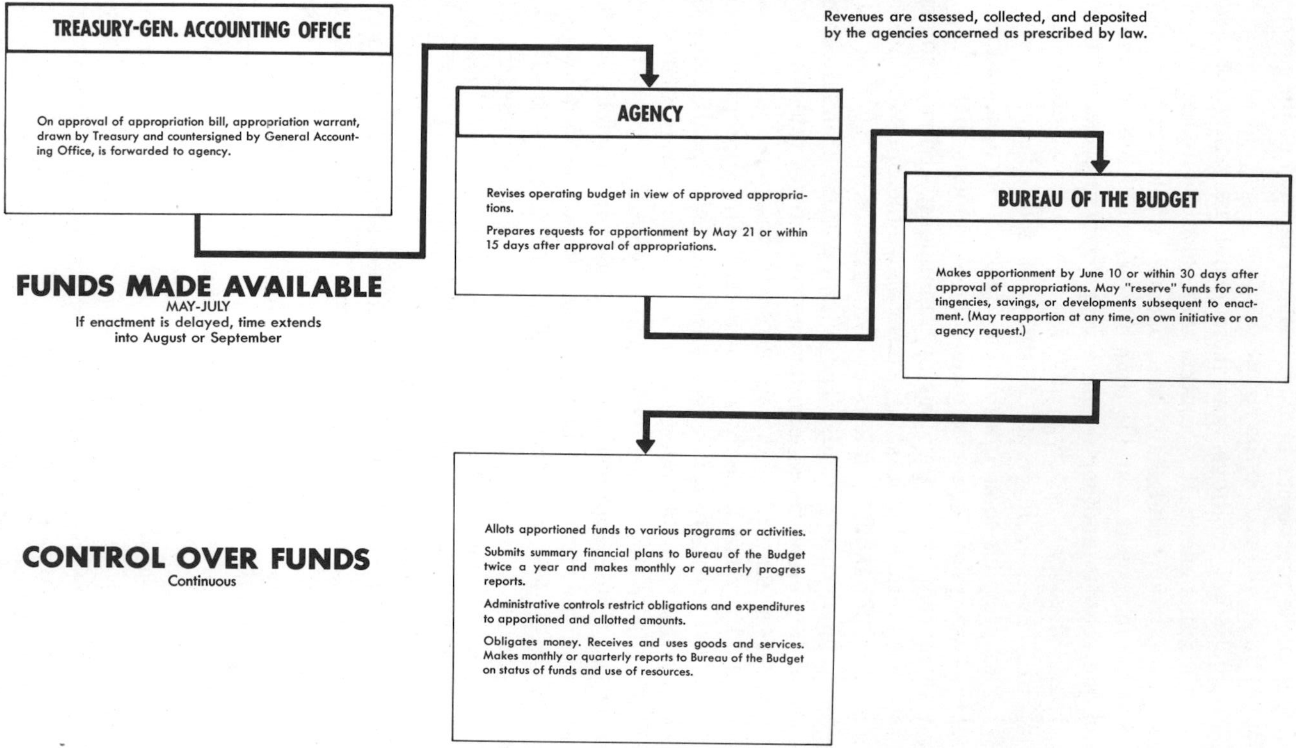

Revenues are assessed, collected, and deposited by the agencies concerned as prescribed by law.

TREASURY–GEN. ACCOUNTING OFFICE

On approval of appropriation bill, appropriation warrant, drawn by Treasury and countersigned by General Accounting Office, is forwarded to agency.

AGENCY

Revises operating budget in view of approved appropriations.

Prepares requests for apportionment by May 21 or within 15 days after approval of appropriations.

BUREAU OF THE BUDGET

Makes apportionment by June 10 or within 30 days after approval of appropriations. May "reserve" funds for contingencies, savings, or developments subsequent to enactment. (May reapportion at any time, on own initiative or on agency request.)

FUNDS MADE AVAILABLE
MAY–JULY
If enactment is delayed, time extends into August or September

CONTROL OVER FUNDS
Continuous

Allots apportioned funds to various programs or activities.

Submits summary financial plans to Bureau of the Budget twice a year and makes monthly or quarterly progress reports.

Administrative controls restrict obligations and expenditures to apportioned and alloted amounts.

Obligates money. Receives and uses goods and services. Makes monthly or quarterly reports to Bureau of the Budget on status of funds and use of resources.

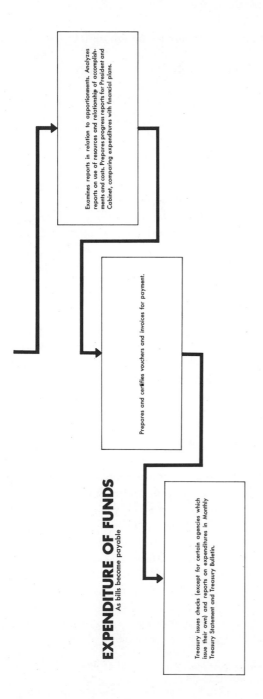

EXPENDITURE OF FUNDS
As bills become payable

Examines reports in relation to apportionments. Analyzes reports on use of resources and relationship of accomplishments and costs. Prepares progress reports for President and Cabinet, comparing expenditures with financial plans.

Prepares and certifies vouchers and invoices for payment.

Treasury issues checks (except for certain agencies which issue their own) and reports on expenditures in Monthly Treasury Statement and Treasury Bulletin.

MANAGEMENT APPRAISAL AND INDEPENDENT AUDIT
Periodic

Bureau of the Budget makes informal review of agency operations. Conducts, or guides agencies in, organization and management studies. Assists President in improving management and organization of the executive branch.

Agency reviews compliance with established policies, procedures, and requirements. Evaluates accomplishment of program plans and effectiveness of management and operations.

General Accounting Office performs independent audit of financial records, transactions, and financial management, generally. "Settles" accounts of certifying and disbursing officers. Makes reports to Congress.

SOURCES: Executive Office of the President, Bureau of the Budget. Reprinted from Aaron Wildavsky, *Politics of the Budgetary Process*, pp. 198–99, by permission of the publisher. Copyright © 1964, by Little, Brown and Company.

ism in state governments is a fixation upon the increment between previously made decisions and the current request. When administrators in state agencies plan their requests, their paperwork requires them to list current and previous expenditures and to compare these figures with their estimates for the coming year. Budget examiners in the executive and legislative branches are most likely to question the funds that would increase appropriations and to cut from these requests in order to minimize budget growth.

If anything can be said about the differences in incremental budgeting at state and federal levels, it is that state personnel seem to be even more fascinated with the dollar-increment of change in an agency's budget proposal. Studies of the federal budgeting process indicate that budget-reviewers often question the substance of programs that are to be purchased with the budget increment. One study of state decision-makers, however, indicates that there is a narrow fixation on the dollar-amount of the increment, with virtually no attention paid to the substance of the program that is at issue.[30] There are several possible explanations for the narrower inquiry of budget-makers. The central budget offices of state governments have fewer investigatory resources than does the U.S. Bureau of the Budget. So their inquiry must be more cursory. State legislators have less staff assistance than do congressmen, and members of appropriations committees are themselves less well-prepared to make a detailed investigation of agency programs. Many state legislatures have high rates of turnover and are without a well-developed seniority system. Thus, the members of state appropriations committees are likely to be inexperienced at their work.

The concern of state budget-makers with their own past decisions is evident in the correspondence between most states' levels of spending in one year and their levels in earlier years. This is not to say that state governments remain at fixed levels of spending. Revenues and expenditures increase in most years. However, the spending in most states increases at about the same rate because their budget-makers show similar disinclinations to move upward rapidly. They cut requests for budget growth. The result is that states tend to remain at the same levels of spending—relative to one another—from one budget period to the next.[31] In 1965, many state governments were spending at positions relative to other states that were similar to their

[30] Thomas J. Anton, *The Politics of State Expenditures in Illinois* (Urbana: University of Illinois Press, 1966), pp. 253–55.

[31] This section draws on Ira Sharkansky, *Spending in the American States* (Chicago: Rand McNally, 1968), Chapter III.

positions in 1903! Despite several major wars and transformations in the economy, together with vast population changes in some of the western and southern states and an increase of many-fold in the magnitude of each state's spending, the basic pattern of states' spending has remained similar throughout the century. States that were high (or low) spenders in 1903 have generally remained high (or low) spenders until the present.

Incremental budgeting is not equally conservative in all fields of government activity. During the 1957–1962 period, spending levels of the states remained most consistent in the fields of education, public welfare, and general government and were least consistent in the highway field. These differences reflect the nature of program changes occurring in these fields during the 1957–1962 period. There were great changes in highway expenditures stimulated by federal money for the Interstate and Defense Highway System. Some states took advantage of these federal funds more rapidly than did others, and the 1962 pattern of spending differed from that of 1957. Spending patterns for general government show the greatest stability over the 1957–1962 period. This reflects the inert nature of activities. The budget for general government supports the legislature and judiciary (22 percent of the funds in 1962), employment and security administration (35 percent), and financial administration (45 percent). Compared to other areas of state government activity, these fields escaped vast substantive changes. Likewise, spending patterns in the field of public welfare remained stable during the 1957–1962 period. This finding may reflect the resistance to innovation among professional welfare administrators which has been cited for the period before 1962.[32] Spending patterns in education also remained stable during the 1957–1962 period. While education budgets increased faster than the average during these years (19 percent increase in education and 15 percent increase in total spending), this did not upset state positions in spending for education. Perhaps educational administrators are sufficiently attuned to new developments so that most states adopt innovations (and increase spending) at about the same rate. Thus, there were great increases in educational expenditures along with stability of interstate differences between 1957 and 1962.

By looking at relationships among the nature of agency requests, the governor's recommendations to the legislature, and the subsequent actions of the legislature, we can see how the governor and the

---

[32] Gilbert Y. Steiner, *Social Insecurity: The Politics of Welfare* (Chicago: Rand McNally, 1966).

legislature actually make their budget decisions in an incremental fashion.[33] Administrative agencies and the governor play the most consistent roles in the state budgeting process. In each of 19 states reported in Table 8–1, the agencies requested a sizable increase (14–53 percent) over their current appropriations, and the governors pared the increase in their recommendations (by 4–31 percent). Agencies requested an average 24 percent increase over their current budgets, and the governors' recommendations trimmed an average 14 percent from their requests. The legislatures' final appropriations typically remained close to the governors' recommendations, but varied from a cut of 8 percent below the recommendation to an increase of 19 percent above the recommendation. Six of the legislatures cut agencies' budgets below the governors' figures, and eleven appropriated more than the governors asked. In only one case, however, did a legislature (in Nebraska) give more money to the agencies than they had requested themselves. The overall average legislative grant for the coming period was 13 percent below the agencies' requests, but was 13 percent above the agencies' current budgets.

When we examine the response of governors and legislatures to the budgets of individual agencies, we find that the *acquisitiveness* of the agency requests plays a crucial role in the decision of other budget-makers. In most of the states examined, the governor and legislature direct the greatest percentage cuts at the agencies that request the greatest percentage increases. However, it is these acquisitive agencies that come out of the legislature with the greatest increases over their previous budgets. Both the governor and the legislature are using similar incremental decision rules: *cut the agencies that ask for a large increase; but do not recommend a budget expansion for those agencies that ask for no increase.* The absolute size of agency budget requests does not appear to influence the decisions made by the governor or by the legislature. Budget reviewers in the governor's office and in the legislature are more likely to respond to the *percentage increment of change that is requested* (i.e., agency acquisitiveness) than to the sheer size of the request. The failure of either the governor or the legislature to impose additional funds on those agencies which do not ask for them illustrates how much the executive and legislative branches let program-initiation pass over to the administrative organization.

---

[33] Ira Sharkansky, "Agency Requests, Gubernatorial Support, and Budget Success in State Legislatures," *American Political Science Review,* 62 (December, 1968), pp. 1220–32.

TABLE 8-1

Annual Percentage Changes by Stages in the Budget Process of Major Agencies, by State

State, Showing Years of Budget Analyzed and Number of Agencies	Agency Request as Percentage of Current Expenditure	Governor's Recommendation as Percentage of Agency Request	Legislature's Appropriation as Percentage of Gov.'s Request	Legislature's Appropriation as Percentage of Agency's Current Expenditure	Legislature's Appropriation as Percentage of Agency Request
Florida 1965–67, n = 39	120%	90%	93%	109%	84%
Georgia 1965–67, n = 26	153	86	100	139	87
Idaho 1967–69, n = 23	119	93	92	109	86
Illinois 1963–65,* n = 37	118	83	102	108	85
Indiana 1965–67, n = 47	123	83	103	112	86
Kentucky 1966–68, n = 28	120	90	93	109	84
Louisiana 1966–67, n = 32	121	90	101	110	91
Maine 1965–67, n = 17	114	85	108	109	92
Nebraska 1965–67, n = 10	122	87	119	124	104
North Carolina 1965–67, n = 61	120	84	105	112	87
North Dakota 1965–67, n = 21	124	74	111	111	82
South Carolina 1966–67, n = 29	117	96	104	116	99
South Dakota 1967–68, n = 25	136	82	98	109	80
Texas 1965–67, n = 41	128	82	104	117	86
Vermont 1965–67, n = 17	121	87	106	115	91
Virginia 1966–68, n = 57	120	92	100	114	91
West Virginia 1966–67, n = 43	125	88	92	101	81
Wisconsin 1965–67, n = 26	115	96	98	111	94
Wyoming 1967–69, n = 13	133	69	109	112	75

SOURCE: Ira Sharkansky, "Agency Requests, Gubernatorial Support, and Budget Success in State Legislatures," *American Political Science Review*, 62 (December, 1968), p. 1223.

* The Illinois data come from the Appendix of Thomas J. Anton's *The Politics of State Expenditure in Illinois* (Urbana: University of Illinois Press, 1966). All other data come from the official budgets and financial reports of the states.

The Sources of Incrementalism

There are several reasons for the popularity of incremental deci-son-making among budgeteers. One reason lies in the appeal of routines in comparison with the rational assessment of the whole budget document. Rather than attempting the impossible task of considering all the issues that are relevant to a budget, officials in administrative units as well as in the executive and legislative branches have grown used to conceding the propriety of expenditures used to finance existing programs; they focus attention on the increment that represents a growth in expenditure (and presumably a change in the agency's program). To do otherwise would continually re-open past accomodations between the parties interested in each item of an agency's program. This would make each item always controversial, would preclude administrators or clients from "counting on" the continuation of current programs, and would require an extraordinary magnitude of investigatory resources just to supervise each part of every agency's program and to prepare the information necessary for an annual decision.[34]

Another reason for incremental decision-making lies in the commitments built into each budget. In some cases, there is relatively little that can be changed in an agency's expenditure from one budget period to the next. Some parts of an agency's budget may represent "earmarked funds." These are moneys that cannot legally be spent for any other than certain purposes and, thus, are not likely to be challenged by either the executive or legislative branches. There are also commitments to government employees and to the clients of public services that limit a serious inquiry into an agency's established level of expenditure. Large numbers of employees cannot be threatened with dismissal or transfer during each year's budget review, and large numbers of citizens cannot be threatened that major components of their public services will be curtailed or shifted in their character. These inflexibilities, reflecting common agreements as to what is "practical," impose real limits on the thorough review of an agency's budget.

A factor that weakens the position of many newly proposed activities—and thereby strengthens the role that incrementalism can play in budgeting—is the lack of acceptable measures of performance. The officials in charge of existing programs have acquired some indi-

---

[34] Allen Schick, "Control Patterns in State Budget Execution," *Public Administration Review*, 24 (June, 1964), 97–106.

cators of their workload, and they can emphasize those which maximize their program's appeal to the reviewers in the legislature and the executive. Those who propose new activities, however, may not be able to offer more than hopes and expectations to the budget reviewers. New programs lack a prior history of experience and have not yet generated a record of success in dealing with clients.[35]

Another reason for incremental budgeting lies in the lack of innovative drive that characterizes many governmental arenas. Budget growth tends to be slow because few major proposals can survive all the veto points in the administrative agencies and in the legislative and executive branches. The constitutional framers set out to design a conservative government, and they seem to have been successful. State governments tend to make only occasional spurts in spending. A period of dramatic growth tends to be short and to be followed by stability or decline. After a surge of innovation in several programs, both the legislature and the executive may tire of the political costs involved in getting lots of people to agree to major changes in programs. Administrators themselves might tire of the expansion necessary to accomodate new programs. Often this means severe competition for new personnel and the need to integrate the new personnel—or perhaps new units—into the existing fabric of supervision, coordination, and control. Programs that grow rapidly may get out of touch with their top administrators; duplications in activities and lack of central control may bring charges of "inefficiency" or "waste." It is often difficult to define these charges with precision. In any case, "inefficiency" and "waste" are powerful accusations in American politics. They may be sufficient to lead some legislators, executives, and administrators to slow or stop the growth in new programs.

Variations in Incremental Budgeting

The rules of incrementalism in government budgeting set outside limits to the percentage of change that is feasible; they do not define precisely the direction and magnitude of the change that will occur. An examination of budget changes in state governments during 11 periods between 1903 and 1965 found only weak relationships between the magnitude of change in each state's spending and its expenditures in an earlier year.[36] It is not possible to predict the level of expenditures in a forthcoming year simply by knowing the current level of expenditure. Although most states' expenditures in year $a + i$

---

[35] Herman Mertins, "Comments," Conference on Public Administration, Meadowbrook Conference Center of Syracuse University, September, 1968.

[36] Sharkansky, *Spending in the American States*, Chapter III.

are close to the same relative positions as they were in year *a*, the direction and magnitude of change is not consistent. Several states go up slightly in their spending; others may drop; a few demonstrate sizable changes in position; and many maintain their same position during the period.

The routines of incremental budgeting lead reviewers to reduce the estimates of growth-oriented agencies and to withhold increases from the agencies that have not sought more funds. Nevertheless, these decision-rules are not uniform. Some governors and legislatures are more or less likely than their counterparts in other states (or in their own states during other years) to grant or withhold increments. In some years, dramatic events, such as war or economic crisis, stimulate officials to be unusually generous—or stingy—in dealing with agency budgets. Sometimes even the "base" of appropriations for existing programs is subject to scrutiny and reduction. By examining the nature of budget relationships among agencies, the governor, and the legislature, in conjunction with several other characteristics of each state in a normal year, we can gain some insight into the elements that influence budget decisions. Actually, the findings are not crystal clear. Although some relationships prevail between the nature of budget decisions and several traits of the state's politics and economy, there are many instances of budget decisions that do not correspond to the general patterns. Deviations from incremental budget routines are not governed by objective forces of economics or politics. Instead, they appear to develop individually in the context of each state.[37]

Two characteristics associated with strong gubernatorial restraint against agency budget-development are his possession of strong formal veto powers and high state government expenditures. The already high expenditures may incline the governor against further large increases in state spending; and the power of a veto may strengthen the governor's resolve to impose a severe review on the agencies when they submit requests to him. In contrast, the governor is unusually generous toward agency requests for budget expansion where there is relatively intense party competition. A competitive party situation may lead him to advance his own career—and his party—by supporting innovative agencies.

Where the legislature is particularly restrictive against agency budget-development there tends to be both relatively high state government expenditure and debt and a low incidence of state adminis-

---

[37] Sharkansky, "Agency Requests, Gubernatorial Support and Budget Success in State Legislatures."

trators who are separately elected. Like the governor, the legislature appears to resist an acquisitive agency in the face of already committed state resources (i.e., high expenditures and debt). With a scarcity of separately elected agency heads, administrators may lack politically independent allies who can promote their budget through the legislature.

Innovative administrators have not rested in the face of incremental budget routines. They have devised several techniques to permit examination of the whole of an agency's budget—including the "base" of its current appropriation—and to compare the usefulness of each component of the budget against the other components of the budget. These changes in budgeting represent the efforts of reformers to replace "satisfactory" procedures with those that are "optimal" or "rational." Program-Planning-Budgeting (PPB) represents a major effort in this direction. It is described in Chapter 3 along with other techniques of decision-making (see pp. 65–68).

SUMMARY

This chapter focuses on the input relations between the legislative and executive branches and the conversion process of the administrative system. The inputs include formal directives and expressions of desire, plus the authority to spend money, hire personnel, and conduct programs. We shall see in Chapter 10 that many of the proposals coming as outputs from administrative agencies provide the substance of the formal decisions that are made by legislators and executives. The circularity of this process testifies to the dependence of elected officials on the administrators' recommendations.

Among the factors that help to make legislators and executives dependent upon proposals coming from the administrators are: the dramatic growth in the scope and complexity of government programs; the fragmentation of institutions and interests that is apparent in the legislative and executive branches; and the related gap in knowledge which separates those legislative and executive officials who allegedly control the policy-making process from the administrators. The legislatures and chief executives of federal, state, and local governments spend much of their time reviewing, modifying, or rejecting proposals that come from the administration.

This is not to say that elected legislators and chief executives are helpless in the presence of demands that come from the administration. The specialized committees in the legislature and the staff aides of the chief executive provide important resources. These facilities—

which seem stronger in the federal government than among states or localities—can subject the administrators' proposals to an intensive inquiry. And they may prompt administrators to focus their own attention on social or economic problems that are selected by legislators or by the chief executive.

In part of this chapter, we examined budget activities among federal, state, and local governments. Budgeting represents the most regular of interactions between legislature, executive, and administrators. Moreover, it is conducted with a medium of exchange that permits a clear description of general patterns of interaction and an identification of unusual activities. Among the findings reported for budgeting are:

1. The legislative and executive branches at the federal level are better organized and better staffed for budgeting than are their counterparts in most state governments.
2. Legislative and executive branches generally grant renewal of existing budget levels. They pay most attention to the increments of new money which are sought, rather than to the base of funds that had been appropriated to support existing programs.
3. Some agencies are more likely to have cuts made in their budget than are others. Acquisitive agencies suffer the most severe cuts in the short term; but an acquisitive strategy seems to be the only route to long-term budget expansion. This is further testimony to the dependence of the legislature and executive on the initiative of administrators. If no initiative is taken by the agencies, elected officials will seldom impose new funds on them.

Part Three

THE OUTPUTS OF THE ADMINISTRATIVE SYSTEM

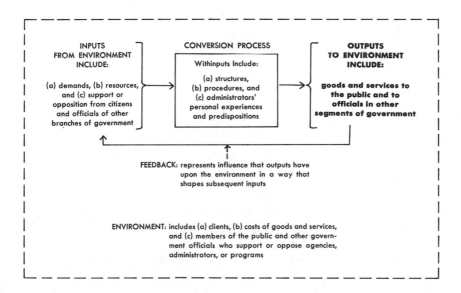

INPUTS FROM ENVIRONMENT INCLUDE:	CONVERSION PROCESS	OUTPUTS TO ENVIRONMENT INCLUDE:

Withinputs Include:

(a) structures, (b) procedures, and (c) administrators' personal experiences and predispositions

(a) demands, (b) resources, and (c) support or opposition from citizens and officials of other branches of government

goods and services to the public and to officials in other segments of government

FEEDBACK: represents influence that outputs have upon the environment in a way that shapes subsequent inputs

ENVIRONMENT: includes (a) clients, (b) costs of goods and services, and (c) members of the public and other government officials who support or oppose agencies, administrators, or programs

This section completes our coverage of the administrative system. Our concern is with the outputs of the system: the transactions that emanate from the conversion process (which we define as the "line" agencies of government) to citizens, politicians, and other government officials. Some of these transactions carry tangible public services: the schools, highways, welfare payments, hospitals, parks, regulation of business practices, and fire and police protection that citizens receive from government. Other transactions carry economic resources from one administrative organization to another: the federal grants to the states and localities and the state aids to local governments represent both the outputs of one administrative system and the inputs to another. Still other outputs are the technical assistance and the program requirements that accompany intergovernmental payments. Another class of outputs includes the information and advice that goes from an administrative agency to the public and to members of the legislative and executive branches. This includes published studies, campaigns to influence the thinking of citizens and politicians, proposals for new legislation, budget requests, and the testimony that administrators give at legislative hearings. These outputs constitute much of the "stuff" that forms the decisions of legislators and the chief executive.

Many outputs of agencies influence persons in the environment of the administrative system and then "feedback" to the conversion process through their effect on subsequent inputs. Citizens respond to the nature of public services or to the public statements of administrators by shaping their own later demands for additional service. Members of legislative and executive branches consider administrators' testimony and use the information to formulate the laws, instructions, and requests that flow from them into the agencies. Feedback is integral to the concept of systems theory: it provides the principal justification for many decisions taken within an agency about the outputs that should be produced. Yet we pay little attention to feedback, aside from noting its importance. The inputs that come to an administrative agency as a result of its earlier outputs look very much like inputs that come in response to other stimuli felt by individuals in the environment. Legislators, executives, and members of the public respond to many other influences besides those coming from the administration. To date, there has been little success in identifying those stimuli going to agencies which reflect the prior influence of the administrators themselves as opposed to those which reflect other influences.

Chapter 9 focuses on intergovernmental relations. These include "vertical" relations among administrators at different levels of the federal structure and "horizontal" relations among the administrators of different states and localities. Through these relations, outputs are carried *from* some administrative units and inputs are carried *to* others. The placement of Chapter 9 in the output section is arbitrary. The reader should recognize that one unit's intergovernmental output is another's input.

Chapter 10 also discusses some features of intergovernmental outputs, along with several other varieties of outputs. Indeed, the focus of that chapter is upon the variety and diversity of outputs and upon the intellectual problems inherent in efforts to classify and analyze them.

9

INTERGOVERNMENTAL RELATIONS

The federal nature of American government means that administrators in most agencies of each level of government must reckon with demands that come from officials in other levels of government. Moreover, these officials are not simply other actors who must be given recognition in the rituals of public administration. Due to certain guarantees that are integral to the meaning of federalism and due to political customs that bolster these guarantees, the spokesmen of other governments have special status.

Every major government in the world has a central unit and local units of government. However, a "federal" arrangement is peculiar in providing certain assurances to both levels of government. It is common to speak of the American national and state governments as "superior" and "subordinate" to one another; but this terminology is inaccurate. On some dimensions, the national government (often called the "federal" government) has prerogatives reserved to it alone. However, the states are not the creatures of the national government. They have a prominent role in any amendments to the basic structure of American government (i.e., the Constitution); and they have important guarantees of equal representation in the Senate, of proportional representation in the House, and of a role in selecting the president.[1]

---

[1] Provisions dealing with elections to the Senate and the House do not guarantee any powers to state governments, *per se,* but provide that spokesmen from a large number of states must accept whatever proposed legislation is enacted into law. The spokesmen for interests that occur in only a few of the states cannot grant the national government major new powers or cannot circumscribe those that are currently held by the states. Likewise is the case of the electoral college. The requirement that a victorious presidential candidate receive a majority of electoral votes (which are allocated on the basis of separate

The constitutional structure of federalism helps to protect the interests of the state governments, but does not protect institutions of local government from either the national or the state governments. The cities *are* creatures of their state governments and are subject to whatever constraints or liberties are found in state constitutions or statutes. However, local governments, as well as states, benefit from the political customs that respect "localism." The respect for localism exists among officials at all levels of government and has been observed in the United States since the early 19th century.[2] These values overlay the structure of federalism and make local governments, as well as the state and national governments, distinct actors in policy-making.

A feature that heightens the importance of federalism for the administrative systems is the mixture of governmental responsibilities. There is no important domestic activity that is manned or financed solely by the federal, state, or local governments.[3] The fields that consume most domestic expenditures—education, highways, welfare, health, natural resources, and public safety—are funded with a combination of federal grants or loans and state and local taxes or service charges. Even when some programs involve *local* implementation with some *federal* funds (e.g., public housing and urban renewal), the *state* legislature and executive also retain a role, i.e., retain the legal prerogative to permit local participation in the federal program and to define conditions under which participation may occur.[4]

THE MEANING OF FEDERALISM FOR ADMINISTRATORS

The combination of a viable federal structure, localistic political values, and the sharing of responsibilities for major domestic services means that administrators at any level of government produce outputs for—and must be alert to inputs coming from—actors at other levels

---

victories in each of the states) gives little real power to state governments, *per se*, but encourages presidential candidates to solicit the support of political leaders in numerous states. This—together with the complementary custom that has grown up in pre-convention politics—may close the presidency to any candidate who would reduce substantially the powers of state governments once he was in office.

[2] See Alexis de Tocqueville, *Democracy in America* (New York: Vintage Books, 1959), p. 282.

[3] Morton Grodzins, "American Political Parties and the American System," *Western Political Quarterly*, 13 (December, 1960), 974–98.

[4] Edward C. Banfield and Morton Grodzins, *Government and Housing in Metropolitan Areas* (New York: McGraw-Hill, 1958).

of government. Often the inputs to an administrative unit are the outputs of an administrative unit at another level of government. Both inputs and outputs go "up" and "down" the relationships among federal, state, and local governments. Federal grants and program requirements are outputs from federal agencies, but are inputs to state and local administrative agencies. The demands and/or intransigent policies of state and local administrators are outputs of their agencies, but are inputs to federal agencies. It is not simply the prominent officials, such as chief executives or legislators of other governments, who might impinge on an administrative unit. The list of important actors includes administrators within one's own field of service at different levels of government, plus the staff agencies of the chief executives and the legislatures at other levels, and the courts of other governments. The federal administrator, for example, must contend with decisions—or anticipated decisions—of administrators, executives, legislators, and judges of each state and local government that draws financial assistance from his agency, that receives information or advice from his agency, or that must adhere to program standards that are developed by his agency. The federal administrator may hear from state and local officials directly or through federal legislators or interest groups who serve as intermediaries. For state and local administrators, intergovernmental relations may take the form of requests, demands, or appeals sent to the federal agency, legislature, executive, or judiciary. In many respects, state administrators stand in similar relations to local agencies as federal administrators stand in their relations with state or local agencies: as providers of funds, information, advice, and program standards. Figure 9–1 depicts in outline form the principal actors and flows of communication that may affect administrative units at any level of the federal structure.

Some intergovernmental relations do not involve units that are "superior" or "subordinate" to one another. These connect administrators of different state governments or of different local governments. These "horizontal" relations transmit information and advice pertaining to one another's experience or establish formal or informal arrangements in which different state or local administrative agencies share resources to attack common problems. The horizontal relations are important in carrying—or blocking—program innovations from one political arena to another. They are vital to an understanding of why some state and local governments provide the types of services they do. Because of the input and output nature of intergovernmental relations with respect to different administrative agencies, this chapter is placed tenuously—and in full recognition of

240

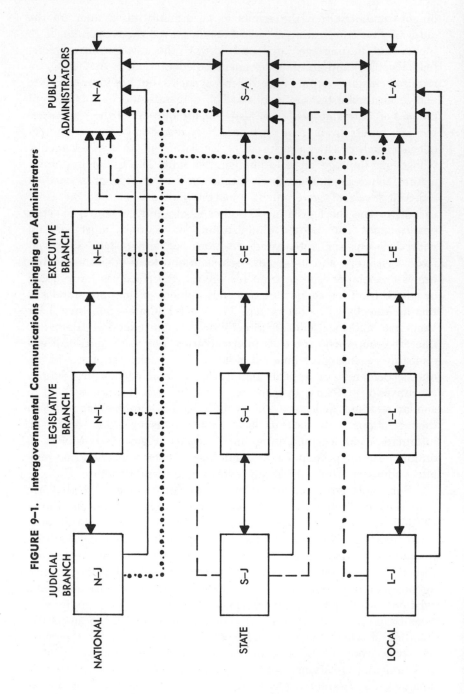

FIGURE 9–1. Intergovernmental Communications Inpinging on Administrators

the arbitrary nature of the choice—in this "output" section of the book.

Here we concentrate on the description of various forms of intergovernmental relations. Additional material in the next chapter deals with the effects of intergovernmental relations on governments that receive them (see pp. 285–92).

TYPES OF INTERGOVERNMENTAL RELATIONS: FEDERAL TO STATE AND LOCAL

Of all the forms of relations among federal, state, and local administrators grants-in-aid have attracted more attention than others. This attention is warranted, insofar as grants probably account for the greatest tangible resources in intergovernmental relations. Yet grants are not the only cause for relations among federal, state, and local administrators. There are other kinds of financial assistance and non-financial relations. Among other financial aids are: federal loans, guarantees of loans that are contracted from normal financial sources, shared taxes, tax credits, and the feature that permits deductions of state and local taxes from federally taxable income. Federal agencies also provide training and other technical assistance for state and local personnel.

Federal Grants-in-aid

Grant-in-aid programs are the single most prominent feature of federal relations with state and local administrators. In 1968, they amounted to $17 billion. In 1965, federal grants were 17 percent of state and local expenditures combined and 36 percent of state expenditures alone.[5] Federal grants have several distinct features, each of which has certain implications for administrators. Each federal program supports a specific state or local program; they do not provide "general support" of state or local activities. They typically require that recipient agencies submit detailed applications for the funds, provide some of their own resources to support the aided activities, and administer the program according to prescribed standards. The "purpose" nature of federal grants and the requirements that come along with the money are frequent sources of conflict between federal, state, and local administrators. It is alleged that the federal carrot leads recipients to undertake activities that are not in their own best

---

[5] This section relies on Deil S. Wright, *Federal Grants-in-Aid: Perspectives and Alternatives* (Washington, D.C.: American Enterprise Institute for Public Policy Research, 1968).

interest and that requirements are frequently inconsistent with their social or economic problems. Federal money is not "free." If the aided program is not uniformly popular in a state or locality, the recipient agency encounters some political costs as well as benefits.

Federal grants are older than the Constitution, although they have reached great heights only since the 1930's. Throughout the late 18th and most of the 19th century, land grants were given to state governments. Of the one billion acres that passed from the control of the federal government during the 19th century, about 230 million acres went to the states. Many land grants were devoted to education. Each new state received a grant for the support of primary education as it was admitted to the Union. The "land-grant" colleges of many states trace their origin to the Morrill Acts of 1862 and 1890.[6] The states were expected to sell or lease the land, with the proceeds used to support educational programs. As the supply of public land dwindled in the late 19th century, the emphasis shifted to money grants. The first regular and continuing money grant began in 1887 for the support of agricultural experiment stations.

The grant-in-aid programs enacted during each decade of the 20th century represented in microcosm the contemporary policy-orientations of American governments. Until World War I, the grants emphasized agriculture and other rural problems. Typical of that period were the Smith-Lever Act of 1914 which established cooperative agricultural extension programs; the Smith-Hughes Act of 1917 which established a program for supporting vocational education (with heavy emphasis in agriculture and home economics); and the Federal Aid Highway Act which authorized the Secretary of Agriculture to cooperate with state highway departments in the construction of rural post roads. This act was supposed to "get the farmer out of the mud."

In the decade of the 1920's, the aura of "normalcy" and the reliance on private enterprise helped retard the development of new grant programs. Increased funds were appropriated under existing grants, but there were no authorizations for new programs. The 1930's emphasized programs to alleviate the personal hardships of the Depression. Among the major grant programs enacted during 1933–1938 were welfare payments for the aged, for the blind, and for dependent children; health services for mothers and children; employment security; and public housing. Some agricultural programs were also begun during the 1930's to cope with economic problems in that sector. Programs were established for surplus commodity distribution, and

[6] W. Brooke Graves, *American Intergovernmental Relations* (New York: Scribners, 1964), Chapter 14.

soil conservation. The period of World War II did not invite major new domestic activities. The total funds provided to states and localities decreased from $2.4 billion in 1940 to $800 million in 1946. With the continuing mobilization of the late 1940's and 1950's, federal aids took on labels that made them part of the defense effort: a program to aid school districts suffering population increases because of federal installations, typically those of the Defense Department and its contractors; the Interstate and *Defense* Highway Act of 1952; and the *Defense* Education Act of 1957. It is debatable as to how important the highway and educational activities were to the defense effort or whether they were merely made more attractive to Congress by being identified as such.

In the 1960's, the program emphasis of new grant programs was urban affairs and education. The Elementary and Secondary Education Act of 1965 was largely responsible for pushing educational grants from $610 million in 1965 to $2.5 billion in 1968. The education category of federal grants increased relative to other categories from 6 to 15 percent of the total. Also during the 1960's, direct grants to cities increased in volume and were joined by grants to private organizations in urban areas.

The emphasis shown by the total amounts of grants spent on various programs has also changed over this century, but the change has been cyclical, rather than unidirectional. Table 9–1 shows the

TABLE 9–1
Federal Grants-in-aid to State and Local Governments,
by Functional Category, 1902–1968
(in percents)

Year	Veterans Service & Benefits	Health, Wel- fare, & Labor	Educa- tion & General Re- search	Agricul- ture & Agricul- tural Resources	Other Natural Resources	Com- merce, Housing, & Trans- portation	Total[a] (per- cent)	Total (billions of dollars)
1902	33.3	—	40.0	26.7	—	—	100	b
1912	22.6	—	47.2	30.2	—	—	100	b
1920	3.2	5.3	13.6	17.4	—	60.5	100	b
1925	.6	1.3	7.5	6.4	.3	84.0	100	.1
1929	.5	1.4	8.6	10.0	1.0	78.5	100	.1
1930	.6	.7	9.6	11.4	1.2	76.5	100	.1
1931	.3	11.5	5.7	7.0	.9	74.6	100	.2
1932	.4	27.4	5.1	5.9	.8	60.4	100	.2
1933	.4	32.7	5.3	6.7	.8	54.0	100	.2
1934	.0	98.7	.5	.7	.1	.0	100	1.8
1935	.0	98.8	.6	.6	.1	.0	100	2.3

TABLE 9–1 (continued)

Year	Veterans Service & Benefits	Health, Welfare, & Labor	Education & General Research	Agriculture & Agricultural Resources	Other Natural Resources	Commerce, Housing, & Transportation	Total[a] (percent)	Total (billions of dollars)
1936	.0	97.2	.6	.9	.1	1.2	100	2.3
1937	.0	95.6	.5	.8	.1	3.0	100	2.7
1938	.0	90.7	1.1	1.5	.1	6.6	100	2.2
1939	.0	90.3	.9	3.2	.1	5.6	100	2.9
1940	.1	86.3	1.0	6.0	.3	6.4	100	2.4
1941	.1	85.0	1.2	5.3	.2	8.2	100	2.1
1942	.1	82.8	1.4	4.3	.2	11.2	100	1.8
1943	.1	70.2	2.0	3.7	.7	23.3	100	1.3
1944	.1	61.4	2.5	6.6	.7	28.6	100	1.0
1945	.1	63.1	2.8	9.1	.8	24.1	100	.9
1946	2.3	63.5	2.8	10.3	.9	20.2	100	.9
1947	3.5	54.0	1.9	3.9	.6	36.0	100	1.7
1948	5.3	63.4	2.3	4.4	.7	24.0	100	1.6
1949	1.7	66.8	2.0	4.7	.8	24.0	100	1.8
1950	.7	70.5	1.7	4.8	.8	21.4	100	2.2
1951	.4	72.9	2.2	4.4	.8	19.3	100	2.2
1952	.3	69.9	5.1	3.5	.8	20.3	100	2.4
1953	.2	65.6	8.4	3.5	.8	21.5	100	2.8
1954	.2	63.7	6.8	7.2	.8	21.2	100	3.0
1955	.2	59.8	7.7	8.0	.8	23.4	100	3.1
1956	.2	58.3	5.8	10.8	.7	24.2	100	3.6
1957	.2	57.1	5.4	10.0	.7	26.6	100	3.8
1958	.2	53.3	3.5	5.9	.7	36.4	100	4.7
1959	.1	44.0	4.7	5.1	.5	45.6	100	6.3
1960	.1	42.7	5.3	4.0	.5	47.3	100	6.8
1961	.1	42.9	5.2	5.4	.5	45.9	100	7.3
1962	.1	45.9	5.2	7.0	.4	41.4	100	7.7
1963	.1	45.6	5.6	6.2	.6	41.8	100	8.4
1964	.1	43.1	4.9	6.6	.5	44.9	100	9.9
1965	.1	42.0	5.7	4.9	1.0	46.4	100	10.7
1966	.1	45.5	12.0	2.9	1.8	37.7	100	12.7
1967[c]	.1	46.6	14.8	3.5	1.7	33.4	100	15.1
1968[c]	.1	47.0	14.6	3.3	2.4	32.7	100	17.1

SOURCE: Deil S. Wright, *Federal Grants-in-Aid: Perspectives and Alternatives* (Washington, D.C.: American Enterprise Institute, 1968), pp. 66–67.

[a] Detail may not add to 100 because of rounding.

[b] Less than $.05 billion.

[c] Estimate.

percentage of total grants provided for each field of service in various years since 1902. Early in the century, benefits to veterans, education, and agriculture dominated the few programs in existence; together they amounted to about $3 million annually. The major educational programs helped support land-grant colleges. As total grants increased, educational grants diminished in relative importance. After World War II, pressures mounted for an increasing scope and magnitude of educational aids. However, some participants in the policy-making process opposed any large increase in federal expenditures; some opposed federally-mandated racial integration that might come along with the grants; some opposed federal grants to schools supported by religious institutions; and some opposed federal grants that would *not* aid schools supported by religious institutions. Although federal aids to education increased somewhat in the 1940's and 1950's, the opposition forced the increases to the circumspect: through the program to aid federally impacted areas[7] and the program for "defense" education.[8] It was not until the breakthrough of Elementary and Secondary Education Act of 1965 (which combined aid to public schools with certain aids to schools supported by religious institutions and which was passed after the courts had resolved the basic problem of racial integration) that education's share of total federal grants moved dramatically upward.

The importance of health, welfare, and labor grants in the Depression is evident in their spurt upward during the 1930's, as shown in Table 9–1. In 1935, grants in this category consumed almost 99 percent of the total federal allocations to state and local governments. They have remained important in the total dollars involved (moving from $2.2 billion in 1935 to $8.0 billion in 1968), but have diminished in relative importance. These programs developed in such a massive way during the 1930's that they obscured other changes taking place at the same time. Grants in agriculture increased by more than 10 times during the 1930's: from about $12 million in 1930 to $143 million in 1940. During the same years, however, their percentage of total grants dropped almost in half: from 11.4 percent to 6.0 percent. Likewise for grants in the fields of commerce, housing, and transportation. They almost doubled in dollar amounts: from $80 million in 1930 to $154 in 1940; but they declined from 76.5 to 6.4 percent of total grants!

---

[7] That is the "impact" on school population due to federal installations or federal contractors.

[8] "Defense education" covered a variety of programs, including foreign languages and natural and social sciences.

Virtually every major department of the federal government provides some grants-in-aid to state and local governments. Table 9-2 shows the number of separate programs authorized by federal administrative units as of January, 1966. At that time, only two of the Cabinet Departments (Post Office and Justice) did not administer grants-in-aid. Since then, however, the Justice Department began to provide grants-in-aid in the law enforcement field; and a new Department of Transportation includes the programs administered by the Federal Aviation Agency. Even such "non-domestic" units as the Departments of Defense and State offer grants-in-aid to state governments.

Changes in program emphases testify to the flexibility of federal grants-in-aid. Because they provide aid to specific kinds of activities rather than general support to state and local governments, policy-makers in the national government can regulate with some precision the kinds of state and local activities that receive funds. Depending on the assessment of need and performance, the funds that are appropriated for each program can be increased in small or large amounts, can be passed over with no increase, or can be forced to endure a decrease. Each program can receive additional features that reflect newly-apparent service problems. For each feature, the matching formula can be adjusted to make the component more or less attractive to potential recipients and, thereby, to affect the speed of adoption. When congressmen are especially anxious to have all states take immediate advantage of a new program, they set the federal-state matching formula at an irresistible height. And in order to elicit cooperation on individual components of a program, new bonus offers of aid can be extended in exchange for compliance with special regulations. When the Interstate Highway program was first enacted in 1953, the federal-state matching formula was set at 90-10; this meant that state highway departments would receive $.90 worth of federal highway money for each $.10 of their own money. By not taking immediate advantage of the program, a state would lose a considerable amount of its citizens' federal tax money that would pay for highways in other states. After the program was underway for several years, Congress added other features (e.g., billboard controls) and auxiliary grants for state compliance. Moreover, the administration has adjusted the flow of highway grants to changes in the economy. Allocations have been speeded during periods of unemployment and slowed at other times to curb inflation. Some observers also claim that presidents have slowed the allocation of highway funds in order to elicit cooperation from Congress on other aspects of their programs.

TABLE 9–2
Separate Authorizations or Program Subcategories of Federal Aid to State and Local Governments, by Administration Unit

Federal Department or Agency	January, 1966
Department of Health, Education, and Welfare:	
Public Health Service	69
Office of Education	68
Welfare Administration	25
Other	22
Total, Department of Health, Education, & Welfare	184
Department of the Interior	35
Department of Agriculture	28
Department of Housing and Urban Development	33
Department of Defense: Department of the Army	15
Department of Commerce	25
Department of Labor	9
Department of State	1
Department of the Treasury	3
Appalachian Regional Commission	13
Atomic Energy Commission	5
Executive Office of the President:	
Office of Emergency Planning	3
Office of Economic Opportunity	15
Federal Aviation Agency	2
Federal Power Commission	1
General Services Administration	8
Interstate Commerce Commission	1
National Foundation for Arts and Humanities	2
National Science Foundation	4
St. Lawrence Seaway Development Corporation	1
Small Business Administration	3
Tennessee Valley Authority	1
Veterans Administration	3
Water Resources Council	2
General authorizations	2
Total	399

SOURCE: I. M. Labovitz, *Number of Authorizations for Federal Assistance to State and Local Governments Under Laws in Force at Selected Dates during 1964–66* (Washington: Library of Congress, Legislative Reference Service, July 5, 1966), pp. 10–11, as reprinted in Deil S. Wright, *Federal Grants-in-Aid: Perspectives and Alternatives* (Washington, D.C.: American Enterprise Institute, 1968), p. 55.

Some recent developments in federal grant programs may affect the relationships that exist among federal, state, and local administrators. There is an increasing use of "project" grants. These require federal approval of state or local applications on a project-by-project basis. They differ from "formula" grants that provide funds to state or local agencies according to a formula established by Congress or the administration. Under a formula grant, the decisions on individual projects are left to the state or local agencies. A study of grant programs that were enacted between April, 1964, and January, 1966, found that individual formula programs increased from 64 to 91, while project programs increased from 126 to 226 programs. The increasing emphasis given to project grants may increase the discretion available to federal administrators and reduce that which is left to state and local administrators.

> The direct, project approach vests far greater discretion in federal administrative officials than the older, formula-grant approach. Such discretion presents the opportunity to accomplish desirable results. But it also places a heavy responsibility on project grant administrators to weigh both the programmatic *and* the political payoffs of their decisions. Another result of the direct [project] approach has been a less important role for Congress in setting policy concerning the allocation of federal grants. This is not to deny that particular committees or congressmen influence grant allocations. It is to say, rather, that legislatively-mandated grant policies have become increasingly ambiguous, or non-existent, guides to administrators who are allocating project funds to diverse applicants.[9]

In a contrary move, there has also been increased support for "bloc" grants. This is a grant to finance a broad function of government which provides the recipient agency with discretion in its application. These grants have wide appeal among state and local administrators, who desire both an increase in federal support and an opportunity to decide their own priorities. Bloc grants are viewed with suspicion, however, by those who feel that many state and local administrators are irresponsible and would use unrestricted funds for purposes that have little social merit. For many years, unrestricted grants were opposed by northern liberals who felt that southerners would use the federal money to reinforce racial inequities. There has been some movement in the direction of bloc grants, but it has not gone as far as some proponents would like, or as far as some opponents fear. In 1966 a group of 16 individual health grants were combined into a single comprehensive program, and recipient agencies were authorized to transfer funds from one category to another. A bloc-grant feature was also included to the Juvenile Delin-

---

[9] Wright, p. 61.

quency Prevention and Control Act of 1967. Here too, however, the money was to be provided within a clearly defined field of service, and there were several standards to govern expenditures.[10]

There is no disputing the fact that federal grants-in-aid have grown over the years; but the appearance of growth varies with the techniques used to measure it. During the 1900–1968 period, the sheer magnitude of federal grants increased by about 5,702 times: from $3 million annually to $17.1 billion. However, these figures do not correct for obvious changes in the value of the dollar, the number of people who are served by federally-aided programs, the pool of economic resources from which federal aids are taken, or the level of state and local government activities which they support with their own funds. When these corrections are made, the magnitude of recent increase appears more temperate. Table 9–3 shows federal grants in 1932, 1936,

TABLE 9–3

Changes in the Magnitude of Federal Grants
to State and Local Governments, 1932–1967

	Total (in millions of current dollars)	As Percentage of State and Local Revenues
1967	$15,505	14.5%
1946	855	5.4
1936	948	10.1
1932	232	2.9

SOURCES: U.S. Bureau of the Census, *Historical Statistics on Governmental Finances and Employment, Census of Governments, 1962* (Washington, D.C.: U.S. Government Printing Office, 1964), Vol. VI, No. 4; and U.S. Bureau of the Census, *Governmental Finances in 1966–67* (Washington, D.C.: U.S. Government Printing Office, 1968).

1946, and 1968 computed in two ways. The two measurements agree in showing a marked increase during the Depression, a fall in magnitude during the Second World War, and an increase since World War II. The growth appears almost shocking when viewed in raw dollar amounts, but corrections for other economic, social, or governmental happenings place the growth in perspective. The role of federal grants in state and local affairs has increased. However, administrative agencies in state and local governments still receive the bulk of their financial resources from their own sources.

---

[10] See Paul R. Dommel, "Confusion over Revenue-Sharing," *New Republic,* November 30, 1968, pp. 12–13.

Other Federal Aids to States and Localities

Grants-in-aid are only one of several devices that federal agencies use to provide resources for state and local agencies. Federal loans, loan-guarantees, tax credits, and the deductibility of state and local taxes from federally taxable income are additional kinds of aid. Some are mixed with grants-in-aid to provide different options within the same basic program. In the public housing program, for example, a federal guarantee for loans arranged in the private market supports the bulk of most projects costs, while an outright grant pays for additional costs. Some programs make available a direct loan from the federal Treasury if a federal guarantee will not help a recipient agency contract for a commercial loan at a desirable interest rate. The unemployment compensation program combines a federal tax credit with a grant-in-aid. Employers are excused for up to 90 percent of a federal payroll tax for the money they pay as state tax to support unemployment compensation; and an amount up to the remaining 10 percent of the federal tax is available to the state employment agency for administrative costs.[11]

Many taxpayers do not realize the federal aid for state and local governments that is written into the income tax code. In computing the income that is subject to federal taxation, a citizen can deduct any amounts paid as state or local income, sales, excise, or property taxes; this provision lightens the burden of state or local taxes and, presumably, allows state and localities to reach higher rates of taxes without encountering severe resistance from their residents. Moreover, any income received from interest on state or local government bonds is not subject to federal taxation; this permits state and local agencies to pay lower than commercial interest rates for the money they borrow.[12]

Several other federal programs provide subtle forms of aid to state or local administrative agencies. The direct provision of federal benefits to institutions or private citizens relieves states and localities of service demands that otherwise would come to them. In this category are both student grants and federal grants, loans, or loan-guaran-

---

[11] See James A. Maxwell, *Tax Credits and Intergovernmental Fiscal Relations* (Washington, D.C.: Brookings Institution, 1962).

[12] Tax deductibility lowers the burden of state and local taxes by excusing the taxpayer of that portion of federal income tax that would be due on the money he pays out in state and local taxes. If he is in an income bracket where 25 percent of his income is paid to federal income taxes, then the federal government pays, in effect, 25 percent of his state and local taxes. The no-tax feature applied to the income on state and local government bonds makes these bonds more attractive to investors than are the bonds of private firms, and they permit state and local agencies to borrow money at lower than commercial rates of interest.

tees to institutions of higher education (both public and private) for the construction of instructional facilities and dormitories. Many federal "research contracts" also provide financial aid to colleges and universities; they allow researchers to hire student assistants (and thereby subsidize the students' education), and to support sophisticated research that enrichens the intellectual climate and the educational offerings of the institutions. The federal social security program is another direct service that may alleviate demands on state and local authorities for welfare and health programs; "social security" is actually the popular designation for a series of programs which provide insurance coverage for old age pensions, disability pensions, and hospital and physician charges.

The Advisory Commission on Intergovernmental Relations (ACIR) is a research agency of the federal government whose purpose is to provide information and technical assistance to state and local governments and to facilitate the administration of federal programs in a way that is most helpful to the states and localities.[13] The Commission itself includes 23 officials of national, state, and local governments, plus 3 members representing the public. A professional staff does detailed analyses and prepares recommendations for review by the commissioners. The statute which established the ACIR outlined its duties as follows:

1. Bring together representatives of the Federal, State and Local governments for the consideration of common problems;
2. Provide a forum for discussing the administration and coordination of Federal grant and other programs requiring intergovernmental cooperation;
3. Give critical attention to the conditions and controls involved in the administration of Federal grant programs;
4. Make available technical assistance to the executive and legislative branches of the Federal Government in the review of proposed legislation to determine its overall effect on the Federal system;
5. Encourage discussion and study at an early stage of emerging public problems that are likely to require intergovernmental cooperation;
6. Recommend, within the framework of the Constitution, the most desirable allocation of governmental functions, responsi-

---

[13] This discussion relies on Deil S. Wright, "The Advisory Commission on Intergovernmental Relations: Unique Features and Policy Orientation," *Public Administration Review*, 25 (September, 1965), 193–202.

bilities, and revenues among the several levels of government; and

7. Recommend methods of coordinating and simplifying tax laws and administrative practices to achieve a more orderly and less competitive fiscal relationship between the levels of government and to reduce the burden of compliance for taxpayers.

The Commission refrains from ideological debates about the "grand alternatives" of American federalism. Instead of papers on the topics of centralization *vs.* decentralization, or assessments of federal court decisions with respect to the sentiments of the original framers,[14] the Commission publishes detailed studies that deal with specific topics of use to federal, state, and local policy-makers, but outside of prominent and highly volatile public controversies. The list of its publications includes: *Coordination of Federal Inheritance, Estate and Gift Taxes; Investment of Idle Cash Balances by State and Local Governments; Interest Bearing U.S. Government Securities Available for Investment of Short-Term Cash Balance by State and Local Governments;* and *Measures of State and Local Fiscal Capacity and Tax Effort.*

There has been some question about the effectiveness of the Commission's work. A 1965 survey found only 16 percent of 900 top-level state administrators had heard of the Commission and could identify it correctly. At the national level, neither Presidents Eisenhower, Kennedy, nor Johnson sought the Commission's recommendations on major policy issues regarding intergovernmental relations. Moreover, the cutback in domestic spending that occurred during 1968 severely hurt the Commission's activities. One staff man reported that several completed studies remained on the shelf because of inadequate printing funds.

STATE AIDS TO LOCAL GOVERNMENTS

The array of state aids to localities includes many of the mechanisms that are found in federal aids to state and local governments. However, state aids emphasize shared taxes and "bloc" grants, rather than grants-in-aid for specified programs. A fixed portion of taxes that are "shared" revert back to the local government in whose jurisdiction they are collected. The bloc grants and shared taxes that are used by most states provide more freedom to local governments than do federal grants-in-aid. They are awarded not for specified projects or in

---

[14] This has been the use to which the "commissions on constitutional government," created by a number of southern states, have put their resources.

response to detailed applications. They go automatically to local governments on the basis of certain criteria and may be used for any programs within a generalized function (e.g., "education," "roads and streets") or for the support of any governmental activities. State aids are generally "free" and do not require matching with a certain proportion of locally-raised revenues. Local governments receive much of their state aid with few application procedures and few limitations on its expenditure.

State governments use a variety of criteria to allocate financial aids to each local government. Some redistribute economic resources from "have" to "have-not" communities; some merely revert to a community a certain proportion of the state tax that was collected there; some reward communities that show some effort in using their own resources in the support of a program; some award funds "equally" on an arbitrary criterion (e.g., population); and some use special considerations that recognize emergency situations or agreements arranged between state and local agencies. Table 9–4 shows the distribution of funds to city governments according to the criteria used in California, Massachusetts, and Pennsylvania. California and Pennsylvania do not offer great rewards for local effort. California distributes almost 70 percent of its funds on the basis of population and another 8 percent on the basis of local sales or licenses or equal amounts to all jurisdictions. Pennsylvania distributes almost 22 percent on the basis of population and another 49 percent on the basis of local sales or licenses and local road mileage. California distributes only 22 percent on criteria that would reward local effort (a ratio of local expenditures for the aided function), and Pennsylvania distributes only 19 percent on this kind of criteria. In contrast, Massachusetts awards almost 59 percent of its aids on the basis of effort formulas. That state also awards a sizable portion of its aids (almost 13 percent) in a way that redistributes economic resources from "have" to "have-not" areas.[15]

The concept of "state aid" is necessarily loose due to the wide variety of programs and techniques in 50 state governments. In many states, the aid rendered to local governments is only a small portion of the services that state governments provide to local residents. State governments vary in the kinds of services they provide directly and

---

[15] The prominence of equalization formulas in Massachusetts' aids to cities does not distinguish that state from the others as much as it seems from Table 9–4. These equalized aids are for education. California and Pennsylvania also provide for equalization in school aids; but because it is school districts—independent from municipalities—that receive such funds, it does not appear in our tabulations.

TABLE 9–4

State Payments to Municipalities: By Percentages
Distributed According to Various Standards, 1962

Standard	California	Massachusetts	Pennsylvania
Population of local jurisdiction	69.9%	0.4%	21.5%
Sales or licenses in local jurisdiction (e.g., sales of alcoholic beverages, tobacco, or other taxed items, the number of auto or drivers' licenses issued locally)	6.7	—	17.1
Road mileage	—	—	32.3
Amount of state-owned land in local jurisdiction	—	0.4	—
Equal aid to all jurisdictions	1.4	—	—
Contractual arrangement with specific cities for services provided to state institutions	0.2	—	—
Specified rate of aid per unit of services provided (e.g., per *patient day* in city hospital)	0.1	1.8	—
Assessed value of certain type of property (e.g., industrial property)	—	22.6	—
Local fiscal ability	—	12.6	—
Ratio to local expenditures for aided function	21.8	58.8	18.9
Need as determined by state agency	0.3	3.1	—
Criteria undefinable by available data	—	0.2	11.0
Total	99.9%	99.9%	100.1%

SOURCE: Computed from: U.S. Bureau of the Census, *State Payments to Local Governments, Census of Governments, 1962* (Washington, D.C.: U.S. Government Printing Office, 1963), Vol. VI, No. 2.

the kinds they leave to local authorities. In the field of education, for example, some state governments pay the entire cost of supporting public junior colleges, while others provide only some of the costs for these to county or municipal governments. In public welfare, some state governments pay for all aid payments that are not covered by federal grants, while other states share these costs with local governments. The most complete record of state involvement in the support of public services shows the percentage of total state and local government revenues that are raised or spent at the state level. Table 9–5 shows this record for each state during 1966.

There is considerable variation in the role that state governments play in raising revenues for themselves and local governments. The

TABLE 9–5
The Use of Intergovernmental Aids by State and Local Governments, 1966

	Percentage of state and local revenues originating at federal level	Percentage of state and local revenues originating at state level	Percentage of state and local expenditures spent by local governments
U.S. average	15.8%	41.6%	63.4%
Alabama	27.6	45.2	50.5
Alaska	44.4	38.2	30.9
Arizona	20.3	44.0	56.1
Arkansas	27.5	47.3	44.0
California	16.4	36.3	73.1
Colorado	19.4	39.2	61.8
Connecticut	12.6	42.9	54.9
Delaware	14.9	60.9	47.6
Florida	14.1	40.6	64.1
Georgia	20.5	45.3	55.5
Hawaii	20.3	56.5	28.5
Idaho	19.8	44.9	50.5
Illinois	12.4	36.0	66.4
Indiana	11.7	46.0	63.6
Iowa	14.3	40.2	58.2
Kansas	14.9	42.2	58.6
Kentucky	24.2	48.3	46.0
Louisiana	21.7	57.2	42.9
Maine	19.4	43.5	44.6
Maryland	12.5	47.1	67.6
Massachusetts	13.6	36.9	67.0
Michigan	12.7	46.3	63.8
Minnesota	16.1	42.0	61.7
Mississippi	23.7	45.8	53.0
Missouri	20.1	38.6	56.4
Montana	24.7	34.7	50.9
Nebraska	16.2	30.2	64.8
Nevada	22.3	36.8	58.9
New Hampshire	16.6	34.2	54.4
New Jersey	10.4	28.5	72.1
New Mexico	29.6	50.7	44.9
New York	8.6	39.8	79.2
North Carolina	17.7	56.9	54.8
North Dakota	18.2	45.6	48.1
Ohio	14.6	36.3	69.7
Oklahoma	23.5	47.7	46.5
Oregon	22.3	39.5	54.5
Pennsylvania	13.8	44.7	58.0

TABLE 9–5 (continued)

	Percentage of state and local revenues originating at federal level	Percentage of state and local revenues originating at state level	Percentage of state and local expenditures spent by local governments
Rhode Island	18.2	44.9	51.4
South Carolina	18.8	57.5	45.5
South Dakota	21.6	35.9	49.1
Tennessee	22.8	43.4	57.0
Texas	16.8	42.2	59.5
Utah	24.6	44.5	51.5
Vermont	26.8	45.6	35.7
Virginia	19.2	44.0	55.8
Washington	16.5	51.7	52.5
West Virginia	27.1	47.5	43.7
Wisconsin	10.4	49.9	70.6
Wyoming	33.7	34.5	48.4

SOURCE: U.S. Bureau of the Census, *Governmental Finances in 1965–66* (Washington, D.C.: U.S. Government Printing Office, 1967).

nation-wide average is almost 42 percent of total state and local revenues coming from the state government. However, the range extends from 60.9 percent in Delaware to 28.5 percent in New Jersey. There is a tendency for low-income states to rely heavily on state-collected revenues. This is evident in the heavy reliance on state revenues in Louisiana, North Carolina, South Carolina, and Vermont. In these states, there are numerous local governments (especially rural counties) that are hard-pressed to support a minimum level of public services with the economic resources that lie within their jurisdictions. Perhaps because many local authorities in these states must rely upon state aid, all local governments in these states are inclined to view the state government as a prime source of funds. It is probably easier for the legislature to pass a state aid bill if there is something in it for the constituents of most legislators. On the other side of the income scale, local governments in the well-to-do states of New York, New Jersey, Massachusetts, and California carry a larger than average share of state and local financing. Seemingly out of step with the general pattern is Delaware. This state has one of the highest levels of personal income per capita in the nation, but is also the heaviest user of state government revenues. In this trait, Delaware reflects the pattern of its southern neighbors. Southern states have been "centralized" historically, owing in part to a colonial experience of diffuse population and a plantation economy that did not nurture the devel-

opment of strong, autonomous towns. Nebraska is another state that
deviates from the normal association between low income and high
reliance on state revenue. Nebraska ranks below the national average
on several measures of economic resources, but it ranks close to the
top in the proportion of revenues that are raised locally. In this case, a
strong localist orientation, together with fiscal conservatism, seems to
have retarded the development of state revenue sources. Nebraska
was one of the last state governments to abandon its reliance on
locally raised property taxes.

One service that state governments provide to local administrators receives little attention from political scientists, but it has important implications for local policy-makers: the definition of municipal
boundaries. This has special importance on the fringes of urban and
metropolitan areas where a proliferation of autonomous municipalities can confound the matching-up of taxable resources and service
demands (see pp. 258–63). In many states, new municipalities are
established when voters in an unincorporated area submit a petition to
the legislature and hold an election to determine local sentiment.
Several states have taken the lead in giving state agencies a strong role
in this process. Their hope is to apply well-reasoned standards to the
applications for new incorporations and to define the borders of new
municipalities in ways that will maximize their efficiency in providing
services. The Minnesota Municipal Commission reviews incorporation
and annexation proposals; Wisconsin divides the responsibilities between the circuit court and the State Director of Regional Planning;
and California has a local agency formation commission in each
county. Some of these units encourage annexations to existing municipalities rather than the creation of new entities; some oppose "gerry-
mandering" that creates odd-shaped jurisdictions that are meant to
include tax-rich areas or exclude nuisance islands; some use man-
made or natural features as boundary lines (rivers, lakes, highways,
railroad tracks); and some oppose boundaries that would divide existing commercial districts or residential areas.[16]

INTERLOCAL AND INTERSTATE "HORIZONTAL" RELATIONS

Vertical associations among federal, state, and local administrators and other officials do not exhaust the catalogue of intergovern-

[16] Clarence J. Hein and Thomas F. Hady, "Administrative Control of
Municipal Incorporation: The Search for Criteria," *Western Political Quarterly,*
19 (December, 1966), 697–704.

mental relations. The presence of 50 state governments and approximately 81,000 local governments gives rise to numerous opportunities for horizontal relationships among administrators at the same level. While vertical relationships focus on the provision and receipt of financial aid, there is no single prominent stimulus for horizontal relations. The formats for horizontal relations vary with the incentives that prompt them. They include "federations" and "compacts" that permit the joint administration of public services; agreements to share information or technical assistance; reciprocal legislation that permits the citizens of one jurisdiction to receive certain services within another jurisdiction; and the membership of government officials in organizations that seek to develop solutions for common problems. Officials in administrative agencies or in legislative or executive branches usually take the lead in formulating intergovernmental arrangements. On occasion, however, the action of aroused citizens impose intergovernmental unions upon officials who are reluctant to surrender their autonomy.

Stimuli of Horizontal Intergovernmental Relations

Metropolitan areas are the most frequent settings for horizontal relations among administrative units. This reflects the high density of people and the demands for policy that they generate, plus the obvious feature of many separate governments, each of which has an administrative organization whose actions depend partly on activities within another's jurisdiction. Some public services can be provided with greater efficiency if administered on an areawide basis than if administered in many separate units. If the service units are sufficiently large, they can employ a variety of specialists needed for complete and competent service. In the case of libraries, zoos, and museums, a large tax base can support a diverse collection in a central location with some smaller collections in branch units. In the case of pollution control, wind and water currents do not respect political boundaries. An enforcement agency must have access to violators throughout the area—likewise in the case of slum control. If a blighted area can spread across a street to another jurisdiction with an inadequate housing code or enforcement program, then one community's slum program will have limited success in controlling the basic problems of crime and disease. In the case of police and fire activities, there is some need for reciprocal rights of pursuit, assistance in apprehending fugitives, or assistance in dealing with major fires. Without these provisions, criminals might evade the law simply by crossing a street, or a community might suffer major fire loss while its neighbor's equipment stands idle.

In some metropolitan areas, there is an unequal distribution of individuals and business firms that are capable of paying high property taxes. One writer calls this the "segregation of resources and needs."[17] If a few communities can support most local costs with taxes paid by merchants, industries, or public utilities, their residents may enjoy high quality schools and extensive municipal "amenities" (frequent garbage collection, well-tended parks, and public recreation programs) with only a low tax rate on private homes. In contrast, the more-purely residential communities must impose heavy taxes on homeowners, but may still provide only poor services. Workingclass residential communities have the further problems of low-incomes combined with lots of school age children; the families may pay abnormally high taxes because there is no industrial or shopping area to share the burden, yet still be unable to support high quality services. Some facilities that pay high property taxes to one community actually draw their own incomes from throughout a metropolitan area. This is particularly true of electrical generating stations, large industries, and shopping centers. They are supported by the entire metropolitan area, but pay their own property taxes to a limited sector.

Although certain problems are widely shared by metropolitan areas, it is an oversimplification to think of *the* metropolitan problem(s). The details differ from one metropolis to another and within metropolitan areas from one local jurisdiction to another. Social and economic segregation is not equally pronounced in all metropolitan areas; and some jurisdictions are better equipped with legal powers that help alleviate some consequences of their social or economic problems. Among the legal powers that distinguish metropolitan areas are the "functional inclusiveness" of municipalities (i.e., their ability to provide services across many fields without relying on special districts); the allocation of service responsibilities between state and local governments; the discretion that local administrators have in shaping their policies; the nature of state financial aids; the income-productivity of the property tax and other revenue sources available to municipalities; the geographical size of local jurisdictions and the incidence of numerous small jurisdictions that divide economic re-

---

[17] Robert C. Wood, *1400 Governments* (Garden City, N.Y.: Anchor Books, 1964), pp. 56ff.

sources and create the segregation of resources from needs.[18] Where state borders divide metropolitan areas, the different state governments are likely to grant different powers and to impose different restrictions on the administrative agencies of neighboring jurisdictions. The policies of one jurisdiction may offer little guidance to its neighbors. According to one discussion of the New York metropolitan region:

> In terms of local expenditures per capita, New York and New Jersey rank considerably ahead of Connecticut, while New York and Connecticut are considerably stronger state-aid states than New Jersey. Connecticut and New Jersey tend to have small general governmental jurisdictions; while the New York system is characterized by a fragmented governmental system with a great deal of overlapping. . . .
>
> Each of these systems carries its own imperatives for the local official administering it. The overlapping situation in New York, for example, might well cause jurisdictions to follow conflicting policies in relation to their common tax base. In contrast, the small functionally inclusive jurisdictions in New Jersey and Connecticut would be able to follow consistent intra-jurisdictional policies. Area-wide consistency in these states, however, would be unlikely while large area coordination is a possibility in New York because of its relatively strong counties. However, even here the lack of zoning power at the county level reduces the potential for such coordination.
>
> The point is simply that it is not particularly useful to try to analyze the decision-making system in metropolitan areas on the assumption that the determinants of the environment are the same in all spread cities (i.e., metropolitan areas) or even are alike in all parts of the same spread city.[19]

Not all instances of horizontal intergovernmental relations are provoked by the problems of metropolitan areas. Some result because features of the environment bring common difficulties to different administrative agencies that are widely separated or are rural in their character. In one form, this is the river or lake which serves as the boundary between different states, yet joins their governments to the problems of pollution and makes the problem more difficult because of the numerous governments involved. The Mississippi River system, for example, (with the Ohio and Missouri as major tributaries) flows through or between 19 states! With numerous governments, it is necessary to appease many actors in negotiations. Interest groups who

---

[18] Alan K. Campbell and Seymour Sachs, "Administering the Spread City," *Public Administration Review*, 24 (September, 1964), 141–53.

[19] Campbell and Sachs, *ibid.*

oppose certain policies have that many veto points where a strategy of intransigence can stall a program. The Great Lakes wash the shores of eight states and present additional problems by involving international relations with Canada. Because Canada as well as the United States has a federal structure, this means that Ontario provincial officials as well as Canadian federal officials take part in negotiations. Two problems requiring intergovernmental coordination along lakes and rivers are pollution and water use. Pollution control requires the cooperation of governments on either side of a stream, as well as those upstream and downstream. The problems of water use involve diversions by one state or community of resources that another state or community desires for its own use. The Great Lakes states have charged that Chicago's diversion of water from Lake Michigan into the Chicago River (and eventually to the Mississippi) lowers shore lines around the lakes and causes much damage and inconvenience to recreational and port facilities. On the Colorado River, conflicts over diversions for irrigation has prompted interstate compacts that portion out the water to Colorado, Arizona, Nevada, and California.

Instruments of Horizontal Relations

The devices that different state or local administrators develop to resolve their common problems are often informal and designed merely to keep them in contact with one another. In this way, they can share information and perhaps coordinate efforts. However, some devices are very detailed and involve formal commitments from several state or local governments and perhaps from Washington or a foreign government.

Several devices attempt to cope with the problems of governmental coordination within metropolitan areas. Some are called "federations" or "consolidations." These terms imply that general-purpose governments provide a full range of services throughout the urban area. In some places, however, these terms denote governmental entities which handle only some local government functions. In Dade County, Florida, for example, the metropolitan government leaves numerous functions to pre-existing municipalities and the county. Most large metropolitan areas have "special districts" that provide individual services to an extensive area. Districts offer elementary and secondary education, water and sewage, refuse collection, police and/ or fire protection, parks, mass transportation, or libraries. Each district may have its own borders that are not coterminous with those of other districts; one district may include several municipalities and parts of other municipalities or the rural fringe and may overlap only partly with the territory covered by another kind of district. Where districts have proliferated, they can provide individual services on an economical basis, but do not reduce the confusion or inequities that arise from numerous separate jurisdictions. Many citizens do not know which districts include their own residence, much less how they can influence policies within their districts.

For many reformers, the "neatest" structure for a metropolitan government is the creation of an extensive general purpose government that eliminates the hodge-podge of distinct municipalities and special districts. Such an entity can extend its taxing powers to the entire business, residential, and industrial community and can respond to the service demands of the whole population. While several of these reforms have been proposed, few have met with any success at the polls. They threaten too many interests. They are opposed by middle-class homeowners who have moved to the suburbs to escape the problems of the central city, by businessmen who created "tax island" municipalities around their properties, and by many government officials who would lose their status as community leaders.

> A radical reorganization proposal is one that involves (or is perceived as involving) substantial change in existing political arrangements for large numbers of people. It may affect elected, appointed, and civil service governmental positions. It may alter the citizenship status of residents of various municipalities. It may realign governmental services and the existing tax structure. In short, it threatens (or is perceived as threatening) the political-governmental world that citizens, governmental employees and officials, and political leaders have learned to live with and like. They know how the system operates, what to expect from it, and how to function within it. Change threatens their very existence. Thus, suburbs threatened with loss of identity and decision-autonomy, suburban businesses threatened with loss of patronage, suburban and county officials and employees threatened with loss of jobs and status, central city political leaders threatened with dilution of electoral support, etc., have usually resisted any and all kinds of metropolitan reorganization attempts.[20]

Where a metropolitan area spills over into more than one state, it may be necessary to formalize intergovernmental agreements as "interstate compacts." These must be defined in legislation that is accept-

---

[20] Thomas M. Scott, "Metropolitan Governmental Reorganization Proposals," *Western Political Quarterly,* Vol. 21, No. 1 (June, 1968), 252–61. Reprinted by permission of the University of Utah, copyright owners.

able to the officials of each state and to the United States Congress. The Port of New York Authority is a product of one such compact. It is an agreement between New York and New Jersey which defines the legal authority and financial procedures for developing and maintaining transportation facilities in the New York City area. The Authority owns bridges, tunnels, airports, highways, and port facilities. It raises money by selling bonds that it pays off with tolls and other revenues earned by its facilities.

Some agreements commit administrators to share information used for enforcement programs. The tax officials of different states and the federal government share information about individuals who move from one state to another or about business firms that deal in many states. Returns filed by an individual or business for state and federal taxes can be checked for consistency, and an audit performed by one agency may produce information that is useful to another.[21]

The national and regional organizations of state and local government officials are important media for informal horizontal relations among state or local governments. These organizations bring their members together for periodic meetings and sometimes provide staff services that compile information and write position papers on topics of common interest. Some attain national publicity. The United States Conference of Mayors includes the chief executives of most large cities; and the Governor's Conference includes all of the state chief executives. Many other organizations exist for the heads of administrative departments. A study compiled in 1966 reported 46 organizations for state and local officials.[22] These organizations provide an opportunity for policy-makers to get together. Some contacts made at these meetings mature into personal friendships. They provide channels that smooth relations between neighboring jurisdictions. When an administrator faces an unfamiliar situation, he contacts colleagues in neighboring jurisdictions to see if they have worked out a policy to deal with similar occurrences. Two organizations publish collections of data that are widely used by state and local administrators to see how their own activities compare with those across the country. The International City Managers' Association publishes *The Municipal Year Book,* and the Council of State Governments publishes the *Book of the States.* Several groups try to maintain communications across func-

---

[21] Clara Penniman and Walter W. Heller, *State Income Tax Administration* (Chicago: Public Administration Service, 1959), Chapter IX.

[22] Jack L. Walker, "The Adoption of Innovations in the American States," a paper presented at the 1968 Annual Meeting of the American Political Science Association, Washington, D.C.

TABLE 9–6
Members of the "1313 Group" in 1964,
Showing Date of Founding

American Public Welfare Association (1930)
American Public Works Association (1894)
American Society of Planning Officials (1934)
American Society for Public Administration (1939)
Conference of Chief Justices (1949—COSGO affiliate)
Council of State Governments (1933)
Federation of Tax Administrators (1937)
Governors' Conference (1908—COSGO affiliate)
International City Managers Association (1914)
Municipal Finance Officers Association (1906)
National Association of Assessing Officers (1934)
National Association of Attorneys General (1907—COSGO affiliate)
National Association of Housing and Redevelopment Officials (1933)
National Association of Juvenile Compact Administrators (1956—COSGO affiliate)
National Association of State Budget Officers (1945—COSGO affiliate)
National Association of State Purchasing Officials (1947—COSGO affiliate)
National Conference of Court Administrative Officials (1955—COSGO affiliate)
National Conference on Uniform State Laws (1892—COSGO affiliate)
National Institute of Municipal Clerks (1947)
National Legislative Conference (1948—COSGO affiliate)
Parole and Probation Compact Administrators' Association (1945—COSGO affiliate)
Public Administration Service (1933)
Public Personnel Association (1906)

SOURCE: W. Brooke Graves, *American Intergovernmental Relations: Their Origins, Historical Development, and Current Status* (New York: Scribners, 1964), p. 588.

tional specialties by maintaining their headquarters in proximity to one another. For many years a "1313 group" maintained offices at 1313 East 60th Street, on the campus of the University of Chicago. The organizations in the 1313 Group as of 1964 are listed in Table 9–6.

As we have noted before, organizations of administrators are important not only as media for intergovernmental communications, but also as interest groups that present the demands of administrators to other government officials. They do not always seek more discretion for state or local administrators. At times they welcome stringent federal requirements and see them as leverage that state or local administrators can use to elicit more funds or better working conditions from their legislative and executive branches.

Regional Similarities in Public Policy

One manifestation of horizontal relations among administrative organizations is policy-copying among geographical neighbors. Copying within regions goes on despite the "nationalizing" features of federal grants-in-aid and program standards, the common national employment markets, high population mobility, and the prevalence of nationwide media of communication (networks and wire-service news). Several features guide officials to their regional neighbors for policy cues: the officials' belief that neighbors have problems similar to their own; the attitude of officials and interested citizens that it is "proper" or "reasonable" to adapt one's own programs to those of nearby jurisdictions; and the structure of organizational affiliations that put officials into frequent contact with their counterparts in neighboring governments.[23] The professional associations of administrators hold both regional and national meetings; and officials report they are more likely to attend and acquire their contacts at regional meetings. Federal agencies also encourage regional communications by virtue of their field offices. The cities of New York, Atlanta, Chicago, Dallas, Kansas City, Denver, and San Francisco have acquired informal status as regional capitals because they contain the offices of numerous Washington agencies. The personnel in these field offices conduct most of the correspondence between the federal agency and state and local units, and they help to pass the news of problems and solutions from one state government to another within their regions. One study of horizontal relations among administrators questioned the budget officers of 67 major agencies in the states of Florida, Georgia, Kentucky, and Mississippi. One question asked:

Have you or any of your colleagues contacted officials in other states in an attempt to learn how they deal with a particular situation that you have encountered in your work?

Where a budget officer answered in the affirmative he was asked:

What states do you feel are the best sources of information?

The 67 officials made 198 nominations of states that were among the "best sources of information." Eighty-seven percent of their nominations were in the region that includes the eleven states of the Confederacy and the Border States of Delaware, Maryland, Kentucky, West Virginia and Oklahoma. Thirty-five percent of the nominations were states that bordered directly on the states of the respondents. A survey conducted among school superintendents in Georgia showed comparable results. The superintendents are most likely to contact their immediate or near neighbors within the state. The choice of a contact is often an uncomplicated one, guided by a notion of friends and

---

[23] This section relies on Ira Sharkansky, *Regionalism in American Politics* (Indianapolis: Bobbs-Merrill, 1969), Chapters 1 and 6.

neighbors within easy reach. One rural superintendent described his daily route as the guide to contacts:

> Well, I live in Macon County, so I have to drive [to work] through Marion and Schley Counties. I talk with those three pretty often.

Although it is conceivable that southerners are more parochial in their reliance on neighbors than are officials in other sections of the country, administrators elsewhere likewise refer primarily to states in the immediate or near neighborhood when questioned about the source of their own policy norms.

The question remains: *Which regional neighbors are the targets of administrators' emulation?* From the comments of several officials, it is evident that agencies which have acquired a reputation for leadership are sought out disproportionately for their advice. There seems to be a two-step communications process: most administrators seek to copy the leading agencies within their region, but the leading agencies either generate their own innovations or take their cues from other leaders outside their immediate region. Jack L. Walker of the University of Michigan has gathered evidence on the timing of innovations in each of the 48 contiguous stages. By aggregating data across several fields of service, he ranked the state governments according to their adoption of programs or policies earlier—or later—than other states. His rankings suggest that agencies in New York and Massachusetts play leadership roles in the Northeast, Michigan and Wisconsin in the middle section of the country, California on the West Coast, Colorado in the Mountain region, and Louisiana and Virginia in the South.[24]

The ambiguous regional location of some states provides their administrators with special opportunities. When a state is situated on the borders between different regions, its officials can choose from among several states as the subjects of comparison. When they face a situation where they must plead for additional funds, they can identify themselves as the poor cousin in comparison with more well-endowed neighbors. But when they find it necessary to defend themselves against public criticism, they can picture themselves as offering better services than other neighbors. Educators in Missouri, for example, often find it necessary to justify their low level of expenditure for public schools. In 1959, the state ranked 38th in per capita expenditures for local schools, but 18th in per capita personal income. When they are on the defensive, Missouri officials can compare their efforts

---

[24] Walker, *ibid.*

to such low-ranking neighbors as Arkansas, Oklahoma, and Nebraska, rather than to high-ranking Illinois. When they are on the offensive, Missouri educators ask for funds to help them attain the standards of Illinois. The best evidence of regional copying shows those policies which are similar in neighboring states, but do not simply reflect the influence of common social or economic conditions. Levels of economic development affect the demands of populations and the resources available to governments, and they have a powerful influence on the nature of services that are provided.[25] Because regional partners tend to resemble one another economically, these economic traits may produce similar levels of revenues, expenditures, and public services. The following discussion identifies some regional policy traits that are not simply reflections of economic conditions, and it suggests some historical features that have guided policy-makers to copy their neighbors.[26]

New England

New England shows several policy characteristics that are different from the expectations associated with its economy. As of 1962, spending for education was lower than expected; road systems were less well-developed; there was less use of the major taxes collected by state governments (retail sales and individual income); and there was slightly more use of the locally collected property tax than expected. Although a recent sales tax enactment in Massachusetts will help to align that state's revenue structure to the national norm, the long struggle preceding the adoption of that tax indicated severe resistance to the innovation. The property-tax emphasis in New England reflects localistic norms that have prevailed since Colonial times. Unlike the colonies further south, those in New England developed a number of viable, quasi-independent towns and cities. This drew its impetus from the relative density of settlement in the northern colonies and from the religious orientation of the settlers. The colonists were Congregationalists whose concern for local autonomy extended to government as well as religion.

The prominence of private schools in New England works against the region's expenditures for public education. Private education was once the domain of elite Yankee schools, but is now the combination

---

[25] Thomas R. Dye, *Politics, Economics, and the Public: Policy Outcomes in the American States* (Chicago: Rand McNally, 1966).

[26] The discussion that follows is meant to illustrate the policies that are shared by neighboring jurisdictions. It is not an exhaustive description of regionally shared policies. See Sharkansky, *Regionalism in American Politics,* Chapter 6.

of these and Roman Catholic parochial schools. In the heavily Catholic states of Rhode Island and Massachusetts, 29.4 and 23.6 percent of the elementary and secondary school pupils attend non-public institutions. In the field of higher education, the status and facilities of Harvard, Massachusetts Institute of Technology, Yale, Brown, and Dartmouth have long stood above the major public institutions in their states. The private-school emphasis occasionally figures in the politics of New England. Supporters of parochial schools argue that public authorities shirk their obligation to support the thousands of students in private schools; and spokesmen for public education feel that opposition from private-school parents weakens the budgetary position of public schools.

In scoring lower than expected on both rural and municipal road mileage, the New England region typifies the low ratio of roads to population that is found in all of the older and more congested sections. Perhaps a combination of deterring costs of new construction, the efficiency of road mileage in congested areas, and a limited concern for highways is the explanation for "underdeveloped" road networks. Each mile of new road is likely to upset existing landowners; urban roads carry lots of vehicles more efficiently than roads in rural areas; and the relatively short distances between population centers may accustom drivers to the problems of heavy traffic and reduce their demands for more roads.

Great Lakes Region

The distinctive traits of the Great Lakes region[27] include lower scores on income taxation and government indebtedness than expected on the basis of its economic traits. For the immediate explanation of these traits, we need look no further than state constitutions for provisions that discourage or prohibit these measures. Those of Michigan and Illinois prohibit the graduated taxation of personal incomes, and those of Indiana, Michigan, Ohio, and Wisconsin put severe restrictions upon government borrowing. Although the Lakes states evade their own constitutional limitations against debt by allowing public corporations to issue "non-guaranteed" bonds (e.g., for college dormitories and toll roads),[28] the restrictions against borrowing hold

---

[27] The region includes the states of Ohio, Indiana, Illinois, Wisconsin, and Michigan.

[28] It is not the state or local governments, per se, that issue these bonds; but it is special corporations that issue them. The bonds are "non-guaranteed" in the sense that the government does not guarantee their payment with its full faith and credit. Instead, the corporation established by the state to construct college dormitories, toll roads, or some other revenue-producing facility pledges the in-

down total indebtedness. The debt limits appeared in the state constitutions of the region during the 19th century, partly in response to a rash of defaulted bond issues that had been used to support turnpikes, railroads, and canals. Because of their over-extended obligations, midwestern politicians wrote fiscal conservatism into their state constitutions, and it became part of the region's policies.

Mountain Region

Despite a reputation for conservatism, state and local governments of the Mountain region[29] show among the highest scores (relative to economic features) on measures of spending, federal aid, and the outputs of public service. An unusually large amount of the land area in the Mountain region is held by the federal government; and western congressmen have won acceptance of the principle that the federal government should give additional support to states with large acreage in the public domain. Upwards of 30 percent of the land in each Mountain state is owned by federal agencies, and this factor earns special recognition in the allocations of several grant programs.

Relative to economic conditions, state and local government expenditures in the Mountain region are the highest of any region in the country. The region also ranks at or near the top on the measures of road mileage and of the generosity of welfare payments. These traits add up to a cultural bias in favor of community-mindedness that stands in odd contrast to the success that right-wing Republicans have recently enjoyed in Montana, Wyoming, and Idaho. Several ingredients of the region's history may shed some light on the "progressive" norms of public services: the radical labor movements that developed in the late 19th and early 20th centuries out of the hardships in mining and lumber camps; the great distances, severe terrain, and isolation of population settlements that might enforce a certain amount of cooperation (at the same time that they provide a rationale for extreme individualism); and the absence of large cultural minorities whose extreme poverty or distinctiveness might have discouraged the dominant population groups from accepting heavy tax levies. Thus, the

---

come from its about-to-be constructed project for the bonds' payment. Nonguaranteed bonds typically require the payment of a higher rate of interest than do bonds guaranteed directly by government agencies; and this higher rate of interest may help to keep borrowing low. See James A. Maxwell, *Financing State and Local Governments* (Washington, D.C.: Brookings Institution, 1965), pp. 194ff. A recently adopted income tax in Illinois (1969) may change this regional trait of low reliance on that source.

[29] This region includes the states of Montana, Idaho, Wyoming, Colorado, and Utah.

cultural homogeneity, the severity of the environment, and the reaction to earlier excesses of a free enterprise economy may have combined to mold the distinct character of policies in the Mountain region.

The Southeast

Southeastern states[30] show a number of traits that are claimed for them by political scientists and historians, even after controlling for their low levels of economic development. They score significantly lower than expected on the provision of services in the fields of education, highways, and public welfare; and they have high scores on sales and excise taxation. The South's performance in the program to aid families of dependent children is especially poor and reflects AFDC's reputation for being a "Negroes' program." The South does score high (relative to economic status) on three educational programs; these receive much of their support from the federal government and threaten the *least* disruptions in the social system: school lunches, vocational education, and vocational rehabilitation. The relatively high use of sales and excise taxes gives a strongly regressive character to southern revenue systems. The extreme poverty of much of the region is partly responsible for its choice of revenue measures. The sales tax wins support partly because it is collected in tolerably small portions. Indeed, Mississippi pioneered in the development of the retail sales tax during the Depression when it sold tokens and collected mil taxes on the very smallest sales. Yet there is also a racial ingredient in the South's reliance on the sales tax. More than one state official in the region told me they favored the levy on retail sales because it "makes the niggers pay their share."

THE MIXED REALITIES OF INTERGOVERNMENTAL RELATIONS

It is misleading to describe "vertical" and "horizontal" relations among administrative agencies and to imply that relations are clearly one type or another. Relationships among administrators of different governments evolve from concrete problems that affect several jurisdictions; they often combine "horizontal" with "vertical" relationships. "Triangular" relations may also develop; these involve two local gov-

---

[30] The Southeast includes the states of Virginia, West Virginia, North Carolina, South Carolina, Georgia, Florida, Kentucky, Tennessee, Alabama, Mississippi, Arkansas, and Louisiana.

ernments with a single federal (or state) agency, or two federal (or state) agencies with a single local government. Neighboring localities may develop a joint project under the prodding of a federal grant. Or an integrated set of local programs may receive support from different federal grants offered by distinct agencies. Beyond this level of complexity, a variety of "polyangular" relations may evolve among a number of federal, state or local agencies that have a common interest in a particular problem.

It is also an oversimplification to assume that the involvement of a "superior" level of administration permits that organization to control its "subordinate" associates. A study of intergovernmental relations in a rural Indiana county found several federal programs controlled by local commissions that operated with substantial discretion. They were extensions of the federal administrative organization,[31] but their mixture of local considerations with federal standards confound any simple equation of federal involvement with federal control. These units included the Selective Service Board, the Welfare Board, County Agricultural Stabilization and Conservation Committee, and the Civil Defense Board. These units were responsible for selecting young men for the armed services; deciding on applications for welfare assistance; distributing crop allotments and payments for conservation activities; and establishing rationing boards, practicing emergency procedures, and securing federal grants for fire-fighting and hospital equipment. Outside the formal boundaries of government, but still able to affect the local administration of federal programs were the banks which exercised their approval on all applications for Federal Housing Administration and Veterans Administration loans.

During the era of massive investment in the Cape Kennedy space facilities, east-central Florida experienced a variety of intergovernmental relations. Between 1950 and 1966, the population of Brevard County increased from 23,600 to 221,000. The economy shifted from one based on citrus, cattle, truck crops, fishing, and forestry to one that was based almost exclusively on the space program. At the end of 1965, the Air Force, the National Aeronautics and Space Administration (NASA), or their contractors employed about 37 percent of the area's labor force. A brief survey of the most prominent interactions provides a rich illustration of the diverse ways in which the administrative agencies of separate governments can come together to make demands on one another and/or to provide one another with benefits. A

---

[31] Douglas St. Angelo, "Formal and Routine Local Control of National Programs," *Southwestern Social Science Quarterly*, 47 (March, 1966), 416–27; see also the discussion of "administrative hybrids" in Chapter IV, pp. 93–95 above.

study of intergovernmental relations that was conducted in 1966 found the following goals motivating intergovernmental relations:

1. An agency's desire to make life more convenient and agreeable for its burgeoning work force;
2. An agency's concern that projects begun by other units would affect its own programs;
3. An agency's desire to support its own projects with the resources controlled by other governments;
4. An agency's desire to protect its constituents' interests from being disturbed by the projects of other governments;
5. The desire of agency administrators to build rapport with other units of government; and
6. The recognition by agency personnel that they had surplus resources that were valuable to other units of government.[32]

NASA officials were most prominent in playing the role of a large employer concerned about the convenience of its employees. The agency wanted community amenities that would help it—and its contractors—recruit personnel to the area; and it wanted convenient travel facilities to insure its employees' promptness and good spirits. It had a special interest in travel problems. The main NASA facilities are separated from the mainland by a wide estuary and occupy a series of islands that had received little use before the space boom. Because the facilities are spread north-south over 50 miles, it is necessary to provide numerous roads, causeways, and bridges between each major work site and the communities that house the workforce. In order to stimulate and guide the state, local, and federal agencies that would provide the necessary roads, NASA's Office of Community Services surveyed the travel habits of its own employees and those of other federal agencies and contractors; and it provided the data to state, county, and municipal officials and to the U.S. Bureau of Public Roads.

The choice of specific locations for causeways and bridges involved the U.S. Army Corps of Engineers. That agency showed the second motivation for intergovernmental relations: projects of other units affect the Corps' own responsibilities. In this case, the Corps had to review the designs of causeways and bridges to see that they did not interfere with navigation in the Intracoastal Waterway and in other streams in the Cape Kennedy area.

The question of money often generates intergovernmental rela-

---

[32] Ira Sharkansky, "Intergovernmental Relations in Brevard County, Florida," a report to the Urban Research Institute of Florida State University, 1966.

tions. In displays of the third motivation for intergovernmental relations, several administrators sought the financial resources of other
agencies for road and bridge improvements. The County Road Department requested extra funds from the State Road Board to acquire
rights-of-way ahead of the normal schedule for receiving state road
funds. In their turn, state officials argued that federal agencies should
pay more than their usual portion for Brevard County road improvements because of the federally induced traffic. Federal agencies did
accept some additional financial responsibility, but they hedged
against the full state demands with the argument that economic
benefits of the space program compensated for state road expenditures.

State and county administrators together approached Washington
officials in the pursuit of extra federal aid. During March of 1965, a
member of the State Road Board said that a delegation led by Governor Burns would meet with Florida Senators and Congressmen and
would try for an audience with President Johnson. This meeting did
not occur, but during April, state officials met with Vice President
Humphrey during his visit to Orlando (for the purpose of honoring
astronaut John Young). Vice President Humphrey then arranged a
Washington meeting between the Governor, members of the State
Road Board, the Chairman of the Brevard County Commission, both
Florida Senators, the Secretary of the Air Force (which operates
Patrick Air Force Base in the Cape area), and the Director and
Associate Director of NASA's Kennedy Space Center. From this meeting there came a state-federal agreement about the division of costs
for certain roads and bridges, an indication of NASA and Air Force
willingness to request a budget allocation for roads based upon military needs, and plans for the submission of a supplementary appropriations bill in Congress.

The Orlando meeting with the Vice President produced an incident that showed some of the tensions that might accompany intergovernmental relations. In displays of the fourth motivation for intergovernmental relations (protecting one's constituents from another
government's projects), local officials and allied newspaper editors
dramatized a *faux pas*. The incident occurred as the meeting began. A
security guard could not find the name of the Brevard County Commission Chairman on the list of guests and insisted that he leave. In
the confusion that preceded the opening of the talks, the Commissioner could not establish his identity. In reporting the incident to the
press, the Commissioner said that he was commanded by the guard:
"Out, out . . . you, out." Local officials and editors viewed the exclu-

sion as depriving Brevard County of a representative at the discussion that might have long-ranging effects upon the county's welfare. Worse yet, the meeting was in Orange County, and its host was the publisher of the *Orlando Sentinel*, an Orange County newspaper. In Brevard County, the Titusville *Star Advocate* quoted a local official as saying: "Brevard County is the ninth most populous county in Florida. We've never asked Orange County for help in the past and we don't plan on asking them for help in the future. . . . I feel Brevard County is due an apology for [the Commissioner's] ouster from that important meeting." Another Brevard County newspaper, the *Cocoa Tribune*, referred to the Orlando publisher as "The Little Emperor of Central Florida," and speculated that he had contrived the exclusion of the Brevard County official in order to emphasize road projects that would benefit Orange County at the expense of Brevard County. The commissioner himself came to see an advantage in his exclusion from the meeting. In the vice presidential embarrassment and apology that followed, the commissioner found other governments more cooperative than he had originally expected.

Road and bridge decisions provide other examples of intergovernmental relations that are motivated by officials' desires to protect their constituents. The Bureau of Sports Fisheries of the U.S. Department of the Interior analyzed the design and location of bridges and causeways with respect to their impact on the health of marine life and on the recreational opportunities of sportsmen. Municipal authorities opposed the choice of certain locations for new roads and bridges because of their likely impact on local restaurants, motels, and retail shops. The administrators of toll-bridge authorities opposed the development of toll-free facilities because of their own obligations to bondholders.

Another display of intergovernmental relations prompted by officials' concern for their constituents surrounded NASA's decision to create a Visitors' Information Center. The Center promised to become the major tourist attraction in the area. A survey by the U.S. National Parks Service predicted that 3.2 million persons would visit the Center annually by 1970. Reacting to this prediction, one county editor wrote:

> Three million people will eat a lot of meals in Brevard County. Many of them will want a place to stay overnight. They will want to buy souvenirs, visit our beaches, perhaps stay over long enough to fish or relax in our fine year-around climate.
>
> Their cars will need fuel and probably some repairs and

maintenance. They may even want to look around with an
eye to choosing a retirement home or looking for a job. . . .
    We'd better be ready to render the services they demand
and will be willing to pay for.[33]

Not only would communities close to the Center glean more from
tourists than communities at the far end of the county, but the
Center's exact location would determine which of several routes the
national automobile clubs and oil companies would recommend for
tourists. If a town did not have convenient access to the Center, it
would lose tourist business. Before NASA made a decision about the
Center's location, several chambers of commerce urged it for their
areas; at least three communities offered free land for the Center, and
one offered a vacant supermarket as a suitable building. To avoid the
honky-tonkism that would surround a location on a public highway
(few major roads in the County are free of strip development), NASA
decided to build the Center inside its reservation, with a federally-
controlled road between it and a major highway. Although this decision did not escape harsh criticism from community newspapers,
NASA tried to minimize the controversy. During the course of public
presentations, NASA asserted that it would not compete with the
private tourist industry. As an appeal to local eateries, the Center
would limit its refreshment stands to snacking, rather than lunching or
picnicking facilities. In order to keep all important communities on
the tourist routes, NASA would make the Center accessible from
various parts of the county; to accomplish this, NASA would allow the
State Road Board to build additional highways through its reservation.
    While intergovernmental competition and conflict were promi-
nent in the relationships generated by road and bridge developments
and by NASA's Visitors' Information Center, most intergovernmental
relations in Brevard County appear amicable. Indeed, that is the
assertion of both federal and local administrators. Both NASA and the
Air Force made a conscious effort to promote rapport with other units
of government. At the Washington level, NASA worked to establish a
subregional office of another federal agency (the Department of
Housing and Urban Development) in Brevard County. The sub-re-
gional office is not a usual component of HUD's organization. Rather,
it is the Department's effort to help area communities cope with their
rapid growth. NASA's involvement came partly from its sense of
obligation for the effects of its own growth, partly from its desire to

---

[33] *Orlando Sentinel* (Brevard County Edition), June 5, 1965.

have good working relations with local governments, and partly from the hope that improved community facilities would help it recruit and hold competent employees. HUD's subregional office provides advice and technical assistance to local authorities who wish to apply for federal grants. Its staff lists and describes the programs of HUD and other federal departments and indicates the criteria that federal officials are likely to consider when they review local applications for grants. Somewhat in the manner of travelling salesmen, they call upon local authorities in order to acquaint them with new or changing programs. The Air Force's major effort in intergovernmental relations is the Civilian-Military Council of Patrick Air Force Base. This provides an opportunity for base commanders and public relations officers to meet with prominent civilians: e.g., the local clergy, retail businessmen, real estate agents, and local government officials. The local government members report that monthly business meetings are typically short and uneventful, but the accompanying social hour provides opportunities to discuss items of mutual concern and to occasionally arrange joint activities. Once each year the members spend several days together—partly at federal expense—visiting other Air Force installations throughout the United States. Members claim this extended period in close contact allows them to understand more clearly the views of fellow members and to comprehend the constraints that influence one another's operations. The members trace several instances of intergovernmental cooperation to the friendships that have developed out of the Council's programs. A public relations officer for the Air Force cited the Council's program as an explanation for the immediate response that he once received from the County Road Department in response to his call for assistance. During the Cuban missile crisis, it was necessary to close the main highway that ran along side of the airstrip. "Within a few minutes" of this official's telephone request, the county had a road grader on the scene to smooth a dirt road detour, and police officers appeared to blockade the highway and re-direct traffic.

Many administrators tell homely stories about the exchange of favors between agencies. Some may reflect high-level decisions to build intergovernmental rapport. However, lower-level employees also exchange favors for less-complex motives. They do so when they are predisposed to cooperation, and when they have a surplus commodity that can benefit another agency in the area. These exchanges have not been significant in terms of money or man-hours, but they make relations tolerable for the personnel of different units. Patrick Air Force Base lent men and vehicles without charge to help a school

construction project that had fallen behind schedule; county personnel and equipment—using materials donated by local businessmen—
helped construct a swimming pool for noncommissioned officers; and
the county donated materials for a refreshment stand on the Air Force
Little League field. NASA and the Air Force donate obsolete missiles
to local authorities for display purposes, and they allow local government personnel to attend in-service training courses provided for
federal employees. On one occasion, Patrick Air Force Base rescued a
local government from embarrassment at the hands of another federal
agency. When the Federal Aviation Agency would not allow a new
airport to commence operations on the day of its formal opening
because its tower operator lacked the proper credentials, the Air Force
loaned a tower operator. Federal and county officials cooperate regu-
larly in making it convenient for federal employees to file requests for
property tax exemptions and to purchase automobile license tags. Both
NASA and the Air Force provide temporary office space for county
officials and allow their own employees release time to take care of
these personal chores.

The preceding descriptions indicate that there is no simple pattern of intergovernmental relations. No formal routines prescribe in
clear terms how administrators of one government should deal with
officials of another unit. Furthermore, each major "instance" of intergovernmental relations is not one event. It is a series of meetings,
telephone conversations, memoranda, informal or formal accords. At
times, a government's decisions may influence another government
when there has been no real contact. An administrator of one unit may
base a decision on his anticipation of the likely response that will be
made by officials of other units. If the officials of different units have
obtained sufficient knowledge of each other's environments and modes
of action, then their anticipation may lead to actions that differ little
from what would occur with formal communications.

SUMMARY

Administrators from all levels of government seek to affect the
decisions of administrative agencies at other levels of government.
Various kinds of intergovernmental aids join the resources of federal,
state and local governments in the support of all major domestic
services. Actors at each level of government feel the impact of decisions that flow from administrative decisions at all levels of government.

There are numerous forms of intergovernmental relations. Many involve financial assistance, and even those which are not overtly financial have economic importance for the participants: grants-in-aid; shared taxes; tax credits; federal income-tax provisions that allow deductions for state and local taxes and the exclusion of income earned on state or local government bonds; the direct provision of services from one government to the citizens of another; technical assistance; and informal ties among personal friends in different agencies or through the media of administrators' professional societies. It is not feasible to estimate the economic value of these relations to the providers or to the recipients. The resources involved in federal grants and state aids to localities are considerable. Federal grants amounted to $17 billion in 1968, and state aids were about $18.5 billion in 1966–1967.

There has been a continuous growth in the magnitude of inter-governmental financial assistance since World War II, although any report of growth is partly a function of the measuring standards that are used. The kinds of programs added during each decade of the 20th century indicate that intergovernmental relations grow with prevailing policy concerns. Recent programs in the fields of education and urban affairs, for example, reflect the preoccupation with these areas of policy during the middle and late 1960's.

Not all intergovernmental relations are vertical. There are numerous horizontal contacts among different states or localities. These arrangements do not emphasize financial "aid," but they often have great economic significance for each of the participants. There are numerous kinds of metropolitan cooperation, interstate compacts, reciprocal agreements on the provision of services and enforcement programs, and informal links on the basis of personal friendships and contacts made through the organizations of government officials. It is often misleading to identify the "type" of intergovernmental relation that prevails at any time or place. Multiple relationships evolve among the officials of different governmental units as their officials or clients perceive their common interest in substantive problems. Individual problems may generate both vertical and horizontal relations among several units. Intergovernmental relations are not without their effects on recipient governments. These effects are discussed—along with other outputs of administrative systems—in Chapter 10.

10

VARIETIES OF ADMINISTRATIVE
OUTPUTS

In Chapter 1, we listed some of the outputs that the conversion processes of administrative systems provide to their environments. Now that we have examined numerous features of the environment, inputs from it to the conversion process, and the conversion process itself, we take a final look at several kinds of outputs. The picture should appear richer—and more complicated—than at our first look.

In discussing the outputs of administrative agencies, we must frequently beg the question as to the origin of these outputs and the influence of administrators upon them. Some only pass through administrative agencies and show little influence from the actions of those agencies. In some cases, an administrative unit may work on a project and "produce" it, but leave no feature on it that is its own distinctive creation. When some state or local agencies provide services that are funded and regulated by federal agencies, for example, the producing units may do nothing more or less than required by the federal manual. Or an agency may simply continue producing a service according to procedures that were devised in the past generation, without the present corps of officials making any alterations in the product. In some cases, administrators might help to create a new program, but primarily as a response to the demands of citizens, interest groups, or members of the executive and legislative branches. These questions about origins are important for a full understanding of the administrative system. We want to know which transactions are originated or shaped in the conversion process, as well as which are shaped primarily by its environment. If we wish to use our knowledge of administration in order to make adjustments in public programs and policies, we should know where to apply our adjustments: to agencies or to other factors in their environment. For the most part, however, this kind of detailed knowledge has not been collected. We can only raise the question about the true origin of administrative outputs, and then proceed to describe several outputs which appear to have some importance for administrators and for actors in their environment.

ADMINISTRATIVE EFFORTS AND PUBLIC SERVICES

Public services include some of the most tangible outputs of administrative agencies, but even they defy clear and unambiguous measurement. We cannot simply equate the policies pursued by administrative agencies with the services that citizens actually receive. Services can be measured in several ways: by the products which are received by clients; by the improvement in the clients' conditions that results from the service; by the popularity of a service among the clients; or by some standards of quality that are set by an organization of professional persons who are concerned with the service at issue. In the case of "services" that are intangible—such as patriotic or religious utterances or other symbolic acts of administrative officials—their output might be gauged by the indications of satisfaction (and dissatisfaction) which appear in the population. Outputs are frequently measured by the efforts directed at services by administrators. Yet some of these outputs may fail to deal with the needs of agency clients. And some may work at cross purposes with one another. Such outputs as agency expenditures, the recruitment and selection of a staff, the design of physical facilities, and the purchase of equipment may not make their expected contribution to the services that an agency renders.

Expenditures are among the most evident manifestations of agency policies. Officials pay a great deal of attention to budget-making, and expenditures are widely viewed as a common denominator with respect to the items that actually produce services. Although spending by itself does not meet popular demands for services, spending appears to buy many of the things that produce services. Sufficient funds may be a *sine qua non* for public services. However, several other determinants of service outputs may be provided in generous or stingy proportions by different jurisdictions whose total budgets are nearly equal. By varying the allocation of funds among different factors, policy-makers may make a budget of a certain total more or less productive of service outputs. Some of the policies that have important effects on service outputs may be independent of spending levels.

Several aspects of an agency's staff may have a bearing on the quality or quantity of service outputs. The nature of the training received by personnel, their sensitivity to clients' needs, and their motivation for professional advancement may each affect an agency's ability to make the greatest use of its funds. The simple factor of staff size and the distribution of personnel among the principal and auxiliary tasks that are to be performed can also affect an agency's service outputs. Professional educators, for example, predict that the consolidation of small districts will add to the teaching skills available for each pupil and will increase the quality of school outputs. If expenditures are used to make salary levels competitive with those in other jurisdictions, they may facilitate the policy-maker's search for the "right combination" of training and motivation for each of the principal jobs within his organization. However, salary alone does not guarantee success in obtaining a good staff. Indeed, the sensitivity of the leadership and its skill in using financial resources may be the key determinant that may (or may not) translate a good budget into a good staff and then into public services that meet the needs and/or desires of the clients.

The crucial dimensions of physical plant and equipment that may affect service outputs include compatibility with contemporary methods of providing service, flexibility with respect to the multiple needs and changing demands of clients, and durability in the face of heavy use. It is probably true that good education can be provided in an inadequate physical plant if the professional personnel are highly motivated and adaptable. But the nature of surroundings and the availability of modern equipment should contribute to the capacity of the staff to perform in a superior fashion. However, attractive plant and facilities cannot guarantee success. If quality facilities are available for only a limited range of the school's task, they may not have their maximum impact on overall performance. If the high school gymnasium sparkles while the library lacks up-to-date science texts, then the money spent on facilities may have a distorted influence on the school's output. The durability of facilities provides yet another dimension that may influence services. If the plant and equipment cannot stand up to the clients, then the cost of maintenance will deplete the investments that can be made on additional facilities or on an improvement in staff. Later in this chapter, we shall return to these questions about the effects that various kinds of administrative outputs have on the services that clients receive.

INFORMATION AS AN OUTPUT

Administrative agencies produce information and ideas for the public and for other branches of government. These outputs often help set the agenda of public discussions, influence the content of "public opinion," and provide the information that legislators and the chief executive use to "supervise and control" the administrators. This is no place to exaggerate the influence of administrative agencies over public opinion. The image to be presented is *not* that of a monolithic government that exercises subtle but irresistible influence over the minds of men. Administrative units are typically as complex and beset with diversity as is the population they serve. This diversity itself is one of the prime defenses that the society has against an overbearing opinion machine: because of this diversity, administrators provide opinion-options to their citizens, rather than public opinion per se.

Administrators use several means to provide information and ideas to the public. Some are formal announcements and other communications designed to influence public opinion; and others are public communications to other government officials which have a secondary function of influencing the public. In many cases it is difficult to separate the primary and secondary targets of administrators communications. They may be addressed to other officials, but delivered in a fashion that guarantees some arousing of public support. Many deliberations are ritualized for the purpose of informing the public about the government's business; thus, the official who routes an in-house communication through the public is only acting according to a format that is well-established in democratic practice. Such procedures as administrative and legislative hearings, legislative debates, court proceedings, reports of special investigatory commissions, and election campaigns are designed to involve the public in governmental affairs. Many of the topics that are discussed in these forums have enough innate importance to attract attention and to make the public receptive to the information and ideas that are offered. The topics of peace and war, economic development and unemployment, inflation and interest rates, testing of new drugs and medical devices, and the provision of education and housing are each vitally important to large numbers of people.

Several kinds of public information come from administrators. Agencies describe ongoing programs in order to advertise their availability and the requirements that prospective clients must fulfill. Some agencies also publicize their needs for new legislation or increased appropriations. An agency may not advertise its needs directly, but inform interest groups of its needs and let them mount the campaign. Agencies also provide much of the information that elected officials use in their public statements and in deliberations about present and proposed activities. Legislators and executives recognize agencies as primary reservoirs of expertise and often use agency speech-writers to compose their own remarks.

Administrators suffer the accusations of those who feel they take unfair advantage of their opportunities to inform the public. They are charged by citizens—and by other government officials—with "managing the news" or with violating "freedom of information." "Managing the news" refers to the selective release of information that benefits the agency providing the information. It is a charge heard frequently during the Viet Nam War. It is alleged that the Defense and State Departments released partial or distorted reports about military engagements or diplomatic efforts. Violation of "freedom of information" is heard frequently in state capitols and city halls, as well as in Washington. It refers to the efforts of government officials to classify controversial documents as "secret" or "confidential." The U. S. Congress and several state legislatures have enacted "freedom-of-information" statutes. They require that certain information be given to any citizen who asks for it, while they protect other documents from public scrutiny. The claim for an individual's "right to privacy" frequently clashes with "freedom of information" and in many states results in withholding from the public the information on tax returns, the records of welfare recipients, and other documents pertaining to individual cases.

With all the possibilities that exist for administrators to supply information and ideas and to regulate some mechanisms of public information, there also are many protections that guard citizens from the opinions of administrators. Perhaps the most important of these protections is the diversity among administrative agencies and personnel. There is no single "administrative line" that is disseminated via the mass media. Spokesmen for different administrative agencies argue publicly with each other's interpretation of a social problem. Individual legislators and the chief executive challenge agency views and provide additional alternatives for the public to consider. There have been numerous public conflicts among the military heads of the armed services, the civilian secretary of defense, the president, and members of Congress. After the Secretary of Defense cuts a budget request, for example, a friendly congressional committee will most likely provide a forum for the service head to accuse the secretary of gambling with the national security.

The citizens also enjoy protection from administrative views by the diversity of non-governmental information. The mass media are themselves a diffuse set of institutions that offer a variety of information and ideas. Individuals also have numerous non-institutionalized sources of information: friends, family, coworkers, and coreligionists, each of whom can provide information and reinforcement for positions counter to those presented by government officials.

Administrators send many of their "informational" outputs to other branches of government. Indeed, many of the inputs that come to administrators from the legislative and executive branches of government actually got their start as the outputs of the administration. As the administration's outputs, these take the form of requests for appropriations or a change in statutes or the form of an administrator's advice to a member of another branch about a proposal that has been developed elsewhere. These outputs of the administration are so important in the deliberations of other branches that—to some observers —they permit administrators to dominate other officials. As noted in Chapter 8, legislators and executives are not as well-prepared as administrators in terms of professional training in the subject matter at hand and in their current opportunities to spend full time on one aspect of public policy. While the other branches fragment their energies to a number of responsibilities beside policy-making, and within policy-making to a wide range of activities, the administrators concentrate their resources on a limited field of specialization. Administrators often bolster their reputation for expertise with the political support offered by interest groups that represent their clientele or with the support of the communities in which their services will be provided. In some cases, these alliances form tightly-knit "subgovernments" that present irresistible demands to the legislature and the chief executive. Perhaps the most well-known "subgovernment" is the alliance of military administrators, defense contractors, and the representatives of communities that have defense plants or military bases. Other alliances are formed among agencies that engage in the construction of public works (Corps of Engineers, Bureau of Reclamation, Bureau of Public Roads) and the construction firms, related industries, local communities, and groups of citizens that benefit from their activities.

The outputs that the administrative agencies provide to executive and legislative branches are not limited to policy proposals and relevant information. The implementation of policies provides outputs that are attractive to elected executives and legislators, as well as to private citizens. These outputs appeal to executives and legislators as the products of their own handiwork in helping to build and supply the administrative organizations. They also appeal to executives and legislators in their roles as purveyors of public service. Voters are thought to identify the services received with the elected executive and legislature. Elected officials look to administrators for outputs that will keep themselves in office.

OUTPUTS TO OTHER ADMINISTRATIVE AGENCIES

Many of the outputs of administrative agencies go directly to administrative units in other jurisdictions. "Intergovernmental relations" are, for the most part, relations between the administrators of different governments. The resources at stake are enormous. They include the $17 billion in federal aids to states and localities (1968), the $18.5 billion in state payments to local governments (1966–1967), plus the undetermined value of technical assistance and administrative cooperation that go "vertically" among administrators at different levels of the federal system and "horizontally" among administrators of separate states or localities. In Chapter 9, we described the various forms of intergovernmental relations. Here we examine several implications of their outputs for recipient units: (1) the character of governments that benefit most from intergovernmental payments; (2) the effects which these payments have on the policies of recipient units; (3) some of the political controversies that intergovernmental relations can arouse in the environment of the recipient units; and (4) the attitudes toward intergovernmental relations that are expressed by officials of recipient governments.

Which Governments Receive Large Intergovernmental Aids?

Generally speaking, the rural states with low-income residents are high users of federal aids. These same kinds of states also rely heavily on state aids to local governments and on state-provided public services.[1] These findings reflect the lack of resources available to local or state revenue officers and the use of intergovernmental payments as devices to redistribute resources from "have" to "have-not" areas. For states with low-income populations, this means taxes that are collected and distributed by the federal government. For local governments in low-income areas, this means state grants and shared taxes.[2]

---

[1] Thomas R. Dye, *Politics, Economics, and the Public: Policy Outcomes in the American States* (Chicago: Rand McNally, 1966), p. 193.

[2] The statutes establishing many federal and state aids are not written in a way to indicate that they will redistribute economic resources from "have" to "have-not" areas. (See Advisory Commission on Intergovernmental Relations,

Several studies identify political characteristics that affect the receipt of intergovernmental aids. J. David Greenstone and Paul E. Peterson examine the adoption of anti-poverty programs in four cities. They find that cities with strong political machines (Chicago and Philadelphia) seek more financial assistance for their citizens and do so more rapidly than do cities without strong party machines (New York and Los Angeles).[3] They explain this in relation to the historic concern of political machines for material benefits and to the speed with which a well-integrated party-government can seek and distribute federal funds.

> Since machines were historically dependent on the efficient payment of material benefits to their various supporters, it is not surprising to find that greater organizational strength increases the mayor's ability to obtain and distribute poverty funds. By contrast, the far greater concern of reform movements for "democracy" and "honesty" in political processes and structures, as opposed to the distribution of material outputs, explain the less effective distribution of funds by poverty agencies in cities with strong reform traditions.

Andrew T. Cowart compares the receipt of anti-poverty funds to characteristics of the state economy, to the incidence of voter turnout, party competition, and equitably districted state legislatures, and to previously established state policies toward welfare, educational, and health services. The factors most closely associated with new anti-poverty programs were the established policies in functionally-related programs.[4] The states that were high users of welfare, health, and educational programs were the first to adopt large-scale anti-poverty programs. Perhaps the populations, administrators, and other officials of these states shared certain norms that affected the earlier adoption of generous welfare, health, and education programs and then of the new federal programs when they became available.

How Do Intergovernmental Aids Affect the Recipients' Policies?

This question has been answered in terms of the "stimulative," "additive," or "substitutive" affects of intergovernmental aids. A stimulative grant is one that increases the level of state or local effort for a

---

The Role of Equalization in Federal Grants [Washington, D.C.: U.S. Government Printing Office, 1964]). However, they are redistributive, in effect, in being used disproportionately by low-income states.

[3] J. David Greenstone and Paul E. Peterson, "Reformers, Machines, and the War on Poverty," in James Q. Wilson, ed., *City Politics and Public Policy* (New York: Wiley, 1968), pp. 267–92.

[4] Andrew T. Cowart, "Anti-Poverty Expenditures in the American States: A Comparative Analysis," *Midwest Journal of Political Science*, 13 (May, 1969), 219–36.

program. An additive grant merely supplements state or local effort on a program, while a "substitutive" grant takes the place of state or local money and actually reduces state or local effort for a program. The features that combine to make a program stimulative, additive, or substitutive include (*a*) the statutory provisions and administrative rules that allocate the aid and (*b*) the policies followed by recipient agencies. Some grant requirements help to stimulate extra financial effort on the part of recipients, while others encourage an additive or substitutive result. Where an agency is required to match the aid with some of its own resources, a grant is more likely to be stimulative than where a recipient need not match the aid. These requirements by themselves do not define recipients' behavior; at the most, they set certain conditions. If a program is sufficiently attractive to the population and officials of a jurisdiction, the grant might have a sharply stimulative effect, even though it requires little or no matching.

Several studies attempt to define the actual impact of intergovernmental aids upon recipient governments. The results are not altogether clear. They vary with the governments, aid programs, or time periods which are studied and with the measurements that are used for "aid received" or "local effort."[5] The evidence indicates that per capita expenditures of state and local governments are high where per capita federal aids are also high. Some writers interpret this to mean that federal programs generally stimulate increased state and local effort. However, the amount of aid that is received for one program may simply replace existing expenditures for that program and, thus, release them for other programs.[6] In this way, one aid program can be substitutive with respect to the activity which it aids directly, but additive with respect to other programs.

Political Controversies as Outputs of Intergovernmental Aids

As might be expected, the huge resources involved in intergovernmental relations produce intense controversy. Individual programs are attacked because of their cost; because of the inconvenience caused to state or local authorities—or to private citizens—by their administrative procedures; or because of their alleged impact on the economy or on politics in the recipient's jurisdiction. The urban renewal program is one intergovernmental activity that provokes strong attacks from both extremes of the political spectrum:

---

[5] Thomas F. Pogue and L. G. Sgontz, "The Effect of Grants-in-Aid on State-Local Spending," *National Tax Journal*, 21 (June, 1968), 190–99.

[6] Jack W. Osman, "The Dual Impact of Federal Aid on State and Local Government Expenditures," *National Tax Journal*, 19 (December, 1966), 262–72.

> For some time now, it's been open season on urban renewal. The St. Georges out to slay this dragon are an odd crew—Socialists and Birchers, civil rightists and segregationists, city planners and people who equate planning with mortal sin. . . . The strident message of all these sallies from the Right is essentially the same: "Let private enterprise do it!" The liberal executioners, in contrast, base their attack on . . . the human dislocations and the hardening of segregated housing patterns than urban-renewal programs have sometimes caused.[7]

It may be endemic to large-scale federal programs that they generate differing kinds of opposition. Their ultimate administration is in the hands of state or local authorities and, in some cases, non-governmental organizations. Administrators differ in their willingness and skill in accommodating different segments of their constituencies. In the diverse ways they design and carry out their projects, administrators seem bound to offend some values in one community, and other values elsewhere.

Federal programs designed for the cities may have special problems. These are said to reflect the rural-yeoman element that has dominated American political culture at the expense of urban programs. Two proponents of this view write:

> Great American cities, unlike such European counterparts as London, Paris, Rome, and Moscow, have not played a dominant part in the history of the nation. American history has not been made by the cities, nor have the cities supplied any of our heroes. European kings and rulers have always been largely urban; in contrast, no American President has been identified with the city. Franklin Delano Roosevelt, whose political power was heavily based on the cities, preferred the image of the Dutchess County gentleman farmer, while John F. Kennedy, instead of being taken for Boston Irish, chose to show his Harvard-Hyannisport profile to the public. Only in the veins of the East Side's defeated Al Smith did the blood of the city course unashamedly. . . .
> At a recent Washington conference, which was given the neighborly title of "Town and Country" to avoid the unpleasant term city, the Secretary of Agriculture seemed not to offend anyone when he spoke of the "garbage can life in the inner city"; nor, on another occasion, did New York State Senator William E. Adams provoke any public ire when he attributed the growth of welfare cases in the suburbs to the spread of "the welfare rot of the central cities." Obviously, the historic "shame of the cities" is still with us, although the

[7] Joseph Epstein, "The Row over Urban Renewal," *Harpers*, February, 1965, pp. 55–61.

"wicked city" has now become the "asphalt jungle" and what was once the slum is now "the rotting cancer" of the inner city.[8]

Some critics of intergovernmental relations see them as generating improper alliances among federal, state, and local administrators. The problem they see is that these cadres of "professionals" undercut elected executives and legislators. According to Deil Wright, who admits to being "concerned about the impact of proliferated federal programs on our federal system":[9]

> Federal grants change the decision-making hierarchy at the state-local level. Their requirements that recipients meet certain conditions and their functional character engender a sense of independence and single-program fixation in local program administrators—who prefer, and often assert, substantial immunity from control by their governors, legislators, and other politically responsible officials.[10]

Another point of view disputes the importance of generalized "state interests" or "local interests" which are guarded by the elected officials and are ignored by administrators. Edward Weidner argues that elected officials line-up on different sides of disputes among administrators and that arguments over particular policies take precedence over their concern for overarching interests of the state or locality.

> While differences on public policy or values are to be expected in a country containing as many heterogeneous elements as are to be found in the United States, it does not necessarily follow that officials in the several states will take one policy position and those of the national government another. Indeed, on an *a priori* basis it would seem surprising if this were the case, given the diversity of conditions in the several states and the fact that the union is made up of all states. "States' rights" is only one of numerous values held by state officials, and it is relatively unimportant to many of them. The prime thing that the states have in common is their existence; it is possible that if an issue were presented that threatened the very existence of the states their political officials might be brought together. In actual fact, a major issue of this kind has not been presented. Consequently, usually national government officials can find many of their state counterparts who support national policy objectives and

---

[8] David Danzig and John Field, "The Betrayal of the American City," *Commentary*, June, 1968, pp. 52–59. Reprinted by permission. Copyright © 1968 by the American Jewish Committee.

[9] Deil S. Wright, *Federal Grants-in-Aid* (Washington, D.C.: American Enterprise Institute, 1968), p. 2.

[10] Wright, p. 48.

many others who oppose. And among the states, differences in values are the rule.[11]

Attitudes as Outputs: Recipients' Views toward Intergovernmental Aids

There are several reports about the feelings of state and local authorities toward intergovernmental relations. These attitudes are part of the outputs of intergovernmental aids from federal agencies. The findings do not reveal anything like a consensus. Some studies cover officials in only one or a few of the states. Others find that very few of the officials contacted actually fill out their questionnaires. A general finding shows acceptance of the basic federal-aid and state-aid programs, but a desire to change certain administrative features. Participants frequently urge an increase in funding or an expansion in the scope of programs that receive federal or state aid. Of the governors who responded to a 1957 survey about federal aids for public welfare, 9 considered the programs adequate, 17 would expand them, and only 2 would reduce or eliminate them.[12] In the highway field, the responses were even more favorable: one governor considered the programs adequate, 15 would expand them, and none would reduce or eliminate them. Similar feelings appear in the resolutions passed by Governors' Conferences over the 1946–1966 period. About one-half of the resolutions about federal grants favored their expansion. The quarrels over administrative procedures seem not so serious as to jeopardize support for the programs. The 1957 survey found that 21 governors cited the federal supervision of welfare programs as "satisfactory," while only 6 found it "unsatisfactory." In the highway field, 19 governors found federal supervision "satisfactory," while only one found it "unsatisfactory." These figures pertain only to the feelings of state chief executives; but they may identify the outside limits of state antagonism to federal programs. Other studies have found that elected officials are more likely to attack intergovernmental relations than are administrators. It is the elected executives and legislators of state and local governments who are least likely to view federal administrators as "cooperative." They lack the close contact with granting agencies that their own administrators experience, and they lack the professional training and program norms that provide a common bond between administrators at different levels of government.[13]

---

[11] Edward W. Weidner, "Decision-Making in a Federal System," in Aaron Wildavsky, ed., *American Federalism in Perspective* (Boston: Little, Brown, 1967), pp. 232–33. See also V. O. Key, Jr., *The Administration of Federal Grants to the States* (Chicago: Public Administration Service, 1939), p. 184.

[12] Wright, pp. 91–97.

[13] Weidner, pp. 232–33.

The general support for existing intergovernmental relations should not obscure the detailed criticisms of administrative procedures. These criticisms focus on a variety of points and—as might be expected in an extensive federal structure—are not equally important to all officials. The criticisms deal with: budget procedures, controls over details of program administration, lack of coordination between federal programs that affect closely-related state and local programs, and the influence of federal grants in "skewing" state and local resources to programs that qualify for federal support. Several quarrels of state officials are mentioned in a speech at the 1958 Governors' Conference. The speaker was Orville L. Freeman, then Governor of Minnesota and later Secretary of Agriculture:

> There are many deficiencies in Federal-State relations. We should seek to identify them and to develop sensible recommendations for their correction.
> We should, in other words, analyze what Professor Grodzins has called the "squeak" points in intergovernmental relations and how they impair the operation of the Federal-State mechanism. We should examine such conditions and problems as the following:
> (1) Because Federal appropriations are voted on an annual basis and many States operate on biennial budgets, the States experience great difficulty in planning their programs involving Federal aid. They do not know how much will be available until Congress has acted.
> (2) The large number of separate Federal aid programs introduces a chaotic note in State budgeting, tending to impair the maintenance of the executive budget. Some kind of coordinated activity at the Federal level would enable the States to participate in Federal-aid programs on a more planned and more integrated basis.
> (3) Federal aid programs tend to skew State financial programs in favor of those activities that have federal support. When a State can, in effect, obtain $2 by the expenditure of $1, such programs obviously will be given preferential treatment. This makes it important to assess at some point the total impact of all Federal aids upon the State's overall financial program.
> (4) Another skewing effect results from the tendency of some Federal aids to favor certain groups of citizens. For example, in the welfare field persons who qualify for Federal aid categories, such as aid to the blind or aid to dependent children, almost everywhere have a favored position over those who qualify for only general relief.
> (5) Some of the worst features of bureaucratic control are manifest in the Federal-aid programs. Some administrative forms are so complex that they make administration unnecessarily unwieldy. Often great amounts of irrelevant

information are required. States frequently experience troublesome delays in obtaining needed decisions from regional and national offices. Sometimes authority to act in behalf of Federal agencies is not clearly spelled out; at times Federal agents will be too indecisive, at other times too arbitrary.

(6) The many Federal-aid programs are conceived, established, and managed independently of each other. No central or single mechanism coordinates programs which often affect each other. The Joint Action Committee might very well consider establishment of an administrative mechanism at the national level that would be responsible for bringing the numerous aid programs into balance with each other and for helping States maximize their participation in the aid programs.

(7) A top-level reviewing mechanism would prevent the sudden springing of a new Federal-aid program without full preparation on the part of both the States and the Federal administering agencies. In 1956 when Congress approved $5 million for aid to rural libraries, the Department of Health, Education, and Welfare was taken by surprise and was completely unprepared for its administration. Aid programs often result from pressures applied on Congress by particular interest groups. States will suddenly discover that still another aid program has been created without their consultation. The legislature must either vote a matching appropriation or face criticism for failing to take advantage of Federal aid.

(8) The scope and complexity of Federal-aid programs, proceeding as they do through the labyrinthian bureaucracy, is making it increasingly difficult for States and their subdivisions to maintain sensible communication and to obtain essential information concerning available aids. Many jurisdictions fail to participate in Federal programs because they do not have personnel who are familiar with the programs or who can master the bureaucratic intricacies.

(9) Federal programs that deal directly with municipalities sometimes unsettle the State's relationship with their subdivisions. Direct Federal-local arrangements should exist only when the State provides no suitable mechanism for the Federal-aid program.[14]

THE EFFECTS OF ADMINISTRATIVE OUTPUTS ON SOCIAL AND ECONOMIC PROBLEMS

After we have identified the diversity of outputs from administrative agencies, we still have questions about their impact on the social and economic problems they are expected to meet. Do the programs

[14] Quoted in Wright, pp. 97–99.

work? What about their *unintended* consequences? Do they generate additional problems that come back to visit administrative agencies in another guise? For someone who is interested in the relation between administrative agencies and their environments, these may be the most important questions.

The policies that are produced by administrative agencies do not by themselves guarantee results. They must interact with whatever social, economic, or political conditions exist in the environment, some of which generate the problems that administrators' outputs are designed to attack.

There are profound difficulties encountered in testing the influence of administrators' outputs on social and economic problems. As observers of government agencies, we have no more certain idea than do their officials about the policies that should be implemented (see pp. 38–40). Like them, we lack a standard of excellence against which to compare the outputs of public service. Not only are there disagreements about what kinds of service levels agencies should strive to attain, but there are related disagreements about the proper units to be used in measuring what the agencies actually produce.

The closest we come to a test of administrative outputs is the examination of statistical associations between one kind of output—government expenditures—and other kinds of outputs that clients expect to receive from administrative agencies. In order to accept the influence of expenditure outputs vis-à-vis the problems they are designed to alleviate, the jurisdictions showing high (or low) levels of expenditures should show consistently high (or low) scores on most measures of service.

Two studies in different contexts show that relationships between government expenditures and levels of public service are neither strong nor pervasive. A study of 163 Georgia school districts shows only weak relationships between measures of educational spending and service outputs.[15] Another study of state and local governments' spending and services across the country found that only 16 of 27 service measures (59 percent) showed sizable relationships with government spending.[16] Some of the spending-service relationships are negative.

---

[15] Ira Sharkansky, "Environment, Policy, Output and Impact: Problems of Theory and Method in the Analysis of Public Policy," a paper presented at the 1968 Annual Meeting of the American Political Science Association, Washington, D.C. That paper uses terminology in a different way than does this chapter. The differences in terminology reflect the different focus of the two writings: this book deals with an abstraction of the "administrative system"; and that paper deals with the "policy process."

[16] Ira Sharkansky, *The Politics of Taxing and Spending* (Indianapolis: Bobbs-Merrill, 1969), Chapter VI. The services in different fields are necessarily

This means that high scores on spending correspond with low scores on the measure of service. In the highway field, the mileage per capita of rural roads and a measure of traffic safety are negatively related with state and local government highway spending. Apparently it is the low-spending states that develop the most extensive systems of rural roads. Low-spending states also experience the most enviable record of highway safety. In the field of crime control, the rates for rape, robbery, burglary, larceny, and auto theft are low where spending is low, while high crime rates coexist with high spending. It is unlikely that high (or low) spending brings about high (or low) crime rates. The incidence of crime probably works upon the spending level. States with little crime feel comfortable with relatively low per capita expenditures for public safety.

The evidence is also discouraging for the expectation that an increase in spending will produce a clear improvement in services. Only 10 out of 27 measures of 1957–1962 changes in services showed sizable positive relationships with 1957–1962 changes in spending. Perhaps the lag between an increase in spending and a change in service levels is greater than five years. Or perhaps an increase in spending is not powerful enough to cope with all of the non-financial elements in bringing about a change in the nature of services.

Several social and economic features of the environment show stronger, and more consistent, relationships with services than does government spending. In the field of secondary education, service levels are highest where there is the greatest incidence of adults with at least a high school education. Perhaps the parents' concern for education makes itself felt on their children and on school personnel; their children may be well-prepared for school, and they may stimulate administrators to provide a high quality program. Highway mileage per capita varies directly with the incidence of motor vehicles; while road safety varies inversely with the incidence of vehicles. Perhaps high levels of traffic produce more accidents and, through intermediate influence on the political process, more road mileage.

---

defined in terms of these fields. Some measurements define the units of service (e.g., miles of highway) in relation to population. Some measures employ the incidence of beneficiaries among people likely to use a service (e.g., the proportion of poor citizens receiving welfare benefits). Others measure the rate at which a program is performed. Others assess services by the frequency with which the population chooses to use a program (e.g., the proportion of a population who attends schools or visits parks). And some assess services indirectly by measuring the continued existence of phenomena (e.g., disease or crime) that administrative outputs are designed to control.

SUMMARY

The "outputs" of administrative systems include the services rendered to the public; agency expenditures and policies concerning staff and physical facilities; the information and advice given to the public and to officials in the legislative and executive branches; and financial and technical assistance given to the administrators of other governments. The outputs of one moment affect the environment and help shape subsequent "inputs." The services rendered to the public satisfy some needs and leave others unsatisfied and thereby influence subsequent demands. Intergovernmental payments likewise meet some needs more than others. They generate some requests for "more of the same" and other demands for additions to or modifications in current programs. Information and advice to other governmental officials often return to administrators in the form of statutes, executive orders, budget authorizations, or committee *Reports*.

Our concern with the administrative system should not end with a simple description of outputs. A curious reader will ask: "What difference do they make?" Present knowledge allows only partial answers to this question. We can list the kinds of information that administrators provide to the public and to other government officials; but we have no systematic information about the impact of this information on the actions of the recipients. We can identify the kinds of governments that make relatively great (and little) use of intergovernmental programs. Our information is not so good, however, that we can predict with any certainty what individual governments will do in response to new programs. Present generalizations are hedged by many deviant cases. In the case of some outputs, we know enough to be skeptical. Government expenditures were long thought to be the key ingredients in the production of public services. Yet we are now aware that numerous other outputs—and some features of the environment—also have effects on the services that actually are made available. We realize that an expenditure—or any other single output —by itself is not likely to produce the kind of service that is intended. This book cannot be read as the final description of public administration or related phenomena. If it is well-written, it should impress the student with the sparse nature of knowledge that is certain and provoke him to discover more.